TOPOGRAPHY OF A HAWK

For definitions of terms, see pp. 10–14.

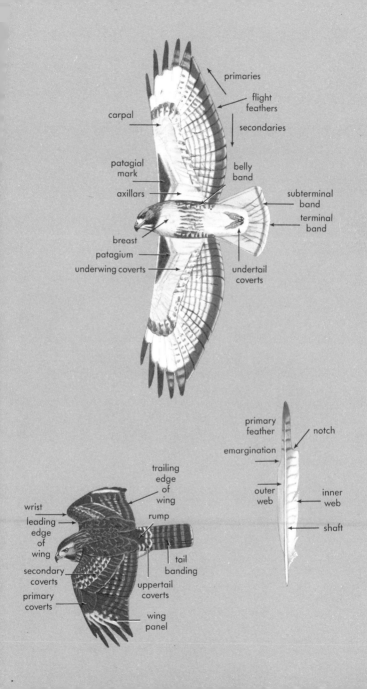

THE PETERSON FIELD GUIDE SERIES®
Edited by Roger Tory Peterson

A Field Guide to
Hawks
North America

William S. Clark

Illustrations by
Brian K. Wheeler

*Sponsored by the National Audubon Society,
the National Wildlife Federation,
and the Roger Tory Peterson Institute*

HOUGHTON MIFFLIN COMPANY   BOSTON   NEW YORK

PETERSON FIELD GUIDES and PETERSON FIELD GUIDE SERIES
are registered trademarks of Houghton Mifflin Company.

Library of Congress Cataloging in Publication Data

Clark, William S., 1937–
A field guide to hawks of North America

(The Peterson field guide series; 35)
"Sponsored by the National Audubon Society
and the National Wildlife Federation."
Bibliography: p. 163
Includes indexes.
1. Birds of prey—North America—Identification.
2. Birds—Identification. 3. Birds—North America—
Identification. I. Wheeler, Brian K., 1955–.
II. National Audubon Society. III. National Wildlife
Federation. IV. Title. V. Series.
QL696.F3C59   1987   598′.916   87-4528

ISBN 0-395-36001-3
ISBN 0-395-93615-2 (pbk.)

Printed in the United States of America

VB 17 16 15 14

Editor's Note

On any clear cold weekend in October, tens of thousands of men, women, and youngsters gaze skyward from the rocky ridges across the land, and from strategic spots along the coast and the Great Lakes. All stare fixedly at black spots in the blue sky; many use expensive binoculars. They are not plane spotters; they are hawk watchers, devotees of an increasingly popular facet of the sport of birding.

When I was a young man, 50 years ago, my friends and I knew of scarcely more than half of dozen good spots where hawk watching paid off—Cape May, New Jersey, Hawk Mountain in Pennsylvania, and Point Pelee in Ontario, to name the three most famous. Neither Wilson nor Audubon knew of the flights at these key places, or if they did, they never wrote about them. But with the explosive growth of birding, and an understanding of the nature of raptor migration, we now know of a great many more hot spots. In fact, Don Heintzelman, in his well-researched book, *Migration of Hawks* (1986), lists more than 1000! There may be even more, yet to be documented.

My first *Field Guide* saw the light of day in 1934, the very year that Hawk Mountain Sanctuary became a reality. In that rather modest first edition with the green binding, I portrayed the flight patterns of hawks as they appear overhead, the first time this had been attempted except for a single black and white plate by John B. May in Volume II of Forbush's *Birds of Massachusetts*. That classic work was published in 1927.

In 1935 the National Audubon Society, under pressure from two or three of its board members, produced *The Hawks of North America*, written by John B. May and handsomely illustrated in color by Major Allan Brooks. As a supplement to the full-page portraits of hawks by the gifted Canadian artist, I was asked to prepare four composite black and white plates showing overhead patterns similar to those in the *Field Guide*. Later these were reprinted, accompanied by food-habit charts, as part of a nationwide educational campaign to the save the hawks, which were then under siege by hosts of gunners.

In more recent years the raptors have enjoyed safe transit past Cape May, Hawk Mountain, Point Pelee, and most of the other slaughter points, largely due to the awakened public awareness and enlightenment.

The original concept embodied in the *Field Guides*—often referred to as the "Peterson System"—was to *simplify;* to make things easier for the tyro. The illustrations, whether of birds perched or in the air overhead, were deliberately schematic, emphasizing shape, pattern, and special "field marks."

It was inevitable that with this basic training behind them, many hawk watchers would want something more in depth. How about the various plumages when a bird is in transition from a juvenile to an adult? How about regional variations and color morphs, particularly in the West? And the effect of air currents and thermals on the silhouette and wing action when the bird was in flight?

This advanced field guide by William Clark is designed to fulfill these desires, while at the same time it does not bypass the neophyte. It is all there. Even beginners, with a little practice, will soon be able to hold their own with most of the others when they join the gatherings of skygazers on the Pennsylvania ridges or at Cape May Point. And the expert will become even more sophisticated in his ability to name things quickly and accurately, and to pick up the unexpected rarity.

As author, William Clark is uniquely qualified because of his years at the Cape May Observatory and elsewhere. He was formerly in charge of the Raptor Information Center at the National Wildlife Federation in Washington. Lately he has become involved with the work of the Israel Raptor Information Center at Elat, Israel, where the spring flights enroute from Africa to Europe and Asia are far more massive than anything we know on our own continent.

A field guide is basically a visual presentation, hence the role of the artist is of equal importance to that of the author. Brian Wheeler, who skillfully prepared the color plates, has long been an associate of William Clark at Cape May and has joined him on exploratory forays elsewhere in the United States and Canada, documenting hawks with his long lenses for reference material. At present Brian Wheeler lives in Colorado, which is an ideal base for an artist who delights in painting raptors.

Enjoy this book, take it with you on field trips, and enlarge your knowledge of these lords of the sky.

ROGER TORY PETERSON

Acknowledgments

We have many people to thank for assisting with the preparation of this book, particularly Bertel Bruun, who provided encouragement and guidance in the early stages. We greatly appreciate the help given us by the staff of Houghton Mifflin: Harry Foster, our editor, and the copy editors, Marcia Brubeck, Virginia Harrison, and Barbara Stratton.

This project greatly benefited from the constructive criticism of the text and artwork of many reviewers, including B. Anderson, J. Arvin, K. Bildstein, R. Blom, P. Bloom, B. Bruun, J. Church, M. Collopy, J. Dunn, J. Enderson, S. Ennett, D. Evans, G. Farquhar, D. Forsman, R. Glinski, A. Harmata, D. Hector, E. Henckel, A. Jenkins, M. Kochert, M. Kopeny, J. Layne, J. Lish, B. Mader, M. McCollough, B. Millsap, D. Mindell, J. Mosher, J. Ogden, L. Oliphant, J. Parker, R. Porter, R. Ridgely, R. Rosenfield, R. Rowlett, J. Schmutz, P. Spitzer, P. Stewart, P. Sykes, C. White, H. Wierenga, C. Wilds, and J. Witzeman. Their input is greatly appreciated. Also appreciated are the many CMP raptor banders who took measurements on eastern raptors. P. Bloom, M. McGrady, and J. Schmutz kindly shared measurement data of western raptors. S. Beissinger, J. Dunning, L. Kiff, and H. Ouellet provided additional data on raptor weight.

Many museums graciously permitted study of their raptor specimens: the American Museum of Natural History, the National Museum of Natural History, the British Museum of Natural History, the Field Museum, the Delaware Museum, the Denver Museum, the Los Angeles County Museum, the Academy of Natural Sciences of Philadelphia, the San Diego Museum of Natural History, the Western Foundation of Vertebrate Zoology, the Alberta and British Columbia Provincial Museums, the Winnipeg Museum, and the museums at the following colleges and universities: Alberta, Arizona, Arkansas, California (Museum of Vertebrate Zoology), Harvard (Museum of Comparative Zoology), Kansas, Louisiana State, Miami (Florida), Michigan, Minnesota (Bell Museum), New Mexico, Oklahoma, Principia College, Puget Sound, Saskatchewan, Southeastern Kansas, Texas A&M, Tulane, Washington, Wisconsin, and Yale (Peabody Museum).

For the loan of specimens used in the preparation of the plates, we thank the staffs of the Peabody Museum, Yale University; the

American Museum of Natural History; the National Museum of Natural History; the University of Michigan; and the Denver Museum of Natural History.

J. Arvin, P. Bloom, H. Darrow, C. Farquhar, D. Hector, A. Jenkins, M. Kopeny, J. Lish, B. Mader, M. McGrady, D. Mindell, the staff of the Santa Ana National Wildlife Refuge, D. Ward, and C. White provided slides for use in the preparation of this guide. Others provided slides for use in the photo section and have been acknowledged on p. xii.

Special thanks go to R. Banks, C. Blake, R. Browning, J. Bull, M. LeCroy, S. Keith, E. Stickney, and G. Watson for freely given assistance and to the Bird Division of the Smithsonian Institution for permitting liberal use of its library.

Virginia and Roger Tory Peterson kindly and eagerly shared with us valuable information used in the preparation of the range maps. We are also indebted to Roger for his personal advice on the plates and for the excellent example of his many field guides.

The following people took Bill into the field to observe raptors: B. Anderson, P. Bloom, M. Call, C. Farquhar, R. Glinski, D. Harlow, L. Hood, A. Jenkins, J. Lish, M. Kochert, M. McCollough, B. Millsap, J. Neal, and L. Oliphant.

L. Boudreau provided technical assistance in the preparation of the range maps by designing the map layouts and advising on their preparation.

Others who assisted Brian in various ways with the illustrations include J. Alhquist, F. Gallo, H. Meng, Frank Nicoletti, D. O'Connell, L. Oliphant, B. Reuter, R. Schwartz, J. Smith, P. Stacey, C. Taylor, the staff of the University of Oklahoma, B. Webb, J. Zipp, and especially F. Sibley.

We are grateful to Ellie Clark for her support and encouragement and to Linda Wheeler, who participated in many of the raptor expeditions and gave her unflagging support.

WILLIAM S. CLARK AND
BRIAN K. WHEELER

Contents

List of Plates

Photo Credits

P. Alden/VIREO: 3b.

C.M. Anderson: 40c

J. Arvin: 3a, 3b.

W. Clark: 2c, 2d, 2f; 4b, 4c, 4f; 8a–8d; 10a–10b (upper and lower), 10c; 11a–11c; 12a–12c; 13b–13d, 13f (right and left); 14c, 14d; 15a, 15c–15e; 16b, 16d–16f; 18a; 19b, 19f; 20a–20e; 21e, 21f; 22a, 22c, 22e, 22f; 26a–26d; 28d; 30e, 30f; 31a, 31c, 31f; 32a; 35c, 35d, 35f; 36a–36f; 38b–38e; 39a–39f; 40b, 40d; 41d, 41f.

W. Clark/VIREO: 28f; 42d.

H. Darrow: 18d; 23e; 33c.

H. Flanders: 9b.

D. Forsman: 34c.

J. Grantham–Nat. Aud. Soc.: 2b.

E. Greaves: 34d.

M.A. Jenkins: 41e; 42a, 42b.

M.A. Jenkins/U.S. Fish and Wildlife Service: 40e.

M. Kahl/VIREO: 39a.

M. Kopeny: 21b.

P. Muuronen: 34a.

D. Roby/VIREO: 42f.

J. Ruos/VIREO: 42e.

C. Servheen: 38f.

N. Smith/VIREO: 22d.

S. Werner: 17f.

B. Wheeler: 1a–1f; 2a, 2e; 3c–3f; 4a, 4d, 4e; 5a–5d; 6a–6d; 7a–7d; 9a, 9c–9f; 10d–g; 11d; 12d; 13a, 13e; 14a, 14b, 14e; 15b; 16a, 16c; 17a–17e; 18b–18c; 19a, 19c–19e, 19g–19i; 20f; 21a, 21c, 21d; 22b; 23a–23d, 23f; 24a–24f; 25a–25f; 27a–27f; 28a–28c, 28e; 29a–29f; 30a–30d; 31b, 31d, 31e; 32b–32i; 33a, 33b, 33e, 33f; 35a, 35b, 35e; 37a–37f; 38a; 40a; 41a–41c; 42c.

D. and M. Zimmerman/VIREO: 33d; 40f.

A Field Guide to
Hawks

Introduction

Hawks, or more properly, diurnal raptors, have been worshiped by many people, even societies, in the past. Nowadays they are still revered, not as deities, but as some of nature's most magnificent creatures. A growing number of people watch, count, hunt with, or study raptors and desire to identify them accurately in the field. Field identification of hawks, kites, eagles, and falcons is notoriously difficult, however, partly because they are wary and difficult to approach and partly because they exhibit a variety of plumages and alter their shape with different flight modes.

The available bird field guides, including those in the Peterson series, constantly incorporate new information and are adequate for the identification of most bird species, but space limitations prevent them from fully describing and illustrating all of the plumage and behavioral variations of the diurnal raptors. Recognition of this problem in Europe led to the publication of the *Flight Identification of European Raptors* by Porter et al. We have used that volume often and have incorporated some of its features in this book.

The purpose of this field guide is to present the latest in tried and proven field marks (see **Field marks,** p. 3) and behavioral characteristics by which the 33 regular and six accidental N. American diurnal raptors may accurately be identified. These field marks and characteristics should enable anyone, with a little practice, to accurately identify most flying and perched diurnal raptors when they are seen clearly.

This work is the culmination of our efforts over the past eight years toward making the art of raptor identification more scientific by identifying new field marks and behavioral characteristics. The original impetus for the book came from a series of raptor identification classes that Bill Clark taught under the auspices of the National Wildlife Federation's Raptor Information Center. These courses were given many times in 16 states in every region of the United States over a period of five years.

We have both spent considerable time in the field watching and photographing raptors in N. America. Many new field marks were discovered when we continued observing raptors *after* they had been identified while asking, "What can one tell beginners about this species that would help them correctly

1

identify it?" We also spent considerable time studying raptor specimens in collections. We visited museums in all regions of N. America, checking field marks, looking for individuals with unusual plumages, and gathering measurement data from labels. Some new field marks came to light as we studied photographs and examined museum skins. All of the field marks presented here have been field tested by us and by others and work in almost all cases, but there will always be the odd raptor that lacks a certain field mark and is thus more difficult to label properly in the field.

Most of the recent N. American ornithological literature, including the regional, state, and provincial journals, was searched for articles on raptor identification, distribution and status, plumages, natural history, behavior, and other subjects. The most important of these are cited in the References. Also included is an Index to References by Species and Topic that is organized by general categories, such as natural history, plumages, or albinism, for the benefit of readers who want to locate more detailed information. Additional pertinent and useful references are cited in the articles listed in the References.

Three or four knowledgeable reviewers critically reviewed each species account presented in the book. In the case of most species, one reviewer was primarily a researcher familiar with the species and its literature, another was an experienced birder or hawk watcher, and a third was a critical editor who was also familiar with birds. Many reviewers fit into more than one category. All of their comments and suggestions were considered; most were used.

Species Accounts

The 39 species accounts appear in the sequence used in the sixth American Ornithologists' Union (AOU) checklist, except that the sea eagles (genus *Haliaeetus*) have been placed with the Golden Eagle. Each account includes the information described below. "Notes" contain important information not easily placed elsewhere.

Common and scientific names: The common names used in this guide came from the sixth AOU checklist except in the case of the Swallow-tailed Kite, where the word "American" was dropped for brevity. The scientific names used in this guide were also taken from the sixth AOU checklist.

Description: An initial brief description of each species indicates range, size, and general type and mentions color morphs, sex- and age-related differences, and field marks common to all plumages. This is followed by a detailed description of each different age, sex, color morph, or geographically different plumage. Diagnostic field marks are italicized.

Field marks: Each species has features, called field marks, that distinguish it from every other species. Examples are the dark mark (patagial mark) on the fore edge of the Red-tailed Hawk's underwing, the red head of the adult Turkey Vulture, and the gull-like wing shape of the Osprey. This guide uses the famous Peterson Identification System of arrows on the plates and photographs to indicate the important field marks.

Plumages: Raptors replace their plumages annually, during the summer in most species. Adult and immature plumages are described and portrayed for all species. All other recognizably different, regularly occurring plumages, such as sexually different and subadult plumages or color morphs, are also completely described and portrayed. The preferred term "morph" is used in this book in place of the widely used "phase," as the latter word implies a character that changes with time.

Similar species: The lists of similar species include cross-references to the appropriate color plates and mention distinguishing field marks.

Flight: The three modes of flight — active, soaring, and gliding — are described. Any other interesting flight mode, such as hovering or kiting, may be included.

Behavior: Behaviors that will help identify each species, such as hunting behavior and prey selection, are described.

Voice: This guide makes little mention of vocalizations because it is difficult to render calls adequately in words. Voice is one of the better field marks used in some field identifications, but vocalizations are best learned from field study or from recordings on disk or tape, such as the bird song guides in the Peterson field guide series. When a species is particularly vocal, that fact is noted in the behavior section.

Status and distribution: Range, including breeding and wintering ranges and migration routes, is presented, together with out-of-range occurrences and relative abundance.

Range maps: The summer and winter ranges are pictured for

summer

winter

permanent
resident

most species. The range maps were produced using published distributional data, personal correspondence from knowledgeable people, and range maps from published bird field guides. Range maps are useful for general distribution but have inherent limitations: they do not show density and habitat preferences, and the precise limits of summer and winter ranges are usually not known and are variable and are thus not best represented by a single line. In all cases the text should be consulted for habitat preferences and exceptions.

Fine points: More detailed information is presented for the more experienced observer.

Unusual plumages: Occurrences of albinism, partial albinism, and dilute plumage are noted.

Subspecies: All of the races in N. America north of Mexico as recognized by the AOU in the fifth checklist are given, together with the approximate breeding range of each. Many species are monotypic. Subspecific labels have not been used with the various recognizably different "forms" of a species because individuals within the range of one subspecies sometimes have the characteristics of another. Furthermore, it is sometimes impossible to separate many subspecies in the field, and some recognized subspecies fail to satisfy the criteria of subspecies (e.g., Krider's Hawk does not occupy a range exclusive of other races of the Red-tailed Hawk but is nevertheless a recognizable form of the Red-tail). In most cases, the forms described correspond to subspecies. In some, however, the subspecies cannot be distinguished in the field and are thus not differentiated in the text or plates.

Etymology: The origins of the common and scientific names are noted.

Measurements: The average and range of values for length, wingspread, and weight are presented in both English and metric units. The total length measurement used is the distance from the top of the head to the tip of the tail. Wingspan is the distance between wingtips of a raptor with the wings fully extended. Weight was taken to the nearest gram. The data are given separately for each sex for some species in which male and female sizes show little or no overlap. Measurements were taken on live birds whenever possible. When few live data were available, we used additional data from museum specimens or, as a last resort, from published sources.

Plates: The 26 plates have been grouped in the center of the book for quick access. Legends on the facing pages contain summaries of the major field marks, most of which are indicated on the plates by arrows. Field marks printed in italics are diagnostic for species identification; those in Roman type pertain to age and sex determination within the species. Some age- and sex-related field marks, however, are also species determining and thus appear in italics (e.g., the red head of the adult Turkey Vulture). The legend pages also include short summaries of status and distribution, cross-references to text and photographs for each species, and a list of similar species with cross-references to plates. The sequence of species on the plate corresponds as nearly as possible to the AOU checklist, but many plates show more than one species.

The plates and the text were produced to complement each other. We worked together closely throughout their production and attempted to show all the important field marks of each species and to picture as many forms of each species as possible, always depicting adult, immature, dark morph, and sexually different plumages.

We have emphasized identification of flying birds, although perched birds have been described and depicted. To save space, drawings of detached heads, wings, and tails were used to show field marks. To facilitate comparison, many comparable species were drawn in the same flight profile on different plates (e.g., the immatures of Red-tailed, Red-shouldered, and Broad-winged hawks on Pls. 9, 10, and 11 are in the upper right corner).

We attempted to group similar species together on the plates. Dark and light morphs of a species were placed on separate plates so that similar species for each color morph could be compared. We were not always able to group the species as we would have liked, however, and in some cases unrelated species had to be placed on the same plate, while in other cases, similar species appear on different plates.

All species on a plate are drawn proportionally (except for the eagles and Northern Hobby on Pl. 25), but perched and flying birds on each plate were drawn to different scales. Seven different scalings were used to draw the raptors of different sizes:

1. Pl. 1. Scavengers
2. Pl. 2. Condor
3. Pls. 6 and 7. Accipiters
4. Pls. 3, 5, and 8–17. Osprey, Harrier, Kites, and Buteos
5. Pls. 18, 19, 20, and 25. Eagles
6. Pls. 21, 22, 23, and 24. Falcons
7. Pl. 26. Dark Raptors—Summary

Photographs: The 42 pages of black-and-white photographs complement the plates by illustrating or emphasizing field marks and depicting a color morph, age or sex class, or position or attitude that is not illustrated on the plates. The photographs are arranged by species in the same sequence as the text.

How to Identify Hawks

Several basic points must be understood for successful identification of raptors. First, in almost all species, females are larger than males—noticeably so in some species. In most species, adult and immature plumages are quite different. Adults usually have blue-gray backs and reddish, barred underparts, while immatures usually have brown backs with noticeable pale feather fringes and pale, darkly streaked underparts. In several species, adult males and females have different plumages. Adults and immatures of some species have different proportions. Adult wings are usually narrower and longer, but in some *Buteo* species, adult wings are wider. In most species the adult tail is shorter. Raptor fledglings are sometimes larger than adults.

Raptor types: All of the raptors treated in this guide can be assigned to one of the general types described below on the basis of wing and tail shape, color, size, and behavior.

Vultures: The three vulture species are large raptors with featherless heads, long wings, and generally blackish coloration. They spend considerable time soaring and gliding.

Osprey: The Osprey is a large gull-like raptor found near water. The distinctive wing shape and dark eye-line are conspicuous.

Kites: The three widespread pointed-wing kites are medium-sized raptors. They are falcon-like in silhouette, but are more buoyant in flight and have unique tails. One is solid white, one is dark and flared, and the last is swallow-like.

Harrier: The single harrier species has long, narrow wings and a long tail, and its buoyant flight is with wings held in a strong dihedral.

Accipiters: The three species of "true hawks," small to large raptors with long tails and relatively short, rounded wings, are found most often in forested areas. Their typical active flight is three or more rapid wingbeats interspersed with periods of gliding. Wingtips reach only halfway down the tail on perched birds.

Buteos: The six species of "buzzards," medium to large raptors with long, broad wings and relatively short, wide tails, are found in open and forested habitats. They all soar frequently, and many sit on exposed perches. Wingtips usually reach to or nearly to the tail tip on perched birds.

Eagles: The two eagle species are very large, mostly dark brown raptors with proportionally longer wings. They soar and glide with wings held nearly horizontal.

Falcons: The five species of regularly occurring falcons are small to large raptors with long, pointed wings, long tails, and large, squarish heads. They are swift on the wing and occur in open habitats. Wingtips usually reach more than halfway down the tail on perched birds.

How to Use This Guide

When you see an unfamiliar raptor, *before* opening the guide, you should determine its general type from the descriptions given above (at first, you may have to open the guide to this section to determine general type). Make written notes of all important field marks observed, including color and contrasting marks (such as a pale superciliary line, shape and color of marks or panels on underwing, and number and relative thickness of tail bands). Also observe and record the raptor's behavior. Make these notes before consulting the field guide because the bird may soon be out of your sight.

Which field marks to look for on any species will depend on whether the bird is perched or flying. On perched birds, note the color and pattern of the back and underparts, the color of the eye, and the head pattern, as well as the presence or absence of tail banding and leg feathering and how far the wingtips extend toward the tail tip. On flying birds, look for the underwing pattern, the shape and relative length of head, tail, and wings, any distinguishing marks (such as belly bands, dark secondaries, and dark patagial or carpal patches), the presence and shape of wing panels, and the pattern of tail banding.

When you have noted all marks and behavior, and only then, open the field guide to the 26 plates. These are arranged in order more or less by the raptor types described above, with the vultures shown on the first 2 plates and so forth. Quickly scan the illustrations of all species of the appropriate type, reading the important field marks for each species (including those referring to age and sex). Note the similar species, and check the plates for these. Also note the short description of status and distribution given for each species on the legend page. Next turn to the pages of black-and-white photographs. Look at those for the species being considered and read the explanatory captions. If a positive identification has not been made, or if more information is desired, consult the text at this stage.

Study the text, color plates, and photos at home to become familiar with the diagnostic field marks to look for on each species. If possible, photograph raptors that you are not able to identify. Be sure to photograph the bird from different angles. Often only one photo of many taken will show a diagnostic field mark.

A word of caution is in order. Even when you use this guide, you should not expect to identify every hawk accurately. Experienced hawk watchers know that they must record a few hawks as "unidentified," most often because they could not see the bird clearly enough. On the other hand, some experienced hawk watchers are able to identify hawks correctly beyond the range where most field marks can be seen. How do they do it? Such people record most identification clues subconsciously; they bring into play the familiarity that comes from experience. They spot subtle differences in shape, proportion, and behavior. This impression of a species is often called "jizz" or "gestalt." It is difficult to teach or describe this ability because the clues are subtle and are subconsciously noted. They also vary from one location to the next and under different wind and light conditions.

We recommend that you continue to watch raptors *after* they have been identified. You will learn more about their identification and will observe the behavior of some of nature's most impressive creatures, a rewarding experience indeed.

Much remains to be learned about raptor identification. We would appreciate any suggestions and constructive criticism for future editions of this book. Please send your comments to the author and artist, c/o Houghton Mifflin Company, 2 Park Street, Boston, Mass. 02108. Good luck in your hawk watching.

Topography of a Hawk

List of Terms

Adult plumage. The final breeding plumage of a bird.
Auriculars. The feathers covering the ears (Fig. 4).
Axillars. The feathers at the base of the underwing, also called the "armpit" or "wingpit" (Fig. 1).
Back. See Fig. 5.
Barring. See Fig. 5.
Beak. See Fig. 5; see also **mandibles.**
Belly. See Fig. 5.
Belly band. See Fig. 1.
Breast. See Fig. 1.
Carpal. The underwing at the wrist, usually composed of all of the primary underwing coverts (Fig. 1).
Cere. A small area of bare skin above the upper mandible (Fig. 5).
Cheek. See Fig. 4.
Coverts. The small feathers covering the bases of the flight feathers and tail both above and below (Figs. 1, 2, and 5).
Crown. The top of the head (Fig. 4).
Dihedral. The shape when a bird holds its wings above the horizontal, further defined as (1) **strong dihedral** (wings held more than 15 degrees above level); (2) **medium dihedral** (wings held between 5 and 15 degrees above

FIGURE 1

primaries
flight feathers
secondaries
carpal
patagial mark
axillars
belly band
subterminal band
terminal band
breast
patagium
underwing coverts
undertail coverts

FIGURE 2

trailing edge of wing
wrist
leading edge of wing
rump
secondary coverts
primary coverts
tail banding
uppertail coverts
wing panel

FIGURE 3

upper mandible
lores
superciliary line
eye-line
nape
lower mandible
hind neck
malar stripe
streaking

FIGURE 4

crown
forehead
cheek
auriculars
ocelli
throat
mustache mark
spotting

FIGURE 5

supraorbital ridge
cere
eye-ring
beak
shoulder
back
lesser coverts
gape
median coverts
belly
greater coverts
barring
primaries
flank
leg feathers
leg
secondaries
tail

FIGURE 6

primary feather
notch
emargination
outer web
inner web
shaft

level); (3) **slight dihedral** (wings held between 0 and 5 degrees above level); (4) **modified dihedral** (wings held between 5 and 15 degrees above level but held nearly level from wrist to tip).

Dilute plumage. An abnormal plumage in which the dark colors are replaced by a lighter, usually creamy color (but not white).

Emargination. An abrupt narrowing on the outer web of an outer primary; see **notch** (Fig. 6).

Eye-line. See Fig. 3.

Eye-ring. The bare skin around the eye, somewhat wider in front of the eye in falcons. See Fig. 5.

Face skin. The **lores** when bare of feathers.

Facial disk. A saucer-shaped disk of feathers around the face, thought to direct sound to the ears.

Feather edge. The sides of a feather. Pale edges usually give the effect of streaking.

Feather fringe. The complete circumference of a feather. Pale fringes usually give a scalloped appearance.

Flank. See Fig. 5.

Flight feathers. The primaries and secondaries (Fig. 1).

Forehead. See Fig. 4.

Glide. Flight attitude of a bird when it is coasting downward. The wingtips are pulled back, more so for steeper angles of descent.

Hind neck. See Fig. 3.

Hover. Remain in a fixed place in the air by flapping.

Immature plumage. First complete plumage, usually different from the adult plumage.

Inner web of feather. See Fig. 6.

Kite. Remain in a fixed place in moving air on motionless wings.

Leading edge of wing. See Fig. 2.

Leg. See Fig. 5.

Leg feathers. See Fig. 5.

Length. Distance from top of head to tip of tail.

Lores. The area of the face between the eye and the beak (Fig. 3).

Lower mandible. See Fig. 3.

Malar stripe. A dark mark on the cheek under the eye (Fig. 3).

Mandible. The upper or lower half of the beak (Fig. 3).

Molt. The process by which a bird replaces its feathers.

Monotypic. Having no subspecies.

Morph. Term used for recognizably different forms of a species, usually color related, as in **dark morph** and **light morph.** See also **phase.**

Mustache mark. A dark mark directly under the eye, appearing on most falcon species (Fig. 4).

Nape. The back of the head (Fig. 3).

Notch. Abrupt narrowing of the inner web of an outer primary (Fig. 6).

Ocelli. Dark or light spots on the nape and hind neck that resemble eyes (Fig. 4).

Outer web of a feather. See Fig. 6.

Patagial mark. See Fig. 1.

Patagium. The area on the front of the wing between the wrist and the body (adjective is **patagial;** Fig. 1).

Phase. Term formally used for color morph. See **morph.**

Primaries. The outer flight feathers (Figs. 1 and 5).

Raptor. Any bird of prey; any member of the Falconiformes or Strigiformes, although the term is sometimes used to refer only to the diurnal birds of prey.

Rump. The lowest area of the back (Fig. 2).

Scapulars. Feathers between back and upperwing coverts.

Scavenger. A bird that eats carrion, offal, and other decaying material.

Secondaries. The inner flight feathers (Figs. 1 and 5).

Shaft of a feather. See Fig. 6.

Shoulder. See Fig. 5.

Soar. Flight attitude of a bird with wings, and usually tail, fully spread. Used to gain altitude in rising air columns.

Spotting. See Fig. 4.

Streaking. See Fig. 3.

Subadult plumage. Intermediate plumage of birds that take more than 1 year to acquire adult plumage.

Subterminal band. See Fig. 1.

Superciliary line. Contrasting line above the eye (Fig. 3).

Supraorbital ridge. Bony projection over the eye, giving raptors their fierce appearance (Fig. 5).

Tail. See Fig. 5.

Tail banding. See Fig. 2.

Talon-grappling. Behavior involving 2 flying raptors that lock feet and tumble with their wings extended.

Terminal band. See Fig. 1.

Throat. See Fig. 4.

Trailing edge of wing. See Fig. 2.

Underparts. Breast and belly (Figs. 1 and 5).

Undertail coverts. See Fig. 1.

Underwing. The underside of the open wing.

Underwing coverts. See Fig. 1.

Upper mandible. See Fig. 3.

Uppertail coverts. See Fig. 2.

Upperwing coverts. Primary and secondary coverts (Figs. 2 and 5).

Wing chord. The distance from the tip of the longest primary to the wrist with the feathers in normal shape (i.e., curved, not flattened).

Wing linings.   Underwing coverts (Fig. 1).

Wing loading.   Weight divided by the wing area; a measure of the buoyancy of flight. The lower the wing loading, the more buoyant the flight.

Wing panel.   A light area in the primaries, usually more visible from below when wing is backlighted (Fig. 2).

Wingspan.   The distance between wingtips with wings fully extended.

Wrist.   Bend of wing (Fig. 2).

Wrist comma.   A comma-shaped mark, usually dark, at the bend of the underwing.

American Vultures

Family Cathartidae

Our 3 species of graceful flying scavengers differ somewhat from Old World vultures, which are more closely related to other members of the family Accipitridae.

Vultures subsist almost exclusively on carrion, which they tear with their strong hooked beaks. Their feet are relatively weak and are not used for grasping prey. While perched in a tree, on the ground, or on a fencepost, all 3 species often spread their wings and face toward or away from the sun. This sunning behavior has been variously interpreted as gathering heat, drying feathers, or straightening feathers. Vultures are somewhat social and gregarious, roosting and eating together, but are solitary breeders. Vultures often defecate on their legs for cooling or disease control or both.

The misnomer "buzzard" was given to the 2 smaller vultures by early settlers, who thought these birds were related to the European buteo with this name. Unfortunately, the name is still in common use.

TURKEY VULTURE *Cathartes aura* **Pl. 1; photos, p. 120**
Description: The widespread Turkey Vulture is a large, brownish black raptor that soars and glides with its *wings in a strong dihedral.* Sexes are alike in plumage and size. Iris is gray-brown.
Adult: Head is red, featherless, and covered with wrinkles and warts. Beak is ivory. Entire body is brownish black, with upperwing coverts and lower breast and belly somewhat browner. Neck and back have a purplish iridescence. From below, flight feathers are silvery and wing coverts are black, forming *two-toned underwing* pattern. Underside of *long tail* is silvery but darker than flight feathers. Legs are pale reddish but are often whitened by defecation.
Immature: Like adult, but head is dusky, lacks wrinkles and warts, and is covered with brown fuzzy down on crown and hind neck. Beak is dusky, often with a light base. Upperwing coverts have buffy feather edges.
Similar species: (1) **Black Vulture** (Pl. 1) is black, not brownish, on back; has a shorter tail and longer neck; flaps with quicker wingbeats; has a white area at base of primaries; and flies with its wings more level. (2) **Zone-tailed Hawk** (Pl. 16) is an excellent Turkey Vulture mimic but has light bands in tail, a dark head, and a dark border and barring on underside of flight feathers. (3) **Northern Harrier** (Pl. 3) also flies

15

with its wings in a strong dihedral and has a similar outline but has a pale body and white rump. (4) **Dark-morph buteos** (Pls. 13–15 and 26) have dark trailing border of underwing and patterned tail. (5) **Eagles** (Pls. 18–20 and 25) can also be all dark but are larger, fly with more level wings, and have different underwing patterns.

Flight: Active flight is with slow, deep, deliberate wingbeats on flexible wings. The Turkey Vulture soars and glides with its wings in a strong dihedral, rocking or teetering from side to side. When the bird is gliding in strong winds, wings are pulled back, with only a slight dihedral. Turkey Vultures often bow their wings downward in a "flex" until the tips almost meet.

Behavior: Turkey Vultures spend much of the day soaring at moderate heights, searching for carrion. Communal night roosts of up to several hundred birds, sometimes including Black Vultures, form on buildings, on radio towers, and in large trees. While carrion is the vulture's usual fare, there are isolated reports of Turkey Vultures' catching live fish and attacking live animals, usually ones that are sick or in some way incapacitated. Turkey Vultures are reportedly able to locate carrion by smell as well as by sight. Studies have shown that Turkey Vultures eat smaller prey than Black Vultures, but Blacks dominate at carcasses by their numbers. Vocalizations reported are limited to grunts and hisses.

Status and distribution: Turkey Vultures are fairly common,

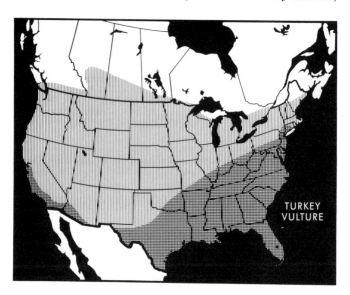

TURKEY VULTURE

breeding over most of the United States and s. Canada. Northern and western birds are migratory, some traveling as far as S. America in winter.

Fine points: One-year-old birds can be aged by their two-toned beaks, which are ivory with a dark tip. Turkey Vultures have shorter, thicker beaks than do Black Vultures. Nestling's down is whitish; Black Vulture's down is buffy.

Unusual plumages: Albinos reported are either all white or all light gray. Partial albinos with some white feathers, including some with only the outer primaries white, have also been reported. There is a report of a hybrid between this species and the Black Vulture.

Subspecies: There are 2 subspecies in N. America, *C. a. septentrionalis* in the East and *C. a. aura* in the West.

Etymology: The Turkey Vulture is named for its resemblance to the Turkey. "Vulture" comes from the Latin *vulturus,* "tearer," a reference to its manner of eating carrion. *Cathartes* is from the Greek *kathartes*, meaning "a purifier," and *aura* possibly derives from the Latin *aurum*, "gold," a reference to the head color of museum specimens, but is more likely a Latinized version of a Latin American word for "vulture."

Measurements:

Length: 62–72 cm (67); 24–28 in. (26)
Wingspread: 160–181 cm (171); 63–71 in. (67)
Weight: 1.6–2.4 kg (1.8); 3.5–5.3 lb (4)

BLACK VULTURE   Pl. 1; photos, p. 120
Coragyps atratus

Description: The southerly distributed Black Vulture is a large, black raptor. Sexes are alike in plumage and size. Iris color is dark brown. *Black tail is short.* Legs are whitish.

Adult: Head is gray and featherless. Beak is dusky with ivory tip. Body and wing coverts are black, with back and upperwing coverts having a purplish iridescence. *Underwing is black with white patch* in primaries.

Immature: Like adult, but head and neck skin are black and are less wrinkled, beak is completely dusky, and body plumage is somewhat less iridescent than adult's.

Similar species: (1) **Turkey Vulture** (Pl. 1) has longer tail and two-toned underwings; is brownish, not black, on the back; and flies with slower wingbeats and with wings in a stronger dihedral. Adult Turkey Vultures have red heads. (2) **Dark-morph buteos** (Pls. 13–16 and 26) have underwings that show silvery flight feathers. (3) **Eagles** (Pls. 18–20 and 25) are larger, have longer tails, and have different underwing patterns.

Flight: Active flight is distinctive, with 3 to 5 shallow, rapid, and stiff wingbeats with the wings thrust forward, followed by a short period of glide. The Black Vulture soars with the wings held level or in a slight dihedral and glides on level wings. Its wing loading is heavier than that of the Turkey Vulture, and so it requires stronger thermals for soaring and therefore does not become active in the morning until an hour or so after the Turkey Vulture. Black Vultures usually soar higher than Turkey Vultures and, like that species, often bow their wings downward in a flex until the tips almost meet. They occasionally fly with legs dangling.

Behavior: Black Vultures are more gregarious and aggressive than Turkey Vultures and subsist on larger carcasses. Blacks are dominant over Turkeys at carcasses mainly because of their greater numbers. They are reported to fish, to attack live prey, especially newborn pigs and other livestock and even skunks, and to eat oil palm fruit. They apparently locate prey not by smell but by watching other scavengers and by frequenting abundant food sources, such as dumps and slaughterhouses. Black Vultures form communal night roosts, often with Turkey Vultures. Breeding is in solitary pairs. Vocalizations reported are restricted to hisses and grunts.

Status and distribution: Black Vultures are common and were formerly abundant residents in the Southeast. They are uncommon to rare elsewhere, occurring north to New Jersey, Pennsylvania, and Indiana and west to n. Texas, with a small population in s. Arizona. They are nonmigratory, but birds have dispersed as far north as Wisconsin, Quebec, and Ontario.

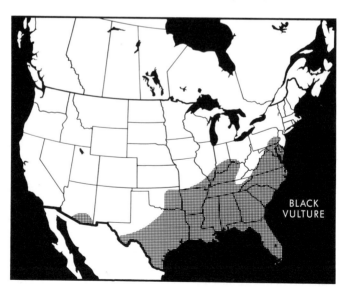

BLACK
VULTURE

Fine points: The down of Black Vulture chicks is buffy; that of Turkey Vulture chicks is white.

Unusual plumages: A sight record exists of an "unmistakable albino." A hybrid between this species and a Turkey Vulture has been reported.

Subspecies: The range of the N. American race *(C. a. atratus)* extends south through the nontropical parts of Mexico.

Etymology: "Vulture" comes from the Latin *vulturus,* "tearer," a reference to its manner of eating carrion. *Coragyps* comes from the Greek *korax,* "raven," and *gyps,* "vulture." The Latin *atratus* means "clothed in black, as for mourning."

Measurements:

Length: 59–74 cm (65); 23–28 in. (25)
Wingspread: 141–160 cm (151); 55–63 in. (59)
Weight: 1.7–2.3 kg (2.0); 3.8–5.1 lb (4.4)

CALIFORNIA CONDOR   **Pl. 2; photos, p. 121**
Gymnogyps californianus

Description: The endangered California Condor is the largest N. American raptor, *much larger than any eagle.* The birds are mostly black, with *bold white triangular patches* on the underside and narrow *white bar* on the upperside of long, broad wings, and have a relatively short, square tail. Sexes are alike in size and plumage.

Adult: *Reddish orange to yellow head* has an unusual tuft of short black feathers between the eyes. Iris color is scarlet. Beak is horn-colored. Neck is reddish in front and pinkish on sides. Black feathers at base of neck form a ruff. Body and upperwing coverts are sooty black. A small vertical area of red skin in center of breast is usually visible on perched and flying birds. Perched birds show a narrow white bar on folded wings. Flight feathers are black. Black secondaries have a silvery wash on upper surface. White underwing coverts form a large triangular patch on underwing. Leg color is whitish. Black tail has square tip.

Subadult: Similar to adult, but head is reddish orange with numerous black areas and appears dark. Neck is reddish orange without black areas, giving bird a ring-necked appearance. White triangle on underwing has some black mottling.

Immature: Similar to adult, but head and neck are dusky; nape and neck are covered with dusky, fuzzy down; and beak is black. Iris color is gray-brown. Whitish area on underwing coverts is more heavily mottled with black.

Note: Most wild condors have white numbered markers on the leading edge of the underwing.

Similar species: (1) **Turkey Vulture** (Pl. 1) is much smaller, flies with wings in a strong dihedral, and has a much longer tail. (2) **Black Vulture** (Pl. 1) does not occur in the range of the California Condor. (3) **Golden Eagle** (Pls. 19–20) is noticeably smaller and in flight has smaller body and proportionally longer tail than Condor. (4) **Bald Eagle** immature (Pls. 19–20) is noticeably smaller, in flight shows white axillary spots and diagonal white lines on underwings, and has a proportionally longer tail.

Flight: Active flight is with slow, stiff wingbeats. Soars and glides very steadily, like an airplane, with wings held slightly upraised. When beginning a glide after gaining altitude in a soar, Condors take 1 or 2 powerful wingbeats, bending their wings below the body until the wingtips almost touch.

Behavior: California Condors are large vultures that subsist entirely on carrion. They prefer large carcasses, such as deer and cattle. They leave night roosts to begin foraging late in the morning after strong thermals form, often returning to a known carcass. Condors spend much time perched and, when thermals are available, begin soaring, both singly and in small groups. Sunning behavior, common among vultures, has been noted. Perched birds spread their wings out and face away from the sun. This species is usually dominant over other scavengers at carcasses. After feeding, California Condors have a curious habit of rubbing their heads on the ground. Adult's head color varies, depending on mood.

Status and distribution: Only a few individuals remain in the wild in their limited range in s. California, a horseshoe-shaped area encompassing the coastal range and the western foothills of the Sierra Nevada. The population has been steadily declining for decades and continues to dwindle despite the recent recovery efforts. Over 20 condors are in captivity for captive breeding. Releases of offspring of these birds are planned.

Fine points: Primary tips of soaring condors are very long and narrow, and in flight are bent upward and appear more brushlike and noticeable than those of other large soaring raptors. This species takes from 13 to 17 seconds to complete a circle when soaring, longer than other raptors. Tails of flying birds sometimes appear to have wedge-shaped tips.

Unusual plumages: No unusual plumages have been described.

Subspecies: Monotypic.

Etymology: "California" and *californianus* refer to the range of this species. "Condor" is Spanish and probably came from the Inca word *cuntur,* the name for the Andean Condor. *Gymnos* is Greek for "naked," a reference to the featherless head; *gyps* is Greek for "vulture."

Measurements:

Length: 109–127 cm (117); 43–50 in. (46)

Wingspread: 249–300 cm (278); 98–118 in. (109)

Weight: 8.2–14.1 kg (10.5); 18–31 lb (23)

Ospreys
Family Pandionidae

The Osprey family contains only 1 species. Ospreys are large, long-legged, eagle-like, fish-eating raptors. They are widespread throughout the N. Hemisphere and Australia. Their outer toes, like those of owls, are reversible; this character and the sharp spicules on the lower surface of the toes allow them to grasp slippery fish. They are anatomically different from other raptors in Accipitridae, Cathartidae, and Falconidae, primarily in their specialized adaptations for catching fish. Ospreys are probably most closely related to the kites in Accipitridae.

OSPREY *Pandion haliaeetus*   **Pl. 3; photos, p. 121**
Description: The Osprey, a large, long-winged raptor, is usually found near water. In flight, the *gull-like crooked wings* are distinctive. Sexes are almost alike in plumage, but females are somewhat larger than males. Cere and legs are dull blue-gray. Perched birds appear long-legged and have wingtips extending just beyond tail tip.
Adult: White head has a darkly speckled crown and *a wide, dark eye-line.* Iris color is bright yellow. Back and upperwing coverts are dark brown. *Underparts are white,* but females usually have some short dark streaks on breast, forming an incomplete necklace that is absent, or nearly so, on males. Underwings show gray flight feathers, *black carpal patches,* and greater underwing coverts that form dark lines between secondaries and white median and lesser coverts. Short tail appears dark with light bands from above but from below appears light with dark bands.
Immature: Similar to adult, but back has a "scaly" appearance because of white feather edges on back and upperwing coverts. Iris color is red to orange. Fledglings have a rufous wash on nape and upper breast that fades by fall. Secondaries appear paler than those of adults. Tail is like adult's but has a wide white terminal band.
Similar species: (1) **Eagles** (Pls. 18–20) are larger, usually have dark bodies, fly with wings flat, and lack black carpal patch (but see subadult Bald Eagle with eye stripe). (2) **Large gulls** are smaller, lack black carpal patch, and have shorter, pointed wings, longer necks and heads, and unbanded tails.
Flight: Active flight is with slow, steady, shallow wingbeats on somewhat flexible wings. The Osprey *soars and glides with the wings crooked in a gull-winged shape,* with wrists cocked for-

ward and held above body level and wingtips pointed down and back. It soars sometimes on flat wings. It hovers frequently while hunting over water.

Behavior: Ospreys are superb fishermen, catching prey with their feet after a spectacular feet-first dive, usually from a hover but sometimes from a glide. They usually enter the water completely. They are able to take off from the surface and, after becoming airborne, shake vigorously to remove water. Ospreys always carry captured fish head forward. Although they are almost exclusively fish-eaters, their diet has been reported to include a few other prey items, such as birds, turtles, and small mammals. They are usually found near water and leave it only during migration. Nest sites are usually in the top of dead trees, but nests are also placed on man-made structures such as duck blinds, channel markers, and navigation aids and even on telephone poles and small wooden docks. Ground nests have been reported, most frequently on islands. Adults vigorously defend their nests but seldom strike humans. The high, clear, whistled alarm call, repeated continuously, is distinctive.

Courtship flights by males are a series of undulating dives and climbs, usually performed while the bird is carrying a fish and calling constantly. Flying adults sometimes swoop down and drag their feet through the water, a practice that is

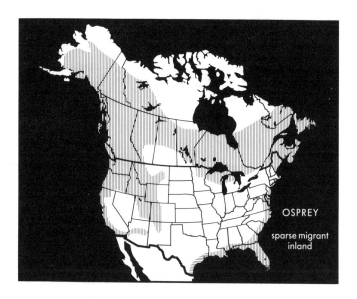

OSPREY

sparse migrant inland

thought to cool or clean their feet but may also be a displacement behavior.

According to much folklore, Bald Eagles rob Ospreys of fish, but they do so rarely in real life. The 2 species cohabit water areas surprisingly peacefully, with only an occasional agonistic encounter, initiated by either species.

Status and distribution: Ospreys are common in the main breeding areas of Florida, along the Atlantic Coast, especially the Chesapeake Bay, and in the Great Lakes; uncommon inland in w. Montana and Wyoming and n. Idaho and along the Pacific Coast south to Mexico; and fairly common from cen. Alaska to Newfoundland on lakes in the boreal forest. They are occasionally encountered on migration in the rest of the United States. The entire N. American population winters in the Caribbean, Cen. America, and n. S. America, except for a few remaining along the Gulf Coast and in s. California. S. Florida birds are resident. All one-year-olds remain south on the winter grounds during their second summer. Two-year-olds return north, some to natal areas, but do not breed. A good number of three-year-olds join the breeding population. Occasionally Ospreys are found at sea far from land. Distribution is worldwide.

Fine points: Ospreys' lack of a supraorbital ridge makes them look pigeon-headed.

Unusual plumages: Birds with a few white feathers replacing dark brown ones have been reported.

Subspecies: The N. American race is *P. h. carolinensis.*

Etymology: "Osprey" came from the Latin *ossifragus,* meaning "bone breaker," but this name probably referred originally to another species. *Pandion* was the name of two mythical kings of Athens; *haliaeetus* is from the Greek *hals* and *aetos,* meaning "sea" and "eagle."

Measurements:

Length: 53–66 cm (58); 21–26 in. (23)

Wingspread: 149–171 cm (160); 59–67 in. (63)

Weight: 1.0–1.8 kg (1.6); 2.2–3.9 lb (3.5)

Kites

Family Accipitridae

The 5 species of kites that occur in our area belong to 3 taxonomic subgroups. The first, characterized by the lack of the supraorbital ridge, a bony projection above the eye, includes the Hook-billed Kite and the Swallow-tailed Kite; the second, characterized by the fusion of the basal joint of the middle toe with the joint next to it, contains the Mississippi Kite and the Snail Kite; and the third, characterized by talons that are flat or rounded below, is represented by the Black-shouldered Kite.

For our purposes, however, it is better to separate the species into 2 types by wing shape: pointed-winged kites and paddle-winged kites. The more widespread species, the Swallow-tailed, Black-shouldered, and Mississippi kites, all have pointed wings. The limited-range species, the Snail and Hook-billed kites, have paddle-shaped wings.

The name "kite" comes from *cyta,* the Old English name of the 2 raptors in the genus *Milvus,* the Black and Red kites. The New World kites were so named because of their light, buoyant flight, which was similar to that of *Milvus* kites. The child's toy made of wood and paper was also named after the *Milvus* kites.

HOOK-BILLED KITE   Pl. 8; photos, p. 122
Chondrohierax uncinatus

Description: The medium-sized Hook-billed Kite of the Rio Grande valley of Texas has a *large hooked beak and paddle-shaped wings.* Sexes are similar in size but have different adult plumages. Plumage of immature is similar to that of adult female. There is a melanistic plumage, but it has not been reported from Texas. This species has unique *greenish lores,* with an orange spot at the top of each. Leg color is yellow-orange.

Adult male: Head is blue-gray. *Iris color is whitish.* Back and upperwing coverts are slate gray. Underparts are medium gray, with narrow white barring, which is not always visible. Underwings show heavily barred primaries and dark secondaries. Dark gray tail usually has 1 wide band visible, gray above and white below, but sometimes 2 bands are visible on widely spread tail.

Adult female: Head has dark blackish brown crown and nape, distinctive *buffy to rufous collar on hind neck,* rufous cheeks, and creamy throat finely barred rufous. *Iris color is whitish.* Back and upperwing coverts are dark gray-brown. Creamy underparts have coarse rufous barring. Underwing shows rufous

24

coverts and heavily barred primaries and outer secondaries. Inner primaries show a rufous wash. Dark brown tail has 2 wide bands, gray above and white below.

Immature: Similar to adult female in pattern, but iris color is medium brown, collar on hind neck is white, and dark brown back and upperwing covert feathers have buffy to rufous edgings. Inner primaries show a rufous wash. Barring on underparts is narrower and darker brown than that of adult female. Underwing shows creamy coverts and heavily barred primaries and outer secondaries. Dark tail has 3 narrow bands that are medium brown above and light below. Some immatures are less heavily barred below. Dark-morph individuals have not been recorded in Texas.

Dark-morph adult: Entire body and coverts are dark slate gray. Flight feathers are black. Black tail has 1 wide white band.

Dark-morph immature: Entire body and coverts are brownish black. Outer primaries are barred black and white. Dark tail has 2 wide white bands.

Similar species: (1) **Gray Hawk** adult (Pl. 8) is more finely barred below than adult male Hook-bill and has a dark eye, more pointed wings, and smaller beak, and its underwing appears paler and lacks boldly barred primaries. (2) **Red-shouldered Hawk** adult (Pl. 9) is very similar in flight, but its wings are narrower and have crescent-shaped wing panels. (3) **Broad-winged Hawk** (Pls. 10 and 13) lacks large hooked beak and collar on hind neck and has dark malar stripe. In flight its wings are pointed, not paddle-shaped. (4) **Roadside Hawk** (Pl. 8) also has pale eye and barred underparts but lacks large hooked beak and collar on hind neck and has solid or streaked breast. (5) **Cooper's Hawk** and **Sharp-shinned Hawk** (Pls. 6 and 7) also have heavily barred primaries but have shorter rounded wings and lack white bands in tail. (6) **Common Black Hawk** adult (Pl. 16) is larger, with broader wings and shorter tail; has a white area at base of outer primaries; lacks barred flight feathers; and is black (Hook-bill appears dark gray).

Flight: Active flight is with slow, languid wingbeats of bowed wings, with wrists slightly cocked up and wingtips down. Soars and glides with wings slightly bowed, usually not very high, often just above treetops.

Behavior: Hook-billed Kites eat tree snails, which they locate by hunting from a perch in thick forest. Their favorite places for snail extraction are marked by piles of snail shells on the ground below. The kites soar for a while on early morning thermals and have been reported soaring in a flock. Call is a distinctive rattling, uttered when the bird is disturbed near its nest and during courtship.

Status and distribution: Hook-billed Kites have recently moved into the Rio Grande valley of s. Texas between Falcon Dam and Brownsville. These breeding birds represent a recent northward range extension of this species for reasons unknown. The 10 to 20 resident pairs breed in mesquite woodlands, especially at Santa Ana National Wildlife Refuge and Bentsen State Park, and in riparian woodlands downstream from Falcon Dam.

Fine points: In parts of its range this species occurs in 2 forms that have beaks of different size, one being much larger. The reason for the difference is thought to be that they eat snails of different sizes. Texas birds all have small beaks. This kite lacks the bony projection above the eye (supraorbital ridge), so it has a pigeon-headed look.

Unusual plumages: No unusual plumages have been reported.

Subspecies: Texas birds belong to the Mexican race *C. u. acquilonsis.*

Etymology: *Chondrohierax* is from the Greek, *chondros,* meaning "composed of cartilage," and *hierakos,* "a falcon or hawk." *Uncinatus* is Latin for "hooked."

Measurements:
Length: 43–51 cm (46); 16–20 in. (18)
Wingspread: 87–98 cm (92); 34–38 in. (36)
Weight: 215–353 g (277); 8–12 oz (10)

SWALLOW-TAILED KITE   Pl. 4; photo, p. 122
Elanoides forficatus
Description: The Swallow-tailed Kite of the Southeast and Gulf Coast is unmistakable in shape and coloration: long, pointed wings, *bold black-and-white pattern below,* and *deeply forked black tail.* Sexes are alike in plumage, but females are larger. Plumage of immature is similar to that of adult. Cere color is dull blue-gray. Leg color is blue-gray.

Adult: Head, underparts, underwing coverts, undertail coverts, and a small area, usually covered, on lower back above rump are pure white. Iris color is red. Back, rump, upperwing coverts, flight feathers, and tail are black. (Black color is actually a blue-black and has a purplish iridescence in good light.) Some tertiaries are white and are visible as white spots on back of perched birds but are usually not visible in flight.

Immature: Similar to adult, but black areas have greenish, not purple, iridescence, and flight and tail feathers have narrow white tips, which usually wear off by spring. Forked tail is shorter than that of adult. Some individuals have fine black shaft streaks on head, nape, and breast feathers. Iris color is brown. Fledglings have rufous bloom on upper breast that rapidly fades.

Similar species: (1) Light-morph **Swainson's Hawk** (Pl. 12),

White-tailed Hawk (Pl. 17), and light-morph **Short-tailed Hawk** (Pl. 4) also have the same two-toned underwing pattern but have dark or mostly dark heads and lack the swallow-tail.
Flight: Swallow-tailed Kite, our most gracefully flying kite, spends much of its time hunting on the wing, riding air currents on steady wings, using its tail as a rudder. Active flight is with slow, flexible wingbeats. This kite soars and usually glides on flat wings but sometimes glides with wrists below body and wingtips up.
Behavior: Swallow-tailed Kites hunt a variety of prey, including flying insects, frogs, lizards, and snakes, all of which are deftly plucked from the ground or from tree branches. They also snatch bird nests, from which the nestlings are extracted. Interestingly enough, they have also been reported to eat fruit. Birds often eat in flight, bending their heads down to bite off a morsel from prey held in the feet. They drink on the wing in a swallow-like manner. During courtship flights, the pair fly in close formation, calling "kee kle klee." Swallow-tailed Kites are especially social and are often seen in groups of up to 50 individuals.
Status and distribution: The Swallow-tailed Kite's breeding range is now restricted to the e. Gulf Coast, most of Florida, and along the s. Atlantic Coast as far north as S. Carolina.

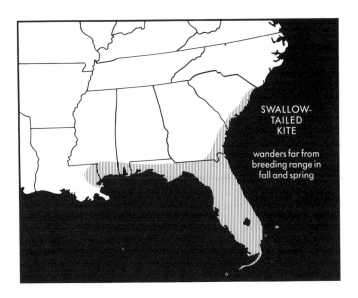

SWALLOW-
TAILED
KITE

wanders far from
breeding range in
fall and spring

Individuals are regularly seen on the Outer Banks of N. Carolina and along the Texas coast during migration. Swallow-tailed Kites prefer to breed in areas near water, marshes, and swamps and along river courses or lakes. During spring migration and after the breeding season in early fall, the birds wander far afield, ranging west to Colorado and north to Minnesota, New York, and s. Canada, and have been recorded casually in the Southwest. Most sightings are of single birds between April and September. The entire population leaves the United States by early September to winter in S. America, returning in early March to its breeding areas, occasionally as early as February in Florida.

Prior to 1900 this species bred over a much larger area of the e. United States, as far north as Minnesota.

Fine points: Swallow-tailed Kites lack the bony projection above the eye (supraorbital ridge) and so have a pigeon-headed appearance.

Unusual plumages: No unusual plumages have been reported for this species.

Subspecies: The N. American race is *E. f. forficatus.*

Etymology: *Elanoides* is from the Greek *elanos,* "a kite," and *oideos,* meaning "resembling." *Forficatus* in Latin means "deeply forked." The AOU has named this species the American Swallow-tailed Kite.

Measurements:

Length: 52–62 cm (58); 20–25 in. (22)

Wingspread: 119–136 cm (130); 47–54 in. (51)

Weight: 325–500 g (430); 11–18 oz (15)

BLACK-SHOULDERED KITE   Pl. 5; photos, p. 124
Elanus caeruleus

Description: The Black-shouldered Kite of California, s. Texas, and the Gulf Coast is a *whitish, falcon-shaped kite* and is *gull-like in color and flight.* Sexes are almost alike in plumage and size. Black upperwing coverts form the *black shoulder of perched bird.* On perched birds, wingtips reach tail tip. Cere and legs are yellow.

Adult: Large white head has a small black area in front of eye. Iris color is orange-red. Back is medium gray (males are paler), and underparts are white. Underwing shows dark primaries, gray secondaries, and white coverts, with *a small black carpal mark. Tail is white* except for light gray central feathers.

Immature: Similar to adult, but crown and nape are brown with white streaks. Iris color is light brown. Gray-brown back feathers have white edgings. Underparts are white with a rufous wash across breast, which fades shortly after fledging. Flight feathers have white tips, and tail has a dusky subterminal band. This is actually a juvenal plumage, and birds are in adult plumage within months after fledging.

Similar species: (1) **Mississippi Kite** (Pl. 5) has dark tail and darker body in all plumages. (2) **Northern Harrier** (Pl. 3) adult male is similar but has gray hood and white rump, and its underwing has black trailing edge and lacks black carpal mark. (3) **Falcons** lack white unbarred tail and black carpal mark. (4) **Gulls** have longer necks and shorter tails and lack black carpal mark on underwing.

Flight: Active flight is with light, steady wingbeats of cupped wings. The Black-shouldered Kite soars with the wings in a medium dihedral, with tips somewhat rounded. It glides with the wings in a modified dihedral. It hovers regularly, sometimes dangling the legs.

Behavior: The Black-shouldered Kite is in many ways like a large Kestrel. The preferred prey is almost exclusively rodents, which the kites hunt most often by hovering but also from high exposed perches. As the birds plunge after prey, they usually hold their wings fully stretched upward. Display flight of adult male is with fluttering wings held in a V above the body and is accompanied by calls. Adults have been observed talon-grappling. This kite is more active just after sunup and before sundown, and groups form communal night roosts of up to several hundred birds, mainly in fall and winter.

Status and distribution: Black-shouldered Kites are fairly common residents west of the Sierra Nevada and deserts of California and in s. Texas and are rare in Florida. They are

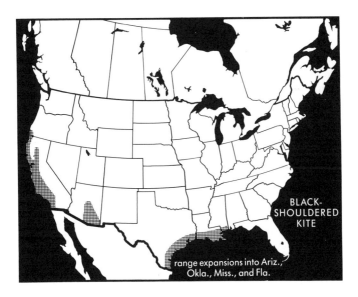

BLACK-SHOULDERED KITE

range expansions into Ariz., Okla., Miss., and Fla.

becoming more numerous and are expanding their breeding range into s. Oregon and Arizona, along the Gulf Coast of Louisiana and Mississippi, and into e. Oklahoma. This species is nonmigratory, but individuals wander far afield and have been recorded in New Mexico, Nevada, Washington, Georgia, and the Carolinas and as far north as Nebraska, Wisconsin, and Minnesota. They prefer grassland, savanna, marsh, and riparian habitats.

Fine points: Adults and immatures have light gray central tail feathers, and the tail appears light gray above on perched birds.

Unusual plumages: No unusual plumages have been described.

Subspecies: The race in N. America is *E. c. majusculus*.

Etymology: Formerly called the White-tailed Kite (*Elanus leucurus*), this species is now regarded by the AOU as conspecific with the Black-shouldered Kite of Eurasia and Africa. *Elanus* is Latin for "a kite"; *caeruleus* is Latin for "sky blue," the back color. *Leucurus* is Greek for "white-tailed."

Measurements:

Length: 36–41 cm (38); 14–16 in. (15)

Wingspread: 99–102 cm (101); 37–40 in. (39)

Weight: 305–361 g (330); 10–13 oz (11.6)

SNAIL KITE   Pl. 4; photos, pp. 122, 123

Rostrhamus sociabilis

Description: The Snail Kite of s. Florida is a paddle-winged kite with a *thin, deeply hooked beak*. Sexes are similar in size but have different adult plumages. Immature plumage is similar to that of adult female. Dark *tail has square tip* and *white base; tail coverts are white*. On perched birds, *wingtips extend beyond tail tip*.

Adult male: Entire body and wing coverts are slate gray, darker on back, head, and upperwing. Iris color is carmine, and *cere and face skin are bright red-orange*. Flight feathers are slaty black. *Legs are bright orange*.

Adult female: Head has dark brown crown and nape and distinctive face pattern of buffy superciliary line, dark eye-line, and buffy cheeks and throat. Cere and face skin are yellow to orange. Iris color is carmine. Back and upperwing coverts are dark brown, with rufous feather edges. Creamy underparts have heavy, irregular dark brown streaking. Underside of wing shows dark brown coverts and barred flight feathers, usually with a light patch at base of outer primaries. Legs are yellow-orange. Older females look somewhat like adult males, with a blackish head that lacks buffy superciliary line, a blackish nape and upper back, and mostly dark underparts with some whitish mottling, but they retain an overall brown cast.

Subadult male: After their second year immature males

gradually change into adult plumage, which is acquired after 3 years.

Immature: Difficult to separate from adult female, but iris color is dark brown, cere is whitish to pale yellow, top of head is streaked, underparts are usually less heavily streaked, and legs are yellow.

Similar species: The **Northern Harrier** (Pl. 3) has longer, narrower wings, flies in a more direct manner with wings in a dihedral, and has white uppertail coverts but no white on tail.

Flight: Active flight is with slow, *floppy wingbeats on cupped wings.* Glides on cupped wings. Soars with wings somewhat less cupped.

Behavior: Snail Kites are highly social and are often seen in large groups. They feed almost exclusively on snails of the genus *Pomacea,* which they deftly pluck from the water surface. They forage by flying slowly above the water with more or less continuous slow flapping at a height of 2 to 10 meters. When a snail is sighted, they brake, swoop down, and pluck the snail from the water with a foot. The snail is transferred from foot to beak in the air. Kites also hunt from perches and perch to extract snails from shells using their specialized beak. Hunting can take place at any time of day. Some prey items other than snails have been reported. Nesting and night roosting are usually colonial. During the middle of the day, Snail Kites often soar, sometimes high enough to be out of sight from the ground.

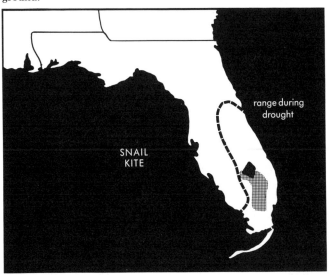

range during drought

SNAIL KITE

Status and distribution: Snail Kites are fairly common but local, restricted to freshwater marshes and other wet areas in s. Florida. During times of drought, however, they are found away from usual haunts. Prior to 1900, the species was recorded from a much larger area of Florida, but draining of surface water has reduced its range. The species is common and widespread in marshlands from s. Mexico, Cuba, and Cen. America south to n. Argentina.

Fine points: Subadult males (2–3 years old) are in transition to adult plumage and are grayer and uniformly darker than adult females. In times of plenty, kites may breed in immature plumage.

Unusual plumages: No unusual plumages have been reported.

Subspecies: The Florida birds form the race *R. s. plumbeus.*

Etymology: Called the Snail Kite because it preys almost exclusively on snails. *Rostrhamus* is from the Latin *rostrum,* "beak," and the Greek *hamus,* "hook"; *sociabilis* is Latin for "gregarious." The Florida race was formerly called the Everglade Kite.

Measurements:

Length: 41–47 cm (44); 16–19 in. (17)
Wingspread: 104–112 cm (108); 41–44 in. (42)
Weight: 340–520 g (427); 12–21 oz (15)

MISSISSIPPI KITE   Pl. 5; photos, pp. 124, 125
Ictinia mississippiensis

Description: The Mississippi Kite of the s. Great Plains, Mississippi valley, the Southeast, and recently the Southwest is a falcon-shaped kite. Sexes are similar in size and plumage. Immatures returning in the spring (subadults) have adultlike gray bodies but retain immature tail and flight feathers. *Outer primary is noticeably shorter than others. Wingtips of perched birds extend beyond tail tip.* Cere is greenish yellow to yellow. Legs are orange-yellow.

Adult: Head is white to pale gray, lighter on males than females, with a small area of black in front of and around eye. Iris color is scarlet. Back and upperwing coverts are slate gray. Whitish upperside of secondaries forms a *pale band on side of perched birds* and a *wide white band on inner trailing edge of upperwing* on flying birds. Underwing is slate gray with a short, narrow white band on inner trailing edge. Underparts are medium gray. *Flared tail* is black.

Subadult: Birds returning their first spring have molted into adultlike gray bodies but have *small, oval white blotches* both above and below, the result of retained immature feathers and whitish bases on first adult feathers. Flight feathers and tail are retained from immature plumage. Subadults lack whitish band on trailing edge of wing.

Immature: Head is dark brown, with fine whitish streaks and a *short buffy superciliary line.* Creamy throat is unstreaked. Iris color is dark brown. Back and upperwing coverts are dark brown with rufous feather edging. Underparts are creamy, with thick dark reddish brown streaking. Flight feathers have white tips. Underwing has mottled light brown coverts and somewhat darker flight feathers, often with a white area at base of outer primaries. Dark brown *tail has 3 incomplete light bands.*

Similar species: (1) **Black-shouldered Kite** (Pl. 5) has white body and tail and black carpal mark on underwing. (2) **Peregrine Falcon** (Pl. 23) is similarly shaped but has dark head and a malar stripe and lacks flared tail. Peregrine's flight is more powerful and purposeful, not leisurely and buoyant.

Flight: Active flight is leisurely, on flexible wings. Flight is light, buoyant, and effortless. Mississippi Kites spend considerable time soaring and gliding on flat wings, rarely flapping. Wingtips often curl up during soaring.

Behavior: Mississippi Kites capture their prey, mainly insects, on the wing. Prey is often eaten in flight. The kites are gregarious and often breed in small colonies of up to 20 pairs and hunt in small flocks. Groups of up to several hundred individuals are encountered in migrating flocks and night roosts. When not on the wing, birds perch inconspicuously for hours. Adults may be aggressive in their nest defense, and attacks on

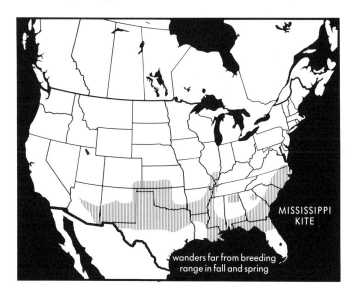

MISSISSIPPI KITE

wanders far from breeding range in fall and spring

humans have been reported. Usually silent, around the nest they utter a double-syllable call.

Status and distribution: The numbers and range of the Mississippi Kite are increasing. The main breeding range is on the s. Great Plains north to cen. Kansas and west to se. Colorado, along the s. Mississippi River north to s. Illinois, along the Gulf coast into n. Florida, and along the s. Atlantic coast north to N. Carolina. Isolated breeding colonies exist in Arizona and New Mexico. On the Great Plains, Mississippi Kites prefer parks and shelterbelts; in the Southeast, Southwest, and along the Mississippi River they prefer to nest in riparian forests.

The entire population is migratory, retiring to S. America in the fall and not returning until spring. The birds are seen on migration in numbers in s. Texas in late August and early September. Individuals wander far outside the breeding area in late spring and late summer and are reported from New York, Wisconsin, and Minnesota as well as from California.

Fine points: The relatively short outer primary extends only four-fifths to wingtip, a character that can be seen on a flying bird. Among perched falcons, only the Peregrine's wingtips reach its tail tip. A few immatures have solid, unbanded dark brown tails.

Unusual plumages: No unusual plumages have been described.

Subspecies: Monotypic.

Etymology: "Mississippi" and *mississippiensis* refer to the state in which the type specimen was collected by Wilson. *Ictinia* is from Greek *iktinos,* meaning "a kite." Species name was originally spelled *misisippiensis,* a printer's error. This form was used until the AOU corrected it in 1976.

Measurements:

Length: 31–37 cm (35); 12–15 in. (14)

Wingspread: 75–83 cm (78); 29–33 in. (31)

Weight: 240–372 g (278); 8–13 oz (10)

Harriers

Genus *Circus*

Circus, a worldwide genus of 10 species, is represented in North America by a single species, the Northern Harrier. Harriers are slender, medium-sized, long-legged, and long-tailed raptors. They have an owl-like facial disk and, in most species, a conspicuous white patch on the uppertail coverts. Adult males and females have different plumages; males are usually gray, females brown. Immatures are similar to adult females in plumage. Harriers have a distinctive hunting flight and are active throughout the day but most often at dawn and dusk.

NORTHERN HARRIER   Pl. 3; photos, p. 126
Circus cyaneus

Description: The widespread Northern Harrier is a slim-bodied raptor with long legs, long wings, and a long tail. In all plumages it has a *white patch on the uppertail coverts* and its *dark head appears hooded.* Sexes have different adult plumages but nearly identical immature plumages. Females are noticeably larger than males. This species has an owl-like facial disk. In spring, birds of all plumages are paler. Cere is greenish yellow to yellow. Legs are orange-yellow. On perched birds, wingtips do not reach tail tip.

Adult male: Head is medium gray. Iris color is bright yellow. Back and upperwing coverts are darker gray. Gray of head extends onto upper breast so that head appears hooded. Rest of underparts are white, with rufous spotting on breast, sometimes heavy and extending onto belly. Underwings are white, except for black tips of outer primaries and dark band formed by black tips of secondaries. Leg feathers and undertail coverts are white, often covered with small rufous spots. *Long tail* is medium gray above and whitish below and is indistinctly banded.

Adult female: Head, back, and upperwing coverts are dark brown, with tawny mottling on head and upperwing coverts. Iris color is brown to yellow (it takes from 2 to 6 years to become completely yellow). Underwings show heavily barred flight feathers and *secondaries and coverts form a dark patch on each wing.* Underparts are white to cream, completely marked with dark brown streaks. Leg feathers and undertail coverts are white with dark brown streaks. *Long tail* is marked with light and dark brown bands of equal width, with central pair of feathers noticeably darker.

Immature: Similar to adult female but appears darker, with

less tawny mottling on head and upperwing coverts. Iris color
of female is chocolate brown, while that of male is light gray or
light gray-brown. Underparts in fall are dark rufous but fade
nearly to white by spring and have dark streaking restricted to
upper breast. Underwing pattern is like that of adult female
but with even *darker secondary patch.* Leg feathers and undertail coverts are unmarked rufous. Tail is like that of adult female.

Similar species: (1) **Rough-legged Hawk** (Pl. 10) light
morph has white at base of tail, not on uppertail coverts, and a
dark carpal patch on underwing. (2) **Turkey Vulture** (Pl. 1)
also flies with wings in a dihedral but is larger, has a dark
body, and lacks white uppertail coverts. (3) **Black-shouldered
Kite** (Pl. 5) resembles adult male Harrier but has small black
carpal mark on underwing and black shoulder and lacks gray
hood, black trailing edge of wing, and white undertail coverts.
(4) **Red-shouldered Hawk** adult (Pl. 9) appears rufous-col-
ored, similar to brown Harriers, when soaring or gliding at
heights but has crescent-shaped wing panels and lacks dark
secondary patches.

Flight: This species' slow, quartering, *harrying flight, with
wings held in a strong dihedral,* is distinctive. Active flight is
with slow wingbeats of flexible wings. Harriers soar usually
with wings in a slight dihedral but also on flat wings; they
appear somewhat buteo-like when soaring and gliding at high
altitudes. A harrier glides with its wings in a modified dihedral
but hunts with its wings in a strong dihedral.

Behavior: Northern Harriers hunt exclusively with their distinctive quartering flight, flying low over the ground and
pouncing quickly when prey is spotted. They occur mainly in
open fields, meadows, grasslands, prairies, and marshes but
usually breed only in wetter habitats. Males prey more on
birds, while females take more mammals. This raptor has been
reported to drown waterfowl. Recent studies have shown that
Northern Harriers can locate prey by sound almost as well as
owls can, suggesting an explanation for the facial disk.

When soaring and quartering in strong winds, harriers rock
somewhat like a Turkey Vulture. Courtship flights of males are
spectacular, involving steep dives and climbs and a series of
rapid loops, with the bird upside down at the top of each loop.

The Northern Harrier is the only N. American raptor that is
regularly polygynous. One male may mate with as many as 3
females. Nest is placed on ground. Harriers usually perch on
the ground but will use fenceposts or other low perches and
occasionally trees. In winter, communal ground roosts of from
a few birds to hundreds are regular, sometimes in company
with Short-eared Owls.

Status and distribution: Northern Harriers are fairly com-

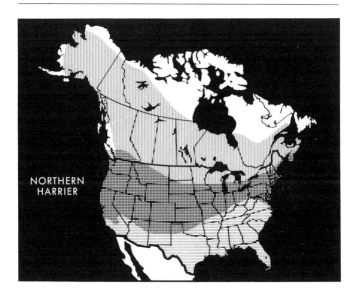

NORTHERN
HARRIER

mon, breeding from midlatitudes of the United States north to
the boreal forests of Canada and Alaska. Northern populations
are migratory and in winter are found throughout the s.
United States.

Fine points: Immature's iris color is dimorphic — chocolate
brown in females, gray to gray-brown in males.

Unusual plumages: Albinism and at least one case of melanism have been reported for the Eurasian race.

Subspecies: The N. American race is *C. c. hudsonius.*

Etymology: "Harrier" comes from the Old English *hergian,*
meaning "to harass by hostile attacks." *Circus* is from the
Greek *kirkos,* "circle," from the bird's habit of flying in circles;
cyaneus comes from Greek *kyaneous,* "dark blue," for male's
back color. This species was formerly called the Marsh Hawk.

Measurements:

Length: Male 41–45 cm (43); 16–18 in. (17)
       Female 45–50 cm (48); 18–20 in. (19)

Wingspread: Male 97–109 cm (103); 38–43 in. (41)
       Female 111–122 cm (116); 43–48 in. (46)

Weight: Male 290–390 g (346); 10–14 oz (12)
       Female 390–600 g (496); 14–21 oz (18)

Accipiters

Genus *Accipiter*

Accipiters are short-winged, long-tailed, forest-dwelling raptors. Three species occur in N. America. They are aggressive, capable of rapid acceleration, and reckless in pursuit of their prey. Because of their preference for forest habitat, especially when nesting, accipiters are less visible than other raptors. During migration they may be conspicuous, however, especially at raptor concentration locations such as Cape May Point, New Jersey; Duluth, Minnesota; and Hawk Mountain, Pennsylvania. All 3 species soar regularly, usually for a while every day. They also frequent bird feeders to try to capture songbirds.

Sexual dimorphism, with females much larger than males, is pronounced in this genus. Contrary to many published reports, there is no size overlap between species (but see species accounts for Sharp-shinned and Cooper's hawks). Nevertheless, since size is hard to judge in the field and they are similar in plumage and shape, accipiters are difficult, though not impossible, to identify in the field.

Accipiter is Latin for "bird of prey." It probably derives from *accipere,* "to take," but also possibly from the Greek *aci,* "swift," and *pteron,* "wing." The word "hawk" comes from the old Teutonic root *haf* or *hab,* meaning "to seize." "Hawk" properly refers only to raptors in this genus but in common usage is applied to all diurnal raptors except eagles, vultures, falcons, and kites.

SHARP-SHINNED HAWK   **Pls. 6 and 7;**
Accipiter striatus   **photos, pp. 127–129**
Description: The Sharp-shinned Hawk, our smallest accipiter, occurs primarily in the northern and mountain forests but is widespread, particularly in winter. Sexes are almost alike in plumage, with females noticeably larger than males. On gliding birds, *head does not project much beyond wrists. Eye is centrally placed on side of small, rounded head.* Outer tail feathers are same length, or almost so, as central pair. *Tail tip is squarish,* with a *thin white terminal band,* and is often notched. Cere is yellow-green to yellow. Sticklike legs are yellow. On perched birds, wingtips reach less than halfway to tail tip.
Adult: *Crown is same color or slightly darker than blue-gray back,* lacking line of contrast with nape. Cheeks are rufous. Iris color is orange to red. Back and upperwing coverts are blue-

38

gray, browner on females. White underparts are finely barred rufous. Flight feathers are heavily barred below. Tail has bands of dark and light brown of equal width and a thin white tip (terminal band) but outer feather on each side has dark bands that are narrower than light ones. Undertail coverts are white.

Immature: Head is dark brown with narrow pale superciliary line. *Back and upperwing coverts are dark brown* with thin rufous feather edging but *with little or no white mottling.* Iris color is yellow. Underparts are white to light cream with *thick reddish brown streaking, becoming thicker and more barred on belly;* sometimes, however, streaking is thin and dark brown, more commonly on males. Undertail coverts are white. Flight feathers and tail are almost like those of adult.

Similar species: (1) **Cooper's Hawk** (Pls. 6 and 7) appears very similar but is larger and more robust; has thicker legs; has a longer, more rounded tail with a wide white terminal band; and has the eye placed farther forward on a squarish head. Its head projects far beyond wrists when gliding, and it often soars with its wings in a dihedral. Adult's crown is darker than nape and back, with a noticeable line of contrast. Immature's underparts are more finely streaked, with less marking on belly; its back has more whitish mottling and cheeks may be tawny (brown on immature Sharpies). (2) **Merlin** (Pl. 22) is also a small dark raptor but has larger, squarish head; dark eyes; pointed wings; and dark tail with thin light bands.

Flight: Active flight is light and buoyant, with rapid, light wingbeats. Soars and glides on level wings, with wrists slightly forward.

Behavior: This shy and retiring species hunts from an inconspicuous perch in wooded areas for small birds, almost its only prey, which are captured after a brief, rapid chase. Hawks are fond of catching birds at songbird feeders and often collide with picture windows. They also hunt by coursing over or through the woods, hoping to surprise their victims. Sharp-shinned Hawks soar almost every day, usually for a while in the morning. On migration they move by active flight until thermals form, thereafter soaring, often up to an altitude of thousands of feet. They almost never raise their hackles, and so their head appears rounded.

Status and distribution: Sharp-shinned Hawks are common in forests throughout n. N. America, moving farther south in winter. The main breeding areas are western mountain and northern forests, but Sharp-shins breed in low densities in most areas except the Deep South, the Great Plains, and deserts. They are seen in greatest numbers during migration. Northern birds move as far south as Cen. America and the Florida Keys during winter.

SHARP-
SHINNED
HAWK

Fine points: Cooper's and Sharp-shinned hawks do not over-lap in size, but western Cooper's Hawks are smaller than east-ern ones. In the Southwest there is a slight overlap in the wing-chord measurements between small male Cooper's and large female Sharpies but no overlap in weight or overall length.

Unusual plumages: An individual with white wings has been reported, and dilute-plumage specimens exist, with cream color replacing dark brown but with rufous color retained.

Subspecies: Two races occur north of Mexico, *A. s. perobscurus* on the Queen Charlotte Islands and *A. s. velox* on the con-tinent south to Mexico.

Etymology: "Sharp-shinned" refers to the raised ridge on the inside front of the tarsus (not actually a "shin"). *Striatus* is Latin for "striped," a reference to the underparts of the imma-ture, which was described prior to the adult.

Measurements:

Length: Male 24–27 cm (26); 9–11 in. (10)
       Female 29–34 cm (31); 11–13 in. (12)

Wingspread: Male 53–56 cm (54); 20–22 in. (21)
       Female 58–65 cm (62); 23–26 in. (25)

Weight: Male 87–114 g (101); 3–4 oz (3.6)
       Female 150–218 g (177); 5–8 oz (6)

COOPER'S HAWK   **Pls. 6 and 7; photos, pp. 127–129**
Accipiter cooperii
Description: The robust Cooper's Hawk, the medium-sized accipiter, has a southerly distribution. Sexes are almost alike in plumage, but females are noticeably larger than males. On gliding birds, *head projects far beyond wrists*. Sometimes soars with wings in dihedral. The *eye is placed well forward on the side of large, squarish head*. Outer tail feathers are progressively shorter than central pair. *Tail tip is rounded*, with a *broad white terminal band*. Cere is yellow-green to yellow. Legs are yellow. On perched birds, wingtips reach less than halfway to tail tip.
Adult: *Crown is dark blue-gray* and *contrasts with lighter-colored nape and back*. Iris color is red to orange. Cheeks are rufous. Back and upperwing coverts are blue-gray, with a brownish cast on females. White underparts are barred rufous. Flight feathers are heavily barred below. Undertail coverts are white. Long tail has bands of dark and light brown of equal width, with a broad white terminal band; dark bands are narrower than light ones on each outer feather.
Immature: Head is dark brown and appears hooded. Many individuals have tawny wash on sides of head. On a few individuals there is a pale superciliary line. Iris color is greenish yellow. *Back and upperwing coverts are medium brown* with *some white mottling and rufous feather edging*. Underparts are white with *fine dark brown streaking, becoming sparse or absent on belly*. Undertail coverts are clear white. Flight feathers and tail are similar to those of adult.
Similar species: (1) **Sharp-shinned Hawk** (Pls. 6 and 7) appears very similar but has a relatively shorter, squared-off tail with a narrow, not wide, white terminal band. Sharpie's head is smaller and more rounded, with eye centrally placed. Head barely projects beyond wrists when gliding. Sharpie is smaller and flies with quicker wingbeats and more buoyant flight. Adult's crown color does not contrast with nape and back color. Immature has darker, less mottled back and thicker, more rufous streaking on underparts, particularly on belly. (2) **Goshawk** immature (Pl. 7) is similar but is larger and has relatively longer and more tapered wings, more heavily streaked underparts, streaked undertail coverts, and paler, more mottled back. Adult Gos (Pl. 6) has light blue-gray breast. (3) **Broad-winged Hawk** (Pl. 10) is similarly colored but has shorter tail with bands of dark and light brown of unequal width, pointed wings, and dark malar stripes and lacks heavily barred underwings. (4) **Red-shouldered Hawk** (Pl. 9) is accipiter-like but has wings shaped like those of a buteo, with crescent-shaped panels and dark malar stripes, and its tail has dark and light bands of unequal width.

Flight: Active flight is with stiff, strong wingbeats. Glides with wings level, wrists cocked forward. Soars with wings sometimes level, sometimes in a slight dihedral, and with leading edge of the wing straighter and more perpendicular to the body than on other accipiters.

Behavior: Cooper's Hawks are mainly still hunters, perching inconspicuously in woods, waiting to attack their prey at an opportune moment. In the West they perch more in the open. They hunt, on occasion, by flying through or over woodlands or along fence rows to surprise potential prey and pursue prey into dense cover, sometimes on foot. The preferred prey of Cooper's Hawks is birds, but many small mammals are taken and, in the West, lizards. Although they are usually secretive, some birds, particularly in the West, will vigorously and vociferously defend their nests. Like most accipiters, this species will soar for a short while almost every day and migrates mostly by soaring. When perched, the birds often raise their hackles, so that the head appears larger and squarish.

Status and distribution: Cooper's Hawks are fairly common to uncommon over most of their breeding range, which covers most of the United States and s. Canada, except for s. Florida and much of the n. Great Plains. Northern birds are migratory, moving as far south as Mexico and s. Florida. In the West they occur at lower elevations than other accipiters and are fairly common in riparian areas.

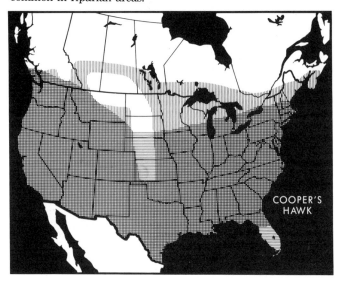

COOPER'S
HAWK

Fine points: Western Cooper's Hawks are overall smaller than eastern ones, thus closer in size to Sharp-shinned Hawks, but there is still no overlap in length or weight.

Unusual plumages: Several dilute-plumage specimens exist, on which dark brown color is replaced by cream and rufous color is retained.

Subspecies: Monotypic.

Etymology: "Cooper's" and *cooperii* after William Cooper, New York ornithologist.

Measurements:
Length: Male 37–41 cm (39); 14–16 in. (15)
        Female 42–47 cm (45); 16–19 in. (18)
Wingspread: Male 70–77 cm (73); 28–30 in. (29)
        Female 79–87 cm (84); 31–34 in. (33)
Weight: Male 302–402 g (341); 10–14 oz (12)
        Female 479–678 g (528); 17–24 oz (19)

NORTHERN GOSHAWK
Accipiter gentilis

Pls. 6 and 7;
photos, pp. 127–129

Description: The Northern Goshawk, our largest accipiter, is found primarily in northern and mountain forests. Sexes are almost alike in plumage, but females are noticeably larger than males. *Tapered wings are long* for an accipiter. Tip of folded tail is wedge-shaped. Cere is greenish yellow. Legs are yellow. On perched birds, wingtips extend halfway to tail tip.

Adult: Head is black with a *thick white superciliary line.* Iris color is deep red to mahogany. Back and upperwing coverts are slate blue; *underparts are pale blue-gray,* with fine black barring and some vertical black streaking. Females usually have coarser, darker barring and more vertical black streaking. Flight feathers are lightly barred below. Tail is dark gray, with 3 or 4 indistinct dark bands. Undertail coverts are white and fluffy.

Subadult: First adult plumage is essentially like that of adult but with more streaking and heavier barring on underparts. Iris color is orange to red. Some brown immature feathers are retained on upperwing coverts, sometimes for 2 years.

Immature: Brown head usually has a pale superciliary line. (**Note:** Many immature Red-shouldered, Broad-winged, and Cooper's hawks also have a pale superciliary line, so this field mark is not diagnostic for immature Goshawk.) Iris color is pale green-yellow, yellow, or light brown. Brown *back and upperwing coverts have extensive tawny and white mottling. Underparts* are cream-colored, sometimes white, with *thick blackish brown streaks. Undertail coverts are streaked* (a few individuals have clear undertail coverts) and are not fluffy like adult's. Underwing shows flight feathers boldly barred with dark brown. Tail has wavy, dark and light brown bands of equal width, with *thin white highlights* at many of the boundaries of these bands, and has a wide white terminal band. Dark bands of each outer feather are narrower than light ones. Wavy tail bands result in a zigzag pattern (however, the tails of some Cooper's and Sharp-shinned hawks show a zigzag pattern on the underside).

Similar species: (1) **Cooper's Hawk** immature (Pl. 7) is similar but has relatively shorter wings and longer tail, darker and less mottled back, tail lacking white highlights, and more lightly streaked belly. Immature Cooper's almost always has clear, unmarked undertail coverts and often has tawny-colored neck. Adult Cooper's (Pl. 6) has reddish breast. (2) **Red-shouldered Hawk** (Pl. 9) immature may also have pale superciliary line but has crescent-shaped wing panels, dark malar stripe, and tail bands of unequal width. (3) **Broad-winged Hawk** (Pl. 10) immature may also have pale superciliary line but has pointed wings, relatively unmarked underwings, dark malar stripe, and light and dark tail bands of unequal width. (4) **Gyrfalcon** (Pl. 23) also has a heavy flight but has two-toned underwing, lacks adult Goshawk's dark hood and pale superciliary line, and lacks immature Goshawk's tail bands of equal width. On perched Gyrs, wingtips extend more than halfway to tail tip. (5) **Buteos** have shorter tails and lack tapered wings and heavily barred undersides of flight feathers. On perched buzzards, wingtips extend almost to tail tip.

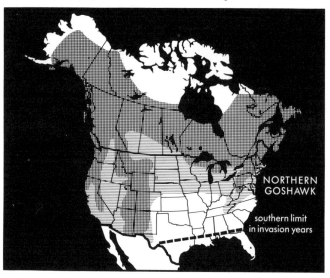

NORTHERN GOSHAWK

southern limit in invasion years

Flight: Active flight is strong, with powerful, stiff wingbeats. The wings may appear rather pointed in active flight. Soars on level wings, appearing much like a buteo. Glides with wings level and wrists cocked somewhat forward.

Behavior: Goshawks are primarily forest dwellers. They prey on medium to large mammals and birds and hunt from a perch or while flying through the forest. They also pursue prey on the ground. Goshawks courageously defend the nest area and will even strike humans, usually on the head or back. Like most accipiters, the Goshawk soars periodically, almost every day, usually in the morning.

Status and distribution: Goshawks are fairly common on their breeding grounds in the northern forests and in the forested mts. of the West. Every 9 to 11 years during the fall and winter, there are periodic movements of this species southward as far as the Gulf of Mexico. A few immatures migrate south of the breeding range every winter or, in the West, to a lower elevation.

Fine points: Immature Goshawks usually have a hint of a facial disk, and 1 or 2 tawny wingbars are visible on perched birds. Goshawk's short tarsus is feathered halfway to feet (only one-third in Cooper's Hawk).

Unusual plumages: Partial albinism, with some white feathers, has been reported.

Subspecies: The 3 N. American races are *A. g. langi* on islands off British Columbia, *A. g. apache* in the mountains of s. Arizona, and *A. g. atricapillus* throughout the rest of the continent.

Etymology: "Goshawk" was derived from the Anglo-Saxon words *gos* for goose and *havoc* for hawk—hence, a hawk that captures geese. *Gentilis* is Latin for "noble." It was named during the era when only the nobility could fly this bird in falconry.

Measurements:

Length: Male 46–51 cm (49); 18–20 in. (19)
       Female 53–62 cm (58); 21–24 in. (23)
Wingspread: Male 98–104 cm (101); 38–41 in. (39)
       Female 105–115 cm (108); 41–45 in. (43)
Weight: Male 677–1014 g (816); 24–36 oz (29)
       Female 758–1214 g (1059); 26–43 oz (37)

Buteoines

Family Accipitridae

The buzzards of the genus *Buteo* and closely related genera are all characterized by robust bodies; long, broad wings; and tails of short to medium length. All soar regularly, and many hover. Underwing and undertail patterns, wing shape, and sometimes behavior help in their field identification. Many species have a dark or melanistic morph, and some occur only in the dark morph. Ten species of *Buteo* and 2 closely related species occur in our area. Six species are widespread throughout e. or w. N. America or both; the other 4 and the 2 related species breed on our southern periphery.

As in most raptor species, the tails of immature buzzards are noticeably longer than those of adults, but the wings are narrower than those of adults in most *Buteo* species.

Buteo is Latin for "a kind of hawk or falcon." "Buzzard" is the proper name for these raptors. It comes from the same Latin root as *Buteo* through Old French and Old English. Early settlers of this continent mistakenly applied the name to vultures.

COMMON BLACK HAWK
Buteogallus anthracinus

Pl. 16; photos, p. 130

Description: The Common Black Hawk of the Southwest is a large, dark buteoine with *wide wings* and long legs. Sexes are alike in plumage; females are larger than males, with much size overlap. Immatures have a different plumage from that of adults and have longer tails and narrower wings. On perched birds, adult's wingtips almost reach tail tip, while immature's wingtips fall somewhat short of tail tip.

Adult: Head, body, and wing coverts are *coal black*. Iris color is dark brown. Underwing is black except for *small white mark at base of outer 2 or 3 primaries*. *Black tail has 1 wide white band* and a thin white terminal band and appears short because of wide wings. Cere, legs, and *face skin are bright orange-yellow*.

Immature: Top of head is dark brown with buffy streaking. *Strong face pattern* is composed of buffy superciliary line, dark eye-line, buffy cheek, and dark malar stripe. Iris color is medium brown. Back is dark brown and upperwing coverts are dark brown, with white and buffy feather edging. Dark brown *upperwings show buffy primary patches* in flight. Underparts are buffy, with *irregular black spotting and streaking,* often heavier and forming a dark patch on sides of upper breast. Underwing is buffy, with a black wrist comma. Buffy undertail coverts have black barring. *White tail has irregular narrow black banding* and a wide, black terminal band. Leg feathers are buffy with fine black barring. Cere is greenish yellow. Legs are yellow.

Similar species: (1) **Zone-tailed Hawk** (Pl. 16) adult perched may also show 1 white tail band on undertail, but band on uppertail is gray. It also has black, not yellow, face skin and shows barring on fore edge of folded wing. In flight, Zone-tail has more slender wings, which are two-toned below. (2) **Dark-morph buteos** (Pls. 13–15 and 26) have two-toned underwings and lack white tail band. (3) **Black Vulture** (Pl. 1) has larger white patches on underwing and lacks white tail band.

Flight: Active flight is with medium slow, strong wingbeats. Soars on flat wings, with tail completely fanned. Glides on flat wings.

Behavior: Common Black Hawks are closely associated with aquatic habitats. They prey chiefly on fish, frogs, crayfish, and reptiles and occasionally on birds and mammals. They are still hunters, sitting quietly on a perch, often low, overlooking a stream or small river, searching for prey. They often wade into shallow water and chase after prey on foot. Calls of this vocal species are a series of staccato whistled notes, very different from calls of other buteoines.

The display flight of the male is a series of undulating climbs and dives, often performed while the bird is dangling its feet and calling. The pair often fly together, with fluttering wings held in a strong dihedral.

Status and distribution: Black Hawks are uncommon but local during the breeding season in riparian areas of e., cen., and s.-cen. Arizona, w. New Mexico, and w. Texas and are rare in s. Utah. There are reports of stragglers in Nevada, California, and s. Florida (in the latter case, probably from Cuba) and casual records elsewhere (Minnesota). Most birds migrate south for winter, but there are winter records from s. Texas and Arizona.

Fine points: White mark on underside at base of outer primaries is most visible when adults are flying away from the observer and may be faint or absent.

Unusual plumages: Partial albinism has been reported from S. America for this species, in one case an immature with some white, some soft brown, and some normal-colored feathers. Adult and immature specimens in dilute plumage have been collected in Panama.

Subspecies: *B. a. anthracinus* is the race in the Southwest.

Etymology: *Buteogallus* is from the Latin *buteo* and *gallus,* "chicken" — literally "chicken hawk" — while *anthracinus* means "coal black" in Latin.

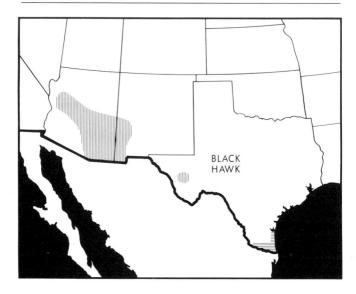

Measurements:
Length: 51–56 cm (54); 20–22 in. (21)
Wingspread: 102–128 cm (117); 40–50 in. (46)
Weight: 630–1300 g (950); 1.4–2.9 lb (2.1)

HARRIS' HAWK   Pl. 17; photos, p. 131
Parabuteo unicinctus
Description: Harris' Hawk, a long-legged, long-tailed, dark
buteoine, inhabits the Southwest deserts. Its wings appear
somewhat paddle-shaped. Immature's plumage is similar to
that of adult; both are dark and have *chestnut thighs and
shoulder patches* and white rumps. Sexes are alike in plumage,
but females are noticeably larger. On perched birds, wingtips
reach only halfway down tail. Iris color is dark brown. Cere,
lores, and legs are orange-yellow.
Adult: Head, body, and greater upperwing coverts are dark
brown. Median and lesser upperwing coverts form a *chestnut
shoulder patch* on perched birds. *Underwing shows chestnut
coverts* and dark gray flight feathers. Greater uppertail and
undertail coverts are white. *Black tail has wide white base and
a fairly wide white terminal band.*
Immature: Similar to adult, but dark underparts are streaked
white, heavier on belly. *Underwing shows chestnut coverts,*
finely barred gray secondaries, and whitish primaries with

dark tips. Chestnut thighs are barred with white. Tail appears dark brown with white base from above but appears light gray with fine dark bands below.

Similar species: (1) **Dark-morph buteos** (Pls. 13–15 and 26) lack chestnut thighs and shoulder patches and white on both tail coverts and tail. (2) **Snail Kite** (Pl. 4) adult male is similar in plumage and shape but lacks chestnut patches and has distinctive thin hooked beak. (Note that its Florida range does not overlap with that of Harris' Hawk.)

Flight: Active flight is more energetic than that of buteos, with quick, shallow wingbeats of cupped wings. Glides on cupped wings, with wrists above body and wingtips pointed down. Soars on flat wings.

Behavior: Polyandry, the mating of 2 males with 1 female, is reported for Harris' Hawks and is apparently more frequent in Arizona than in Texas. Harris' Hawks prey mainly on mammals and birds, but lizards and insects are also eaten. They hunt on the wing and from perches, but hovering, a characteristic of some buteos, is not common. Harris' Hawks perch more horizontally than other raptors and are often seen in groups of up to a dozen individuals, especially in winter. Cooperative hunting has been reported. Vocalization most often heard is alarm call, rendered as "iirrr."

Status and distribution: Harris' Hawks are fairly common in

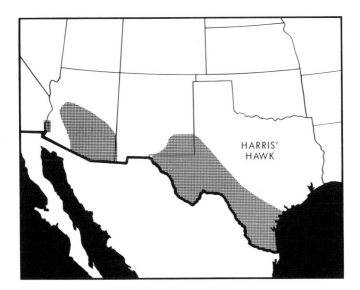

HARRIS' HAWK

coastal scrub prairies of s. Texas and mesquite deserts of sw. Texas and se. New Mexico, and mesquite and saguaro–palo verde deserts of s. and cen. Arizona. They formerly bred in se. California along the Colorado River, where reintroduction efforts have resulted in a few nesting pairs. There is a breeding record for Kansas. The species has been casually reported in Nevada, Utah, and Oklahoma.

Captive-bred Harris' Hawks are popular in falconry, and escapees can be expected almost anywhere in our area.

Fine points: The belly of some immatures is mostly white with some dark streaking, but immatures are almost always dark-breasted, usually with a sharp dividing line between dark breast and lighter belly.

Unusual plumages: No unusual plumages have been described.

Subspecies: The race in the Southwest is *P. u. harrisi.*

Etymology: Named after Edward Harris, a friend of Audubon. *Parabuteo* is from the Greek *para,* "beside or near," hence, "similar to *buteo.*" *Unicinctus* is from Latin *uni,* "once," and *cinctus,* "girdled," a reference to the white band at base of tail. This species is also called the Bay-winged Hawk.

Measurements:
Length: 46–59 cm (52); 18–23 in. (20)
Wingspread: 103–119 cm (108); 40–47 in. (43)
Weight: 568–1203 g (890); 1.3–2.6 lb (2.0)

GRAY HAWK *Buteo nitidus*　　　　**Pl. 8; photos, p. 132**

Description: The Gray Hawk of Arizona and s. Texas is a small, long-tailed, accipiter-like buteo. Sexes are alike in plumage; females are noticeably larger. *Greater uppertail coverts form a white U above base of tail.* Wingtips reach halfway to tail tip on perched birds. Leg color is yellow.

Adult: Head, back, and upperwing coverts are medium gray. Iris color is dark brown; cere is bright yellow. *Underparts are finely barred with white and medium gray.* Whitish underwing is lightly barred gray. Undertail coverts are white. Black tail has 2 white bands, 1 wide and 1 narrow.

Immature: Top of head, back, and upperwing coverts are dark brown, with much rufous edging on coverts. *Striking face pattern* consists of creamy superciliary line, dark eye-line, creamy cheek and throat, and dark malar stripe. Iris color is medium brown; cere is yellow. Creamy to white underparts are heavily streaked with dark brown. Underwings appear whitish. *Creamy leg feathers are barred dark brown. Long, medium brown tail has 5 or more dark brown bands,* subterminal widest.

Similar species: (1) **Broad-winged Hawk** (Pl. 10) immature is similar but has more pointed wings; has streaked, not barred, leg feathers; has 4 or fewer dark bands in tail; and lacks strong face pattern and white U above base of tail. Adult Broad-wing has rufous breast. (2) **Accipiter** (Pls. 6 and 7) immatures have 4 or fewer dark and light tail bands of equal width and more boldly marked flight feathers below and lack white U above tail base. (3) **Hook-billed Kite** (Pl. 8) adult male is similar to Gray Hawk adult but has white eyes and paddle-shaped wings that appear dark below.

Flight: Active flight is rapid and accipiter-like, with quick wingbeats followed by short glides on flat wings. This hawk soars on flat wings, although usually at a lower altitude than do other buteos. Its courtship flights are similar to those of other buteos.

Behavior: Gray Hawks are dashing raptors. Their relatively short wings and long tail allow them to maneuver in dense cover in pursuit of prey, mainly lizards and small birds but occasionally insects and small mammals. They hunt from perches, from low glides, and by rapid stoops from soar.

Status and distribution: Gray Hawks are uncommon and local in riparian areas of s. Arizona, usually occurring where there is permanent running water. There are approximately 45 known breeding pairs. A few pairs reside along lower Rio Grande valley in Texas. There are breeding records from w.-cen. New Mexico. The Arizona population is migratory, leaving by October and returning in late March or early April. Texas birds are sedentary.

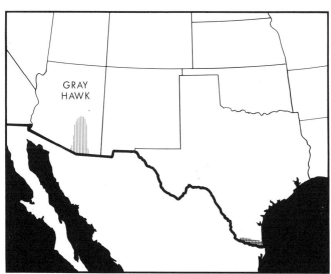

Fine points: When soaring, Gray Hawk's wingtips appear more rounded and tail longer than those of the Broad-winged Hawk. Immature Gray's outer primaries are barred to the tips; immature Broad-wing's are not.

Unusual plumages: No unusual plumages have been reported.

Subspecies: The race in the Southwest is *B. n. plagiata.* Amadon (1982) has assigned this species to the genus *Asturina.*

Etymology: *Nitidus* in Latin means "bright, shining."

Measurements:

Length: 36–46 cm (42); 14–18 in. (17)

Wingspread: 82–98 cm (87); 32–38 in. (34)

Weight: 378–660 g (524); 13–23 oz (18)

ROADSIDE HAWK   Pl. 8; photos, p. 133
Buteo magnirostris

Description: The tropical Roadside Hawk is a small, long-legged, and long-tailed buteo accidental in lower Rio Grande valley of Texas. Adult and immature plumages of this accipiter-like raptor are similar. Sexes are alike in plumage, with females somewhat larger. Northern Mexican birds lack the rufous wing patches characteristic of this species elsewhere. Buffy greater uppertail coverts form a buffy U above tail base, visible on flying birds. Cere and leg colors are yellow-orange to orange. Wingtips reach just over halfway to tail tip on perched birds.

Adult: Head is gray to gray-brown; iris color is pale lemon yellow. Back and upperwing coverts are dark brown, sometimes with a grayish cast. *Breast is medium brown, forming a bib.* Belly is creamy, with prominent rufous barring. Flight feathers are strongly barred below. Leg feathers are creamy, barred finely with rufous. Undertail coverts are white to creamy. *Long tail has dark and light brown bands of equal width.*

Immature: Similar to adult, but head is browner, with noticeable *creamy superciliary line* and orange-yellow iris color. Breast (bib) is heavily marked with whitish streaks. Tail has more and narrower bands than that of adult.

Similar species: (1) **Gray Hawk** (Pl. 8) immature has bold face pattern, dark iris color, tail bands of unequal width, and whiter, more extensive U above tail base and lacks bib on underparts. (2) **Broad-winged Hawk** (Pl. 10) has more pointed wings, tail bands of unequal width, and dark iris color and lacks bib on underparts. (3) **Red-shouldered Hawk** (Pl. 9) has crescent-shaped wing panels, tail bands of unequal width, and dark iris color and lacks bib on underparts. (4) **Cooper's** and **Sharp-shinned hawks** (Pls. 6 and 7) have shorter, more rounded wings and lack bib on underparts. (5) **Hook-billed**

Kite (Pl. 8) also has pale iris color but has large hooked beak, collar on hind neck, and underparts entirely barred.

Flight: Active flight is accipiter-like, with 3 to 5 rapid, stiff, shallow wingbeats followed by a glide. Soars with wings level; soaring is usually not very high, most often just above the forest. Glides with wings somewhat cupped, with wrists up and wingtips down. Does not hover.

Behavior: Roadside Hawks are conspicuous because of their habit of perching in open places, often on poles and wires along roadways. They are a general feeder, eating mainly insects and reptiles but also rodents and sometimes birds. They hunt from perches and glide down to the ground to capture prey.

Pair in courtship flights glide together with fluttering wings held in a V, loudly calling. Voice is a shrill scream and once heard is seldom forgotten.

Status and distribution: Roadside Hawks are accidental in the Rio Grande valley of Texas. One overwintered at Bentsen State Park in 1982–1983. A specimen exists from Cameron County, Texas. The extensive neotropical range of this hawk extends northward to cen. Tamaulipas, where much of its habitat has been lost in recent years.

Fine points: Adults usually have 4 dark tail bands; immatures have 5. Outer primaries are barred to tips.

Unusual plumages: No unusual plumages have been reported.

Subspecies: The n. Mexican race is *B. m. griseocauda.*

Etymology: *Magnirostris* is from the Latin *magni,* "large," and *rostrum,* "beak."

Measurements:
Length: 33–38 cm (36); 13–15 in. (14)
Wingspread: 72–79 cm (75); 28–31 in. (30)
Weight: 230–440 g (318); 8–15 oz (11)

RED-SHOULDERED HAWK   **Pl. 9;**
Buteo lineatus   **photos, pp. 134, 135**
Description: The Red-shouldered Hawk is a medium-sized, long-legged, long-tailed, slender buteo usually found in wet woodlands or savannas. There are four recognizably different plumage forms: Eastern, Florida, Texas, and California. All forms can be identified in flight as Red-shoulders by *crescent-shaped wing panels.* Sexes are alike in plumage; females are larger, but there is considerable size overlap. Wingtips do not reach tail tip on perched birds. Legs and feet are pale yellow.

Eastern adult: Head is medium brown with tawny streaking. Iris color is dark brown. Cere is bright yellow. Back is dark brown with rufous feather edges. Lesser upperwing coverts are rufous and form *red shoulder of perched birds. Flight feathers are boldly barred with black and white* above, not as boldly barred below, with a *white crescent-shaped panel* near the black outer primary tips. Secondaries and inner primaries have white tips. *Underwing appears two-toned;* rufous coverts are darker than flight feathers. Underparts are rufous, with dark brown streaks and white barring. Leg feathers are creamy with fine rufous barring. *Tail is black* with *3 or 4 narrow white bands.*

Eastern immature: Head is medium brown, usually with buffy superciliary line and dark brown malar stripes. Iris color is light to medium gray-brown. Cere is greenish yellow. Back is dark brown with some tawny mottling. Upperwing coverts are dark brown with some tawny and whitish mottling and often a hint of the red shoulder. Primaries are dark brown with a *crescent-shaped tawny area* on upper surface adjacent to black tips. White underparts are marked longitudinally with dark brown blobs. Underwing is uniform white to cream and shows crescent panel when backlighted. Leg feathers and undertail coverts are white and spotted with dark brown. *Tail above is dark brown* with *many fine light brown bands,* often with a rufous wash above on the basal half.

Florida adult: Like Eastern adult but smaller and paler, with *pale gray head* and grayish back. Its tail has fewer (2 or 3) white bands.

Florida immature: Similar to Eastern immature but smaller. Underparts are more heavily streaked and somewhat barred, leg feathers are usually barred, and tail has fewer bands with little or no rufous.

Texas adult: Similar to California adult but on average not as brightly colored.

Texas immature: Similar to Florida immature but larger, and streaked breast has little or no barring.

California adult: More richly colored and smaller than Eastern adult. Breast color is solid rufous and tail has fewer (2 or 3) and wider white bands. Similar to Texas adult.

California immature: Different from all other immature forms; more *adultlike.* Its *underparts* are heavily marked, *more barred than streaked. Underwing coverts are rufous,* and so underwing appears two-toned like that of adult. *Crescent-shaped area* of upperwing similar to, but less bold than, that of adult. Secondaries and inner primaries have white tips. *Leg feathers and undertail coverts have thick rufous barring.* Tail resembles that of adult but is dark brown with whitish light bands.

Similar species: (1) **Broad-winged Hawk** (Pl. 10) immature perched is difficult to distinguish from perched immature Red-shoulder (see **Fine points**). In flight, Broad-wing is smaller and has more pointed wings, with square, not crescent-shaped, wing panels. Adult tail has 1 wide white band (but may show another narrower white band near tail base). Adult underwing coverts are creamy, not rufous. (2) **Goshawk** immature (Pl. 7) is similar but has tail bands of equal width; heavily barred, tapered wings; and streaked undertail coverts and lacks crescent-shaped panels and malar stripes. (3) **Cooper's Hawk** (Pls. 6 and 7) has tail bands of equal width and heavily barred, short, rounded wings and lacks crescent-shaped wing panels and malar stripes. (4) **Red-tailed Hawk** (Pl. 11) has unstreaked breast and lacks crescent-shaped wing panels (panels, if present, are square or trapezoid-shaped). (5) **Northern Harrier** (Pl. 3) immature also has rufous body and underwing coverts but has dark secondary patches and lacks crescent wing panels.

Flight: Active flight is accipiter-like, with 3 to 5 quick, stiff, shallow wingbeats, then a period of glide. Soars with wings flat and pressed forward. Glides with wings bowed; wrists up, tips down. While gliding, bird flaps occasionally. Does not hover.

Behavior: Red-shouldered Hawks are vocal, and their distinctive call, especially evident during courtship, should be learned (however, Blue Jays are good at mimicking this call). Hunters of wet woodlands, the hawks sit quietly on an inconspicuous perch, searching for prey — mammals, birds, frogs and toads, snakes and lizards, and occasionally crustaceans, fish, and insects. In winter they are seen in more open areas, but they select lower and less open perches than Red-tails. Birds in Florida, along the Gulf Coast, in Texas, and in California use more exposed perches, including telephone poles and wires. Red-shouldered Hawks are fond of soaring and often vocalize while in the air. They sometimes join a group of crows mobbing large owls and have been observed eating suet at bird feeders. This species nests in suburban neighborhoods.

Status and distribution: Red-shouldered Hawks were probably somewhat reduced in numbers by pesticides, but loss of habitat is most likely the cause of any long-term decline. Birds are now being recorded in good numbers in areas where habitat is still available.

   Eastern form is fairly common east of the Great Plains in river bottom habitat, ranging north into s. Canada. Northern birds are migratory, especially immatures, moving as far south as Florida and Mexico in winter. Recorded casually in Colorado.

   Florida form is common to abundant in peninsular Florida, where it occurs in almost all habitats except pine woods and coasts.

   California form is fairly common in California west of deserts and the Sierra Nevada in riparian and oak woodland habitat, ranging barely into s. Oregon. Recorded casually in Arizona, Nevada, and Utah.

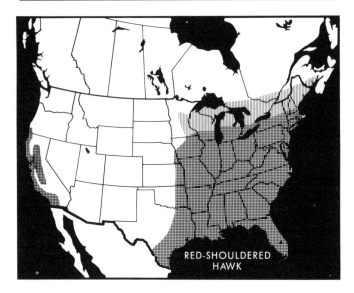

RED-SHOULDERED
HAWK

Texas form is fairly common in riparian areas of s. Texas south to the Nueces River valley. New Mexico records are most likely this form.

Fine points: Immature Red-shouldered Hawk's upper tail is dark with light bands; Broad-wing immature's is light with dark bands.

Unusual plumages: Albinism and partial albinism have been reported. One bird was all white with yellow eyes and faint tail banding.

Subspecies: The AOU recognizes 5 races: *B. l. lineatus,* e. N. America north of Florida and the Gulf Coast; *B. l. alleni,* Gulf Coast and most of Florida except southern tip, where *B. l. extimus* occurs; *B. l. texanus* in s. Texas; and *B. l. elegans* in California and Oregon.

Etymology: "Red-shouldered" refers to the rufous patch on upperwing coverts. *Lineatus* is Latin for "striped," a reference to the tail.

Measurements:
Length: 38–47 cm (42); 15–19 in. (17)
Wingspread: 94–107 cm (101); 37–42 in. (40)
Weight: 460–930 g (629); 1.1–1.9 lb (1.4)

BROAD-WINGED HAWK   Pls. 10, 13, and 26;
Buteo platypterus   photos, pp. 134, 135
Description: The crow-sized Broad-winged Hawk is an east-

ern forest buteo. Rare dark-morph birds breed only in Alberta. Sexes are alike in plumage. Females are larger than males but with some size overlap. Iris color varies from light to dark brown. *Wings are relatively pointed for a buteo.* Cere is greenish yellow to yellow; legs are pale yellow. Wingtips do not reach tail tip on perched birds.

Light-morph adult: Head, back, and upperwing coverts are uniform dark brown. Underparts are white, with medium to heavy rufous barring, lighter on lower belly, and undertail coverts are white. *Unmarked underwings are white to cream,* and primary and secondary tips are dark, forming dark band on trailing wing edge. *Dark brown tail has 1 wide white band* and another narrow one usually visible only when tail is fanned.

Light-morph immature: Top of head, nape, back, and upperwing coverts are dark brown, with some white or rufous edging. Brown face has pale superciliary line and black malar stripe. White underparts are lightly to heavily marked with brown streaks, but some individuals are almost clear-breasted. *Underwings are unmarked,* like those of, adult, except that trailing edge band is not as dark. Leg feathers are usually clear, sometimes spotted, rarely barred. Light brown tail has 4 or 5 dark brown bands; subterminal band is widest.

Dark-morph adult: Entire body and upperwing and underwing coverts are uniform dark brown. Iris color is dark brown. Underwing is two-toned, with silvery flight feathers and uniform dark brown coverts. *Tail is identical to that of light-morph adult.*

Dark-morph immature: Similar to dark-morph adult except that most birds have rufous and white mottling on underparts and underwing coverts. A few have solid brown bodies and underwings. *Tail is identical to that of light-morph immature.*

Similar species: (1) **Red-shouldered Hawk** (Pl. 9) in flight shows crescent-shaped wing panels in all plumages (see **Fine points**). Adult has 2 or more light tail bands of equal width and red shoulder patch. Perched immature Red-shoulder is difficult to distinguish from perched immature Broad-wing (see **Fine points** under Red-shouldered Hawk, p. 56). (2) **Cooper's Hawk** and **Goshawk** (Pls. 6 and 7) have dark and light tail bands of equal width and wider, more rounded wings that are heavily barred below; these hawks lack malar stripes. (3) **Gray Hawk** (Pl. 8) immature is similar to immature Broad-wing but has bold face pattern, barred leg feathers, and diagnostic white U above tail base. (4) **Dark-morph buteos** (Pls. 13–15 and 26) of other species are larger, have different tail patterns, and except for Short-tailed and Swainson's hawks, do not have pointed wings. (5) **Swainson's Hawk** (Pls. 13 and 26) dark morph has dark gray, not silvery, flight feathers and light undertail coverts.

Flight: Active flight is with strong, stiff wingbeats. Soars and glides on flat wings. Does not hover.

Behavior: Broad-winged Hawks are forest birds except during migration and prey on small mammals, birds, frogs and toads, snakes, and insects. They are still hunters, searching for prey from a perch along a forest edge or, more often, in the forest. On migration, large numbers of Broad-winged Hawks are often seen soaring together.

Broad-wings can be aggressive in their nest defense and have struck humans climbing to their nests. Vocalization is a two-noted, high-pitched whistle.

Status and distribution: Broad-winged Hawks are common in forested areas east of the Great Plains and in the boreal forest from Nova Scotia west to Alberta. They are irregular on the e. Great Plains. The entire population is migratory, with most going into Cen. and S. America, some as far as Chile and Argentina. They are common to abundant on fall and spring migration in the East and along the s. Texas Gulf Coast and casual throughout the West. Some birds winter in the subtropical areas of Florida, the Gulf Coast, and California. All winter sightings outside these areas are most likely immature Red-shouldered Hawks.

Rare dark morph is restricted to the far western portion of the breeding range in Alberta but is regularly encountered on migration on the e. Great Plains, less frequently in West.

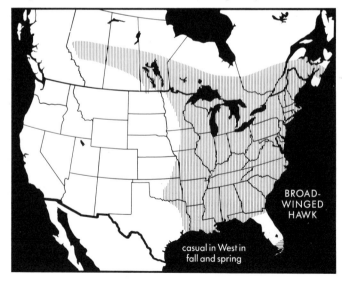

BROAD-WINGED HAWK

casual in West in fall and spring

Fine points: Immature in flight usually shows pale wing panels and could be confused with the Red-shouldered Hawk. Its panel, however, is square or trapezoid-shaped, not crescent-shaped like that of the Red-shouldered. Red-tailed Hawk immatures also show a square or trapezoid-shaped panel but have dark patagial marks on underwings. Immature Broad-wings returning in late spring show a gap in the middle of the trailing edge of wing because of molted inner primaries.

Unusual plumages: There are reliable sightings of a completely albino adult and of an immature with many white feathers in the back and wings.

Subspecies: The N. American race is *B. p. platypterus*.

Etymology: *Platypterus* is from the Greek *platys,* "broad," and *pteron,* "wing."

Measurements:
Length: 34–42 cm (37); 13–17 in. (15)
Wingspread: 82–92 cm (86); 32–36 in. (34)
Weight: 308–483 g (401); 11–17 oz (14)

SHORT-TAILED HAWK   **Pls. 4 and 13; photos, p. 137**
Buteo brachyurus
Description: Florida's Short-tailed Hawk, a small, long-winged buteo, is an aerial hunter of birds. It is most often seen in flight, when a *small white spot on the lores* is noticeable. There are both light and dark color morphs. Sexes are alike in plumage; females are larger. Immature plumages are similar to adult's. *Wingtips reach tail tip* on perched birds. Cere and legs are yellow.

Light-morph adult: Head is dark brown. *Solid dark cheeks* and narrow white throat are noticeable in flight. Iris color is brown. Back and upperwing coverts are dark brown. Underparts are white. *Underwing is two-toned,* with coverts white and flight feathers darker, but *primaries are paler than secondaries.* Grayish tail has a dark subterminal band and several indistinct, often incomplete narrow dark bands.

Light-morph immature: Similar to light-morph adult, but breast has a few fine streaks on each side. Dark cheeks have pale streaking but are still noticeable. Iris color is beige. Recently fledged birds have rufous wash on breast. *Grayish tail has dark bands of equal width.*

Dark-morph adult: Head, body, and wing coverts are dark brown. Iris color is brown. Flight feathers are silvery below, with *secondaries darker than primaries. Tail is same as that of light-morph adult.*

Dark-morph immature: Similar to dark-morph adult, but belly and underwing coverts are mottled with white, and unmottled breast forms *dark bib.* Iris color is beige. *Tail is same as that of light-morph immature.*

Similar species: (1) **Broad-winged Hawk** (Pl. 10) immature is similar to light-morph Short-tail but is usually streaked on underparts, has uniform light underwing, has wide dark subterminal tail band, and lacks dark cheeks. Wingtips do not reach tail tip on perched birds. (2) **Broad-winged Hawk** (Pls. 13 and 26) dark morph is similar to dark-morph Short-tailed Hawk but has silvery secondaries (same shade as primaries), is browner, and has different tail pattern. Dark-morph Broadwing has apparently not been recorded in Florida. (3) **Swainson's Hawk** (Pl. 12) light morph also has two-toned underwing, but its primaries and secondaries are the same dark gray color. They fly with their wings in a strong dihedral and have dark breasts (adult) or usually more heavily streaked underparts (immature). (4) **Swainson's Hawk** (Pls. 13 and 26) dark morph has light undertail coverts. (5) **Red-tailed Hawk** (Pls. 15 and 26) dark morph (rare in Florida) is much larger, and adult has rufous tail. (6) **Red-shouldered Hawk** (Pl. 9) has crescent-shaped pale wing panels.

Flight: Active flight is with stiff, strong wingbeats. This hawk soars with its wings held in a slight dihedral. It glides on flat wings, often with tips turned up. The Short-tailed Hawk is best identified by its characteristic hunting behavior, kiting on stiff, flat wings with primaries upturned and head down.

Behavior: Short-tailed Hawks are specialized aerial hunters

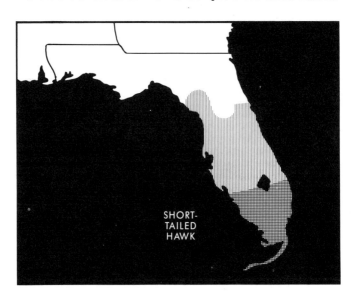

SHORT-TAILED HAWK

of small birds. They soar up to heights of 50 to 300 meters, sometimes higher, and face into the wind and hang stationary on outstretched wings and fanned tail, with their heads down, searching the forest canopy or field below. On light winds they hunt by soaring slowly upwind. When prey is spotted, they fold their wings and stoop rapidly. Sometimes, to get a better look at potential prey, they lower themselves slowly on raised wings and then stoop. Often, after an unsuccessful stoop, they alternately flap and sail over the canopy, apparently hunting. Short-tailed Hawks usually perch to rest and preen inside the canopy. They have been reported sitting on treetops with only their heads visible, apparently hunting, most often early in the morning.

Status and distribution: Short-tailed Hawks are uncommon to rare, but sometimes overlooked, in peninsular Florida in summer. The preferred habitat is mixed woodland savanna or wooded edge. The population retreats in winter to southern third of the peninsula and Florida Keys, becoming more obvious. Dark-morph birds are more common than light-morph ones in Florida. Oberholser (1974) mentions a hypothetical sight record from s. Texas.

Fine points: Light-morph adults may have small rufous areas on sides of upper breast.

Unusual plumages: No unusual plumages have been reported.

Subspecies: The Florida race is *B. b. fuliginosus.*

Etymology: *Brachyurus* is from the Greek *brachys,* "short," and *ourus,* "tail."

Measurements:
Length: 39–44 cm (41); 15–17 in. (16)
Wingspread: 83–103 cm (93); 32–41 in. (37)
Weight: 342–560 g (426); 12–20 oz (15)

SWAINSON'S HAWK
Buteo swainsoni

Pls. 12, 13, and 26;
photos, pp. 138, 139

Description: The Swainson's Hawk, a slender buteo with long, pointed wings and a long tail, is a common summer inhabitant of western grasslands. *Two-toned underwing* of light morph is distinctive. There is much plumage variation, but most individuals are recognizable. Unlike most other buteos, adults and immatures have similar wing and tail proportions. Sexes are almost alike in plumage, with females larger than males, but there is much size overlap. On perched birds, wingtips reach tail tip.

Light-morph adult: Head is brown, with small white spot on forehead and large white throat patch. Iris color is dark brown. Back and upperwing coverts are brown, sometimes with grayish cast, with greater uppertail coverts forming a light ∪ above tail base. *Rufous to dark brown breast forms a bib* that contrasts with lighter-colored belly, which is sometimes barred (more often on females). A few lightly colored adults have incomplete bibs that are broken up by a pale area in the center of breast. Usually there is a large white throat patch. *Underwing is two-toned;* white coverts contrast with dark gray flight feathers. Light gray-brown tail has numerous fine dark bands, with subterminal band thicker. Cere and legs are yellow.

Light-morph immature: Head is brown, with white forehead, streaked crown, buffy superciliary line, dark eye-line, buffy cheeks and throat, and dark malar stripes. Iris color is pale brown. Back and upperwing coverts are brown, with broad buffy feather edgings and a pale U above tail base. Underparts are white to creamy, lightly spotted to heavily streaked with dark brown, often with a hint of bib. *Underwing is two-toned,* but with less contrast than adult's. Some individual's underwings appear uniformly pale and mottled. Tail is like adult's. Cere is greenish yellow to yellow. Legs are pale yellow.

Eye, cere, and leg color and tail pattern of dark-morph birds are same as those of light-morph birds of similar age.

Dark-morph adult: Body and upperwing coverts are dark brown, rarely jet black, often with small white areas on throat and forehead. Underwing can be all dark, but most often underwing coverts are buffy or rufous or mottled white. This is the only buteo with dark gray flight feathers. White U on rump sometimes noticeable. *Undertail coverts are light,* often barred.

Dark-morph immature: Similar to light-morph immature, but underparts and underwing coverts are even more heavily streaked, and back has little or no buff feather edging. Underwing is somewhat less two-toned because coverts are nearly as dark as flight feathers.

Rufous-morph adult: A variation of dark-morph adult, with belly, underwing coverts, and leg feathers medium to dark rufous. Underwing is two-toned; rufous coverts contrast with dark gray flight feathers. *Light undertail coverts are barred with rufous.*

Similar species: (1) **Red-tailed Hawk** (Pl. 11) immature may appear similar to immature Swainson's but is told by wing shape and dark patagial mark. (2) **Dark-morph buteos** (Pls. 13–15 and 26) of other species have dark undertail coverts and silvery flight feathers except for immature White-tailed Hawk. (3) **Prairie Falcon** (Pl. 22) perched is similar to pale immature Swainson's but has dark eyes, white area between eye and dark ear patch, and wingtips that do not reach tail tip.

Two species share light-morph Swainson's Hawk's underwing pattern of light coverts and dark flight feathers — Short-tailed Hawk in Florida and adult White-tailed Hawk in coastal Texas — but only Swainson's has all flight feathers dark gray.

Flight: Active flight is light, with wingbeats of medium speed. This hawk soars with its wings in medium to strong dihedral; glides with wings in a modified dihedral. It hovers and kites often, especially in strong winds.

Behavior: Swainson's Hawks hunt from perches as well as on the wing. They prey on small mammals but also eat many insects. They follow tractors and mowers, capturing disturbed rodents, insects, and even birds. Vocalization is a drawn-out "keerrr," less wheezy than Red-tailed Hawk's.

This species is very kite-like in flight. The birds soar effortlessly for long periods and often hunt from a soar or glide. On migration they are often seen in small to large flocks, flying or descending en masse to feed on grasshoppers.

Sometimes aggressive in nest defense, especially if they have chicks; Swainson's Hawks have struck human intruders. They will sometimes abandon the nest if disturbed prior to egg hatching.

Status and distribution: Swainson's Hawks are fairly common and obvious during summer in most grassland areas of West, from Great Plains westward; they occur east to nw. Illinois and sw. Wisconsin, north rarely into e.-cen. Alaska. Although California and Oregon populations have been reduced, other populations seem stable. The entire population is migra-

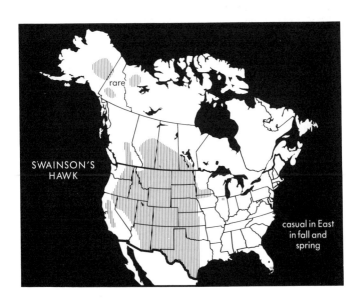

SWAINSON'S HAWK

rare

casual in East in fall and spring

tory, and most birds move into s. S. America, but a few winter in s. Florida, and winter specimen records exist for s. Texas and s. California. There are no valid winter records (late December through February) from N. American temperate areas, but valid December records exist for Alaska, California, and other areas.

Dark morph is usually rare, from 1% to 10% of local populations, but constitutes 35% of that in n. California. Birds of each color morph tend to mate preferentially with their own morph.

Swainson's Hawk is a rare but regular fall and spring visitor to e. N. America. There are many sight, specimen, or banding records from almost all states.

Fine points: Unlike other buteos, Swainson's Hawks take 2 years to acquire adult plumage; immature plumage is worn for 2 years. They have only 3 notched primaries, a character shared with Broad-winged and White-tailed hawks; all other buteos have 4 notched primaries.

Unusual plumages: Individuals with some white feathers have been reported.

Subspecies: Monotypic.

Etymology: Common and scientific names after William Swainson, English naturalist.

Measurements:
Length: 43–55 cm (49); 17–22 in. (19)
Wingspread: 120–137 cm (128); 47–54 in. (51)
Weight: 595–1240 g (849); 1.3–2.7 lb (1.9)

WHITE-TAILED HAWK
Buteo albicaudatus

Pls. 17 and 26;
photos, pp. 140, 141

Description: The White-tailed Hawk of Texas's coastal prairies is a large buteo with long legs and *distinctive wing shape—long, pointed wings* that *pinch in abruptly to the body on the trailing edge.* Adult and immature plumages are distinctly different. Subadult plumage is intermediate between them. Sexes are almost alike in plumage; females are darker and somewhat larger. Immature's tail is longer and wings are narrower than are those of adult and subadult. On perched birds, wingtips of adult and subadult extend beyond tail tip, while those of immature reach or just surpass tail tip. Cere is greenish yellow.

Adult: Top and sides of head are medium to dark gray, with small white areas above each lore. Note *dark cheeks.* Iris color is brown. Throat is usually white but may be dark on birds with darker backs. Back is medium to dark gray, darker on females. Lesser upperwing coverts form a *chestnut shoulder patch* on otherwise dark gray upperwing coverts. Uppertail coverts and rump are white. Underparts are white, often with fine dark barring on belly, heavier on females. *Underwing is two-toned; white coverts contrast with darker flight feathers,* with *primaries darker than secondaries.* There is almost always a white area at base of outer primaries. *White tail* has a *thick black subterminal band* and 5 or more fine black bands. Legs are yellow.

Subadult: Head, throat, and back are blackish brown. Lesser upperwing coverts form a *chestnut shoulder patch* on otherwise blackish brown upperwing coverts. Rump is whitish. *Breast is white,* and *belly is heavily barred and mottled with dark reddish brown.* Underwing is mostly dark, with some whitish mottling on dark coverts; gray flight feathers are several shades lighter and have a dark border. White leg feathers have dark reddish brown barring. Undertail coverts are whitish, with some dark mottling. Tail is variable but is usually grayish with fine dark banding and wide dark terminal band. Legs are yellow. (Subadults are variable in plumage, as there is a gradual, continuous transition in plumage from mostly dark immature to white-bodied adult.)

Immature: Head, back, and upperwing coverts are blackish brown. Iris color is dark brown. Back and upperwing coverts (feathers) have tawny edgings. White greater uppertail coverts form a *white U* above tail base. Blackish brown underparts have a variably sized creamy to white breast patch and whitish feather edging on belly feathers. Underwing coverts are dark, with some white mottling and usually with 1 or 2 white diagonal lines. Flight feathers are several shades lighter; underwing appears two-toned but only when seen in good light. Outer primaries often have white bases. Undertail coverts are white with some dark mottling. Leg feathers are creamy with blackish brown mottling. Light gray tail has many fine indistinct bands. Legs are pale yellow.

Similar species: (1) **Swainson's Hawk** (Pl. 12) light morph also has two-toned underwing, but dark gray primaries and secondaries are the same color. It also has either a dark bib (adult) or spotted or streaked breast (immature). (2) **Ferruginous Hawk** (Pl. 12) light morph is similar to adult White-tail but has white cheeks, completely light underwing, and dark rufous leg feathers (adult) and lacks rufous shoulder patch and thick black subterminal tail band. (3) **Short-tailed Hawk** (Pl. 4) light morph also has two-toned underwing but occurs only in Florida, is smaller, lacks the black subterminal tail band, and has secondaries darker than primaries, opposite of coloration on White-tailed Hawk. (4) **Swainson's Hawk** (Pls. 13 and 26) dark morph is similar to immature White-tail but is smaller; has more prominent tail banding, dark unbarred leg feathers, and less distinct white U above tail base; and lacks white breast patch. (5) **Harlan's Hawk** (Pls. 14 and

26) is similar to immature White-tail but has dark undertail coverts, silvery flight feathers with dark border, and dusky tail tip and lacks white U above tail base. (6) **Dark-morph buteos** (Pls. 13–15 and 26) of other species, except for Swainson's Hawks, lack white U above tail base and have silvery flight feathers.

Flight: White-tailed Hawks are similar to Swainson's Hawks in flight and silhouette. Active flight is heavier than that of Swainson's, with slow, steady wingbeats. This hawk soars with its wings in a strong dihedral; glides with wings in a modified dihedral. It hovers and kites frequently.

Behavior: White-tailed Hawks hunt both from perches and on the wing, while either gliding or hovering. They prey on lizards, snakes, and insects as well as on birds and mammals. They gather at prairie fires, sometimes in numbers, to feed on disturbed prey. Talon-grappling has been observed. Nest is usually placed in a single low tree or bush.

Status and distribution: Fairly common but local in relatively undisturbed Texas coastal prairie and chaparral from Brownsville to Galveston. This species is sedentary, but local concentrations, particularly of immatures, have been noted during winter. Casual in Louisiana, Arizona, and New Mexico.

Fine points: Immature has one or more pale spots on side of face, noticeable when viewed at close range.

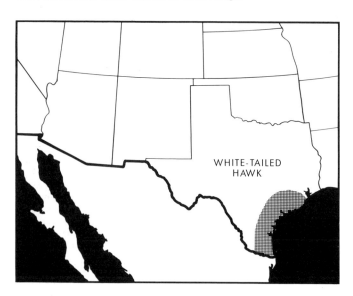

WHITE-TAILED
HAWK

Unusual plumages: No unusual plumages have been described, but subadult plumage has not previously been described in bird field guides.

Subspecies: The Texas birds belong to *B. a. hypospodius.*

Etymology: *Albicaudatus* is from the Latin *albus,* "white," and *caudatus,* "tail."

Measurements:

Length: 46–58 cm (50); 18–22 in. (20)

Wingspread: 126–135 cm (129); 49–53 in. (51)

Weight: 880–1235 g (1022); 1.9–2.7 lb (2.3)

ZONE-TAILED HAWK
Buteo albonotatus

Pls. 16 and 26;
photos, p. 141

Description: The Zone-tailed Hawk of the Southwest is a dark, slender-winged, and long-tailed buteo. In all plumages its coloration, silhouette, and *flight habits are similar to those of the Turkey Vulture.* Sexes are almost alike in plumage, but females are noticeably larger. On perched birds, wingtips reach tail tip. Cere and legs are bright yellow.

Adult: Head, body, and wing coverts are *black* (but have a grayish bloom when seen in good light). Iris color is dark brown. Face skin is light gray. Flight feathers from above are black and from below are light gray with heavy dark gray barring. *Underwing below appears two-toned. Black tail has 1 wide band* and *either 1 (male) or 2 (female) narrow bands,* which are gray above and white below.

Immature: Similar to adult but somewhat *browner,* with *white spotting on body,* heavier on underparts. Flight feathers are whiter below than those of adult. Tail is dark brown above, with black banding, and whitish below, with 5 to 7 narrow dusky bands and a wide dusky subterminal band.

Similar species: (1) **Turkey Vulture** (Pl. 1) is very similar but has a smaller, unfeathered head and unbanded tail and lacks dark trailing edge on underwing. (2) **Common Black Hawk** (Pl. 16) adult has broader wings, all dark underwings with a small white mark at base of outer primaries, orange-yellow face skin, and unbarred flight feathers. Its tail band is white above. (3) **Dark-morph buteos** (Pls. 13–15 and 26) of other species have silvery flight feathers below and, except for the Broad-winged Hawk, lack the wide white tail band. (4) **Broad-winged Hawk** (Pl. 13) dark-morph adult has a similar tail pattern but is dark brown, not black, and is smaller.

Flight: Active flight is with medium slow, flexible wingbeats. Soars and glides like a Turkey Vulture, with *wings in a strong dihedral.* It may also soar with flat wings and a spread tail, then resembling a buteo.

Behavior: Zone-tailed Hawks hunt on the wing, apparently mimicking the Turkey Vulture so that they can approach prey closely enough for capture before it can flee. They sometimes fly with Turkey Vultures, showing their true identity and rapid flight only when potential prey is sighted. Then they stoop rapidly to snatch a bird, mammal, or lizard. Zone-tailed Hawks are often overlooked because of their similarity to Turkey Vultures.

Talon-grappling between individuals of this species has been reported. Vocalizations are typical of a buteo: a drawn-out, whistled "keeer." This species can be very brave in defense of its nest and has on numerous occasions swooped at, and even soundly smacked, human intruders.

Status and distribution: Zone-tailed Hawks are uncommon in hilly riparian habitat and mountain coniferous forests and canyons of w. Texas and New Mexico and Arizona. They are casual in s. California and s. Texas. Some individuals may be resident, but most migrate south during winter. Small numbers have recently been reported in winter in se. Texas.

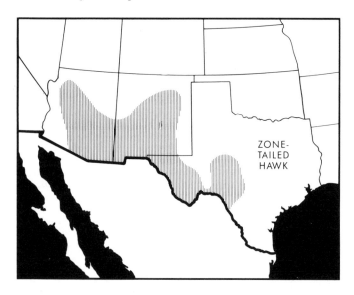

ZONE-
TAILED
HAWK

Fine points: The underside of folded tail appears like that of Common Black Hawk, with 1 white band visible, as undertail coverts cover the narrow bands. When perched, however, Zone-tails show barring on leading edges of primaries, visible at a reasonable range and lacking on Black Hawk. The gray color on upper tail bands is on outer feather web only; bands are white on inner web and appear white when tail is fanned.

Unusual plumages: No unusual plumages have been reported.

Subspecies: Monotypic.

Etymology: Named "zone-tailed" for its tail markings. *Albo* and *notatus* are Latin for "white" and "marked."

Measurements:

Length: 48–56 cm (51); 19–22 in. (20)

Wingspread: 121–140 cm (129); 48–55 in. (51)

Weight: 610–1080 g (830); 1.3–2.4 lb (1.8)

RED-TAILED HAWK
Buteo jamaicensis

Pls. 11, 14, and 26;
photos, pp. 142–145

Description: The Red-tailed Hawk is our most common and widespread buteo. Its plumages are highly variable, but the *rufous tail* of adult or *white mottled or barred tail* of adult Harlan's Hawk (see p. 71) and the *dark patagial marks on underwing* of light-morph birds are diagnostic field marks. Immatures do not have the rufous tail. Although numerous subspecies have been described and there is considerable individual variation, 4 light-morph and 3 dark-morph forms can be distinguished in the field with some reliability: The light-morph forms are Eastern, Western, Fuertes', and Krider's. The dark-morph forms are Western dark morph, Western rufous morph, and Harlan's Hawk. Sexes are alike in plumage and overlap considerably in size. Adults have shorter tails and broader wings than do immatures and thus have different flight silhouettes. On perched adult birds, wingtips reach tail tip in Western, Fuertes', and Harlan's adult forms but do not in other forms. Adult's iris color is medium to dark brown; that of immature is light gray-brown. Cere color is yellow to greenish yellow for both adults and immatures. Leg color varies from pale yellow to yellow.

Eastern adult: Head is medium brown, with dark brown malar stripe, and appears hooded. Throat is white. Back and upperwing coverts are dark brown, with white mottling often forming a V on back. Underparts are white, often with a light rufous wash on sides of upper breast and with an incomplete belly band of short dark streaks and bars, occasionally with little or no belly band. Underwing is white, sometimes with coverts lightly washed with rufous and with a *dark patagial mark* and a dark comma beyond wrist. Blackish tips of flight feathers form a dark band on trailing edge of underwing. Undertail coverts and leg feathers are white. *Rufous tail* has a narrow dark brown subterminal band and can appear pinkish from below. Whitish tips of otherwise dark uppertail coverts form a white U above tail base.

Eastern immature: Head is medium brown, paler than adult's. Back and upperwing coverts are dark brown, with white mottling forming a V on back. Upper surfaces of primaries are somewhat lighter colored than secondaries; seen from below they appear as square or trapezoid-shaped wing panels. Underparts are clear white, with belly band more distinct than adult's. Recent fledglings have a rufous bloom on breast that fades quickly. Underwing has *dark patagial mark;* band on trailing edge is paler and narrower than that of adult. Undertail coverts and leg feathers are white. Tail is light brown with many narrow dark brown bands of equal width. There may be a white area at base of upper tail like that of adult.

Western light-morph adult: Like Eastern adult, but brown colors are darker, and there is a heavier rufous wash on underparts and underwing coverts. Dark patagial marks on underwings are larger and darker. Belly band is usually wider and more pronounced but may be absent. Leg feathers have brown barring. Tail has wider dark subterminal band and may have 7 to 10 additional, usually incomplete narrow dark bands.

Western light-morph immature: Like Eastern immature, but brown colors are darker. Belly band is more pronounced, and leg feathers have brown barring. Tail may have rufous wash.

Fuertes' adult and immature: Like Eastern adults and immatures but darker above, with less mottling, and less heavily marked below. Dark patagial marks on underwings are present. Adults have little or no belly band.

Krider's adult: Similar to Eastern adult but overall much whiter (see also partial albino under **Unusual plumages**). *Top of head is pure white* to mostly white, with darker nape. There is often a dark line through eye. *Brown back and upperwing coverts* are *heavily mottled with white.* Dark patagial marks on underwing are reduced or absent. Underparts are mostly white, with belly band reduced or absent. *Tail is pinkish to whitish,* often washed with rufous near tip, and usually with a narrow dark subterminal band. Many intergrades with a mixture of both adult Krider's and adult Eastern characteristics are encountered.

Krider's immature: Like Krider's adult, but *white tail has 3 or more narrow dark bands,* sometimes with no banding on basal half. Tail can also be like that of Eastern immature. Primaries are whitish but have dark tips; underwing shows square or trapezoid-shaped wing panel. There is usually a white U above tail base.

Western dark-morph adult: Head, entire body, and upperwing and underwing coverts are dark chocolate brown to (rarely) jet black. Underwing shows silvery, heavily barred primaries and secondaries, with a dark band on trailing edge. Undertail coverts are usually rufous, somewhat paler than color of rest of underparts. *Tail is rufous* with a wide dark subterminal band and 7 to 11 narrow dark bands.

Western dark-morph immature: Like dark-morph adults but mottled with buff or rufous on underparts and underwing coverts. Sometimes has a brown color overall without mottling. Tail is like that of Western light-morph immature but has wider dark bands.

Western rufous-morph adult: Like dark-morph adult but breast, underwing coverts, undertail coverts, and leg feathers are rich dark rufous. Undertail coverts and leg feathers are heavily barred with dark brown. Wide belly band is solid dark chocolate brown.

Western rufous-morph immature: Not rufous; like Western light-morph immature, except that it has *heavily streaked breast, heavily mottled belly band* and underwing coverts (which mask dark patagial mark), and heavily barred leg feathers and undertail coverts. Tail is like that of Western light-morph immature.

Harlan's Hawk adult: Head, entire body, and upperwing and underwing coverts are black, usually with *much white speckling on breast and underwing coverts*. Underwing shows barred or *mottled silvery flight feathers*, with a dark band on trailing edge. Note barred tips of outer primaries. Undertail coverts have some white mottling. They have *3 types of tails: dirty white with dark gray longitudinal mottling, usually with a terminal band;* similar but *dark gray with darker mottling and terminal band;* or *off-white with a wide black subterminal band and 6 to 8 wavy narrow black bands, sometimes with dark mottling.*

Harlan's Hawk immature: Head, back, and upperwing coverts are blackish brown, similar to those of dark-morph adult. Underparts are blackish, usually, but not always, with white streaking on breast and white mottling on belly. Underwing shows white mottling on blackish coverts (not always) and moderately barred flight feathers without thick dark band on trailing edge. Outer primaries usually have barred tips. Undertail coverts are barred black and white. Tail is similar to that of dark-morph immature Red-tail, but dark bands are usually wavier. Separated in the field only with difficulty from immature dark-morph Red-tail.

Harlan's Hawk light-morph adult and immature: Very rare; similar to adult and immature Krider's Hawk but with more heavily marked underparts and adult with whitish Harlan's Hawk tail (described above for dark morph).

Intergrades between adult Harlan's Hawk and Western Red-tails occur and belong to 1 of 2 types:

Intergrade dark-morph adult: Similar to Harlan's dark-morph adult, but tail has varying amounts of red infused and sometimes a completely rufous tail with dark longitudinal mottling.

Intergrade light-morph adult: Similar to Western light-morph adult, but tail has varying amounts of dark longitudinal mottling and white coloring.

Similar species: (1) **Ferruginous Hawk** light-morph adult (Pl. 12) may also have a belly band, rufous tail, or dark marking on underwing coverts but has dark rufous leg feathering down to feet; its tail does not have a dark subterminal band; and underwing markings, if present, are chestnut and are not restricted to fore edge of patagium. (2) **Ferruginous Hawk** dark-morph adult (Pl. 15) may also have white mottling on breast like adult Harlan's but lacks wide dark band on trailing edge of underwing and dusky subterminal tail band. (3) **Ferruginous Hawk** light-morph immature (Pl. 12) is similar to Krider's Hawk immature but has legs feathered to toes, has little white mottling on back and upperwing coverts, and lacks dark banding on tail. (4) **Light-morph buteos** of other species lack dark patagial marks on underwing. (5) **Rough-legged Hawk** dark-morph adult (Pls. 15 and 26) has tail pattern similar to dark-morph adult Harlan's but has mostly dark upper side of tail, little or no white mottling on breast and underwing coverts, and legs feathered to toes. (6) **Dark-morph buteos** (Pls. 13, 15, and 26) of other species have different tail pattern.

Flight: Active flight is with slow, steady, deep wingbeats.

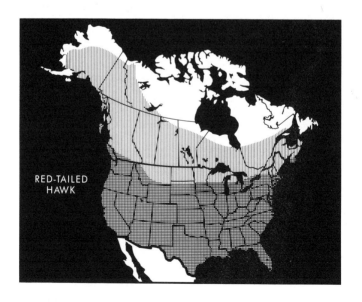

RED-TAILED
HAWK

Soars with wings raised slightly above horizontal. Glides with wings level or in a slight dihedral. Hovers and kites on moderate wind, especially using deflection updrafts from wood edges and cliffs. Red-tails soar often.

Behavior: Red-tailed Hawks are birds of both open and wooded areas, particularly wood edges, and are often seen perched conspicuously on a treetop, a telephone pole, or other lookout while hunting. Red-tails prey mainly on rodents but also on insects and their larvae, fish, and larger mammals, such as rabbits and squirrels. They often pursue prey into dense brush, pirate prey from other raptors, and eat carrion. The most frequently heard vocalization is a long, wheezy "kkeeeeer," somewhat like the sound of escaping steam.

Courtship displays are a series of steep dives and climbs and include glides by both adults together with their feet down. Talon-grappling has been reported and could be either courtship or aggressive display.

Status and distribution: Red-tailed Hawks are widespread and common, occasionally abundant, and occur in every N. American habitat except high Arctic and extensive tracts of dense forest. Northern birds are migratory.

Eastern Red-tail is found from the Great Plains east. The Florida peninsula has a resident subspecies similar to but smaller and more rufous than Eastern birds.

Western Red-tail is found west of the Great Plains and north of the Fuertes' form, ranging north to cen. Alaska. It occurs in winter on the Great Plains and, rarely, in the East. Alaskan and Pacific Northwest Red-tails are darker and more rufous. Eastern and Western forms intergrade on the western edge of the Great Plains. Dark-morph birds are relatively rare but can constitute as much as 10% of a local population.

Fuertes' is found from Oklahoma and Texas west through New Mexico and Arizona. It intergrades with Eastern and Western forms on northern edge of its area.

Krider's is found in summer on n. Great Plains, where it is greatly outnumbered by Eastern form. It winters south to Texas, Oklahoma, Arkansas, Louisiana, and Kansas.

Harlan's Hawk is found in summer in wooded areas of cen. and w. Alaska. Its range overlaps with Western form in e. and cen. Alaska and n. British Columbia. It is fairly common on migration on the n. Great Plains. Main area in winter is w. Arkansas and e. Texas, Oklahoma, and Kansas, but it is encountered in widely scattered locations from Washington, California, and Arizona east to Wisconsin and Tennessee.

Fine points: When viewed flying head-on, many Red-tails show light areas, somewhat like headlights, on the leading edge of each wing.

Unusual plumages: Partial albinos, varying from almost all white birds to some with just a few white feathers, are fairly common and are reported from almost all areas. Most birds are from half white to mostly white. Mostly white individuals usually have a dark area on the nape. All individuals seen, reported, and in collections are adults. A dilute-plumage immature specimen is mostly cream-colored, with some faint rufous bars and streaks. There is an adult specimen, which is normal in every way except for its greenish gray, not rufous, tail.

Subspecies: The AOU recognizes the following races: *B. j. borealis* in e. N. America except the Florida peninsula, where it is replaced by *B. j. umbrinus;* and *B. j. calurus* in w. N. America, except where it is replaced by *B. j. fuertesi* in s. Texas, New Mexico, and Arizona; and cen. and w. Alaska, where *B. j. calurus* is replaced by *B. j. harlani.* The range given for *B. j. krideri* is the n. Great Plains.

Etymology: Krider's Hawk was named for John Krider, who collected the first specimens in Iowa. Fuertes' Red-tailed Hawk was named by George Sutton and Josselyn Van Tyne for Louis Agassiz Fuertes, the bird artist. Audubon named the Harlan's Hawk for Dr. Richard Harlan (he did not coin the common name but only used *harlani;* he called the bird "Black Warrior"). *Jamaicensis* indicates where the first specimen was collected.

Measurements:

Length: 45–55 cm (49); 17–22 in. (19)
Wingspread: East 110–132 cm (120); 43–52 in. (47)
      West 120–141 cm (130); 47–56 in. (51)
Weight: 710–1550 g (1082); 1.5–3.3 lb (2.4)
Note: "East" includes Eastern and Krider's forms; "West" includes others.

FERRUGINOUS HAWK
Buteo regalis

Pls. 12, 15, and 26;
photos, pp. 146, 147

Description: The Ferruginous Hawk of the arid West is our largest buteo and has long, tapered wings, *a large head,* and a *robust chest.* Sexes are alike in plumage, but females are noticeably larger than males. Upperwing shows whitish primary patch (see **Fine points**). Legs are feathered down to toes. Wingtips almost reach tail tip on perched birds. Cere and feet are yellow.

Light-morph adult: Top of head is dark brown with rufous or creamy streaking, nape is lightish, and there is a dark line behind eye. *Cheeks are white with no dark malar stripe.* Iris color is light to medium brown. Back is dark brown and rufous. Upperwing coverts are more rufous than dark brown. Underparts are white, sometimes with belly band of rufous barring like that of Red-tailed Hawk. Underwings are white with a black wrist comma and, usually, *rufous patches on coverts* (more often on females). *Leg feathers are rufous* and barred with dark brown but also sometimes white with rufous barring. *Unbanded tail is white, light gray, light rufous,* or some mixture of these and with fine dark mottling.

Light-morph immature: Top of head is dark brown with creamy streaking, nape is lightish, and there is a dark eye-line. *Cheeks are white with no dark malar stripe.* Iris color is light brown. Back is dark brown, with little or no rufous. Upperwing coverts are dark brown, with some rufous feather edging. Underparts are white, with darkish areas on each flank and sometimes either a chest band or a belly band of dark spots. Recently fledged birds have rufous wash on breast that fades by fall. *Underwing is clear white* with black wrist comma. Leg feathers are white with black spots. Tail above is grayish brown with basal third white; below it is silvery with a dusky subterminal band.

Dark-morph adult: Back and upperwing coverts are mostly dark brown, with rufous feather edges and rufous patches on the patagials and uppertail coverts. Underparts are dark rufous, sometimes dark brown, with some white streaks on breast. Iris color is light to medium brown and obvious. Underwing is two-toned; silvery primaries contrast with dark coverts. Note *white comma at wrist.* Trailing edge of underwing has dusky border. Undertail coverts are dark rufous. Solid gray tail is unbanded but may have some dark mottling.

Dark-morph immature: Entire body and wing coverts are dark brown, sometimes with rufous on breast. Iris color is light brown. Underwing is two-toned; silvery flight feathers contrast with dark coverts. Note *white comma at wrist.* Trailing edge of underwing has a dusky border. Tail above is dark brown, with faint dark bands; below it is silvery with a dusky subterminal band.

Similar species: (1) **Red-tailed Hawk** light morph (Pl. 11) has dark patagial marks on underwing. Adult's rufous tail has dark subterminal band. (2) **Krider's Hawk** (Pl. 11) has heavily spotted back, wingtips that do not reach tail tip, and unfeathered tarsi. Immature Krider's has narrow dark bands in white tail. (3) **Harlan's Hawk** (Pls. 15 and 26) also has white breast streaking and grayish tail but has wider, darker band on trailing edge of underwing and lacks white wrist commas. (4) **Rough-legged Hawk** light morph (Pl. 10) has dark square carpal patch, heavily marked underparts, and usually a solid dark belly band. (5) **Rough-legged Hawk** dark-morph immature (Pls. 15 and 26) has same tail pattern as dark-morph immature Ferruginous but lacks white wrist comma and has smaller head and gape. (6) **Dark-morph buteos** of other species (Pls. 13–15 and 26) lack white wrist comma and have different tail patterns.

Flight: Active flight is with slow strong wingbeats, much like that of a small eagle. This hawk soars with its wings in medium to strong dihedral and glides with its wings in a slight or modified dihedral.

Behavior: Ferruginous Hawks are adept flyers and hunt by coursing rapidly low over open ground, soaring at height, hovering, or swooping down from a perch. Cooperative hunting of pairs has been reported. The main prey is ground squirrels and jackrabbits, but Ferruginous Hawks occasionally take other mammals and birds.

Nest site is small tree or rock outcropping, but the hawks also nest on the ground when no tree or outcropping is available, and they sometimes use haystacks. Adults are strong in their nest defense against ground predators and chase away even coyotes by their relentless attacks. Vocalization is typical of a buteo—a drawn-out "keerrr," less wheezy than that of the Red-tailed Hawk. Ferruginous Hawks occasionally form communal night roosts in winter, sometimes with other species, including Bald Eagles.

This species has a large gape, thought by some researchers to be used for thermal regulation by allowing rapid air exchange, especially for nestlings, which may be in direct sunlight all day.

Status and distribution: Ferruginous Hawks are fairly com-

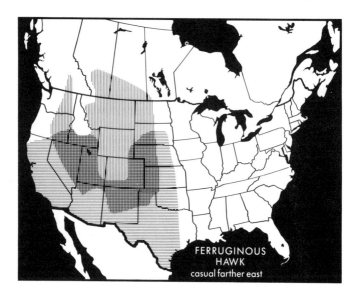

FERRUGINOUS
HAWK
casual farther east

mon but shy and retiring, breeding on undisturbed plains, sagegrass, high deserts, badlands, or edges of pinyon-juniper from w. Great Plains west to cen. Washington, Oregon, and nw. Nevada, north into s. Canada, and south to n. Arizona and nw. Texas. In winter some birds move southward, eastward, and westward. They are casual in the East during migration and in winter, with many records from Minnesota and Wisconsin but some also in Ohio, Tennessee, Virginia, New Jersey, and Florida. Dark-morph birds are not uniformly distributed and represent from 1% to 10% of local populations.

Fine points: Ferruginous Hawks have an extensive light area on upper surface of primaries in most plumages. This feature is not diagnostic, as other buteos have a similar area. Immature light-morph birds have large black spots on white uppertail coverts.

Unusual plumages: No unusual plumages have been reported.

Subspecies: Monotypic.

Etymology: "Ferruginous" comes from the Latin *ferrugo,* "rust," for rufous color in adult plumage. *Regalis* is Latin for "royal," a reference to the bird's large size.

Measurements:
Length: 50–66 cm (59); 20–26 in. (23)
Wingspread: 134–152 cm (143); 53–60 in. (56)
Weight: 980–2030 g (1578); 2.2–4.5 lb (3.5)

ROUGH-LEGGED HAWK
Buteo lagopus

Pls. 10, 15, and 26; photos, pp. 148, 149

Description: The Rough-legged Hawk of the arctic tundra is a large, long-winged, and long-tailed buteo. Both light and dark morphs have an immature and 2 adult plumage types. Plumage characters can be used to determine sex for most adults, but some adults occur in the plumage of the other sex. Females are larger than males. Dark-morph individuals are more common than in other *Buteo* species. Legs are feathered completely to feet. Light-morph birds have a *square black carpal patch* on light underwing. On perched birds, wingtips reach tail tip. Cere is yellow and feet are orange-yellow.

Light-morph adult male: Head is whitish to light brown, with streaked crown, a dark eye-line, and lightish nape. Iris color is dark brown. Back is dark gray-brown, with white and tawny mottling. Upperwing is dark without white primary patches. Underparts are white, with breast heavily marked, appearing as a *solid dark bib* at a distance, and belly more lightly marked, sometimes clear white. Usually there is *clear U-shaped area between breast and belly.* Adult underwing has heavily spotted white coverts, *black carpal patch* with much white mottling, some barring on secondaries and inner primaries, and dark trailing edge. Leg feathers are white with dark barring. *White tail* usually has *2 or 3 incomplete narrow dark bands* and *a wide dark subterminal band* but *may have many bands.*

Light-morph adult female: Similar to adult male type, but belly is more heavily marked than breast, sometimes with a solid wide dark belly band, usually with a *creamy U between breast and belly.* Back is browner than adult male type's. Upperwing is dark without white primary patches. Underwing is like adult male type but with carpal patch more prominent. *White tail* has *wide dusky tip* with *black subterminal band on it.*

Light-morph immature: Head is creamy with brown streaking and a dark line behind eye. Iris color is light brown. Back is brown with little mottling. In flight a whitish patch is visible on upperwing primaries. Creamy breast has some brown streaking, and *belly has thick solid dark band.* Underwing has clear creamy to white coverts with little mottling, prominent *black carpal patch,* and dusky trailing edge. Leg feathers are clear creamy, sometimes lightly spotted but never barred. *White tail* has a *wide dusky terminal band.*

Dark-morph adult male: Overall color is jet black except for silvery, heavily barred underside of flight feathers, which have dark tips, forming dark trailing wing edge. There is often a light area on nape. Iris color is dark brown. Dark tail has 3 or 4 narrow white bands.

Dark-morph adult female: Overall color is dark brown except for silvery, moderately barred underside of flight feathers. Underwing has dark trailing edge like adult male type's and sometimes has rufous coverts, which contrast with dark carpal patch. Iris color is dark brown. *Tail is all dark above* (dusky with darker tip) and *silvery below,* with a *dark terminal band.*

Dark-morph immature: Overall color is medium to dark brown, often with rufous intermixed, sometimes with light-colored head. Iris color is light brown. In flight a whitish patch is visible on upperwing primaries. Silvery flight feathers are lightly barred, with dusky tips forming a less boldly marked trailing edge of underwing than on adult. Underwing coverts are dark brown or rufous; when they are rufous, black carpal patch is noticeable. Tail above is dark, with faint darker bands; below it is silvery with a dusky subterminal band.

Note: Some dark-morph immatures and adult female types have light-colored heads and whitish and tawny mottling on upper breasts.

Similar species: (1) **Northern Harrier** (Pl. 3) has white on uppertail coverts, not on base of tail. (2) **Turkey Vulture** (Pl. 1) has unbarred silvery tail, lacks dark trailing edge on underwing, and flies with wings in a strong dihedral. (3) **Ferruginous Hawk** dark-morph immatures (Pls. 15 and 26) are very similar to Rough-leg immatures but have a white comma on underwing at wrist and longer, more tapered wings. (4) **Harlan's Hawk** (Pls. 14 and 26) is similar to dark-morph Rough-leg but has white mottling on breast and underwing coverts, white on top of tail, and often mottling on underside of flight feathers. (5) **Dark-morph buteos** of other species (Pls. 13–15 and 26) have different tail patterns except for adult Harlan's Hawk and immature Ferruginous Hawk. (6) **Eagles** (Pls. 18–20) lack silvery flight feathers.

Flight: Active flight is with slow, flexible wingbeats. This hawk soars with its wings in a medium dihedral. It glides with its wings in a modified dihedral. It hovers frequently; sometimes with deep wingbeats, sometimes with fluttering wings.

Behavior: Rough-legged Hawks are birds of open country, breeding above treeline on open tundra. The entire population moves south and in winter frequents open areas, such as farmlands, marshes, and airports. The birds hunt from lower perches, hover in lighter winds, and perch on smaller trees and limbs than do Red-tailed Hawks. Rough-legged Hawks prey almost exclusively on small to medium-sized mammals. Communal night roosts are formed in winter. On migration at concentrations caused by water barriers, Rough-legs appear less hesitant than other buteos to cross open water.

Status and distribution: Rough-legged Hawks breed on arctic tundra and in mixed tundra–boreal forest from the Aleutian Islands and w. Alaska to Newfoundland. They are a com-

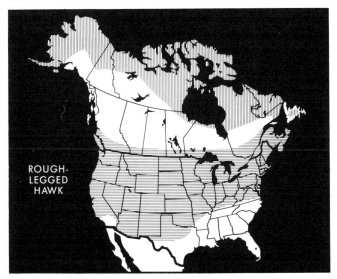

ROUGH-
LEGGED
HAWK

mon winter visitor across N. America from south of the boreal
forest to cen. United States and to Mexico in the Southwest.
Large numbers are encountered in spring migration around
Great Lakes. A few immatures linger into June in n. United
States and s. Canada.

Fine points: Many individuals of both color morphs show a
white area with a central dark spot on the nape. The Rough-
legged Hawk is the only species in N. America to have this
mark.

Unusual plumages: No unusual plumages have been reported.

Subspecies: The N. American race is *B. l. sancti-johannis.*

Etymology: Named "rough-legged" for the completely feathered legs. *Lagopus* is from the Greek *lagos,* "hare," and *pous,*
"foot."

Measurements:
Length: 46–59 cm (53); 18–23 in. (21)
Wingspread: 122–143 cm (134); 48–56 in. (53)
Weight: 745–1380 g (1026); 1.6–3.0 lb (2.2)

Eagles

Family Accipitridae

Two eagle species are widespread in North America, the Golden Eagle and the Bald Eagle. Two other species, the White-tailed Eagle and Steller's Sea Eagle, occur accidentally. All four are large and dark, with proportionally longer wings than the smaller buteos, which they resemble in flight. Golden and Bald eagles are similar in size; in both species, females are larger than males and northern birds larger than southern ones. Both species have longer tails and wider wings in their first (immature) plumage than in subadult and adult plumages.

"Eagle" comes from the Middle English *egle* and the Old French *egle* or *aigle,* which in turn derived from the Latin *aquila,* "eagle."

BALD EAGLE   **Pls. 18–20; photos, pp. 150, 151**
Haliaeetus leucocephalus
Description: The widespread but local Bald Eagle is a large, dark soaring bird usually found near water. Adults with *white head and tail* and dark brown body and wings are distinctive. Immature and subadult plumages are different from adult's and are similar to those of the Golden Eagle. Sexes are alike in all plumages. There are no plumage differences between northern and southern birds. In flight *head and neck protrude* beyond body *more than half of tail length.* Trailing edge of wing is nearly parallel to leading edge, more so on wing of adult than on that of immature. Legs are orange-yellow.

All nonadult plumages have *white axillary spots* and *diagonal white lines on underwings* (but the latter may not be noticeable on birds that have mostly white underwing coverts). Tails in these plumages vary greatly, from mostly darkish to mostly *dirty white,* with *dark edges* and tips. Plumage molts are not completed annually; most birds show signs of molt all year. Plumage transitions are gradual.
Immature: In the first full plumage, head is uniform dark brown. Beak and cere are black, and iris color is dark brown. *Back and upperwing coverts are tawny brown* and *contrast with dark flight feathers,* which may have a whitish wash on some feathers. Breast is dark brown and usually contrasts with belly, which varies from pale to dark tawny. Some individuals have some white streaking, usually where breast and belly meet but sometimes sparsely on entire underparts. Tail is noticeably longer than in subsequent plumages and is sometimes

81

solid dark, a character usually not found in later plumages.
White-belly I: In their first spring, when they are almost a
year old, Bald Eagles begin molting into the White-belly I
plumage. Brown head has a *buffy superciliary line,* which contrasts with dark brown patch behind eye. Iris color lightens to
light brown or amber, and beak and cere fade to a slaty color,
with cere a bit lighter in color. Some white feathers appear on
upperwing coverts and back, the latter forming an *upside-
down white triangle on back,* which is most visible on flying
birds. Upper breast remains mostly dark brown, appearing as *a
dark bib* contrasting with newly acquired white belly, which
has few to many short dark streaks. Body and tail molt are
complete, but only a few of the flight feathers are replaced.
New secondaries are noticeably shorter. Wing now appears ser-
rated on trailing edge and as wide as that of immature. New
flight feathers have more whitish areas; new whitish secondaries have dark tips.
White-belly II: Bald Eagles that are 2 years old appear similar to one-year-olds, but *superciliary line is larger and whitish;*
dark line behind eye is narrower; and cheek and throat are
whitish. Iris color is pale whitish yellow, beak has lightened to
horn-colored with a few dirty yellow spots, and cere is yellowish. *Upside-down white triangle on back* is retained. Bib on
upper breast is still usually distinct. All but 2 or 3 immature
secondaries have been replaced by shorter feathers; wing now
appears narrower than on immature or White-belly I, with a
few longer old secondaries visible protruding on the trailing
edge.
Adult transition: This plumage is acquired at approximately
the age of 3 and is highly variable. From White-belly II plumage, head lightens and body darkens. Bird usually acquires an
Osprey-like dark eye-line. White on head does not extend onto
neck as far as it does on adult. Iris color is pale yellow, and
cere and beak are orange-yellow, with dark smudges on beak.
White spot on underwing usually remains until the bird is
nearly in adult plumage, while white diagonal line fades early
in transition. Subadult tail is retained until spring of fifth year
(when bird is almost 4 years old).
Adult: This plumage is first acquired at 4 years of age. *Head is
white,* sometimes with a few brown or black spots even in older
birds. First adult head plumage is not solid white but white
with streaks of brown or black and often retaining the Osprey-
like dark eye-line. *Beak and cere are bright orange-yellow;* iris
color is pale lemon yellow. Body and wing coverts are dark
brown with paler feather fringing. Flight feathers are dark
brown. Tail coverts and *tail are white.* Tail in first adult plumage often has dark terminal band.
Similar species: (1) **Golden Eagle** (Pls. 18–20) in flight has

head that protrudes less than half tail length: head of Bald
Eagle protrudes more than half the tail length. The trailing
edge of wing is straighter on Balds. Immature and subadult
Goldens have white on underwing restricted to base of flight
feathers; white on Balds is on underwing coverts and axillars.
White axillar spot on nonadult Balds can be seen from a great
distance. White in Golden's tail extends out to the edges, while
nonadult Balds always have dark edges on whitish tails that
are otherwise similar to those of the Goldens. Tawny greater
upperwing coverts of adult and subadult Goldens form a
tawny bar on upperwing, visible on flying and perched birds
and lacking on all Balds. Perched Goldens show the golden
nape and yellow cere and bicolored beak, Balds usually have
cere and beak uniformly colored. Bald's tarsi are bare, while
Golden's are completely covered with buffy feathers. (2) **Osprey** (Pl. 3) in flight shows all-white body and black carpal
patch on underwing. On perched birds the small white head
with dark eye-line is distinctive. (3) **Turkey Vulture** (Pl. 1)
flies with wings in pronounced dihedral; has small head and
two-toned underwing.

Flight: Active flight is with slow wingbeats, similar to that of
Great Blue Heron but more powerful. Soars usually on flat
wings but sometimes with a small dihedral. Glides on flat
wings with wrists cocked forward. This eagle soars often, many
times with other eagles.

Behavior: Bald Eagles are usually found near water where
they can find their favorite food, fish. Breeding areas are almost always near water. In winter, when fish may be scarce,
they also eat carrion and waterfowl. They regularly pirate food
from other raptors, especially other Balds and occasionally Ospreys. The Bald Eagle is a superb fisherman and an agile raptor but prefers to find food in the easiest possible way.

This social species forms communal night roosts, most commonly in winter, of several birds or more and, rarely, several
hundred. Individuals often spend considerable time perching.
Some birds remain perched in night roosts for a day or two.
Balds are vocal, particularly around other eagles, and 2 eagles
often lock talons and whirl with each other (talon-grapple)
while in flight.

Status and distribution: Bald Eagles are locally common
during the breeding season in Florida; Chesapeake Bay;
coastal Maine through Maritime Provinces; Great Lakes; the
boreal lake region from w. Ontario through to coastal British
Columbia; most of Alaska, where they are abundant on the se.
coast; Washington south to n. California; and the greater Yel-
lowstone areas of w. Wyoming, s.-cen. Montana, and e. Idaho.
Small local breeding populations exist along the Gulf Coast of
Texas and Louisiana, coastal S. Carolina, along the Mississippi

River, and in cen. Arizona. There are a few widely scattered pairs in many other states. Most individuals leave inland northern breeding areas in winter. Large winter concentrations have been noted along Chilkat River in Alaska, in Klamath basin in Oregon, and along the upper Mississippi River. Some wintering and migrant Bald Eagles are found far away from water in areas of the West. Many nonbreeding birds from Florida and the Southeast disperse north and west throughout e. N. America during summer.

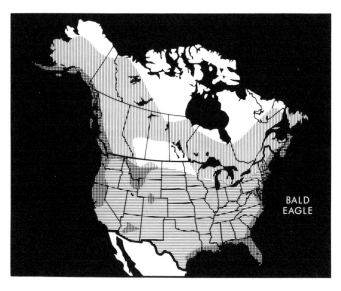

BALD
EAGLE

Fine points: Immature (first-plumage) flight feathers are noticeably pointed on the tips, giving the trailing edge of immature and White-belly I wings a sawtoothed appearance. Bald Eagles have unfeathered tarsi for about 1½ inches above the feet. Most nape feathers in immature and subadult plumages have buffy tips but are much less noticeable than golden nape of Golden Eagle. Bald's wrists during a glide are more forward and primaries are more folded than are those of the Golden. **Unusual plumages:** Several dilute-plumage adults have cream-colored body and covert feathers. Partial albino nestlings and nonadults have been seen in the West. **Subspecies:** The AOU recognizes 2 races, *H. l. alascensis* in Alaska and Canada and *H. l. leucocephalus* in the lower 48 states.

Etymology: In Old English *balde* means "white"; "Bald-headed Eagle" meant "white-headed" and later became just "Bald Eagle." *Haliaeetus* is from the Greek *halos*, "sea," and *aetos*, "eagle." *Leucocephalus* is from the Greek *leucos*, "white," and *kephalus*, "head."

Measurements:
Length: 70–90 cm (79); 27–35 in. (31)
Wingspread: 180–225 cm (203); 71–89 in. (80)
Weight: 2.0–6.2 kg (4.3); 4.4–13.6 lb (9.5)

WHITE-TAILED EAGLE   Pl. 25; photos, p. 153
Haliaeetus albicilla

Description: The accidental White-tailed Eagle has adult, subadult, and immature plumages similar to those of the Bald Eagle. It is approximately the same size as the Alaska Bald Eagle (which is larger than more southern Balds). Adult White-tailed Eagle is distinguished from Bald Eagle by creamy, not white, head; shorter, more wedge-shaped tail; and *dark brown undertail coverts*. Immatures and subadults are similar to Bald Eagles of like age but appear somewhat darker on underwing, with less prominent white axillary spots and diagonal white lines; the *tips of their tail feathers have white spikes*. Sexes are alike in plumage, with females noticeably larger than males. In flight, head and neck project more than half the length of tail. Immatures have wider wings and much longer tails than adults do. Trailing edge of wing, as on Bald Eagle, is nearly parallel to leading edge, more so on adults than on immatures.

Immature: In the first plumage, head is uniform dark brown, iris color is dark brown, and beak and cere are black. Upperparts appear patterned, with tawny upperwing coverts and back contrasting with blackish flight feathers. Breast is dark brown with white or tawny streaks; belly is dark tawny with dark brown streaks. Dark brown leg feathers contrast with tawny belly. Tail is much longer and less wedge-shaped than adult's and appears whitish from below, with dark brown outer webs on each feather and a triangular black area at tip of inner web, so that white area on each *tail feather tip appears spiked.* Some birds have tails that are mostly dark with some whitish mottling. Leg color is pale yellow.

Subadult: The next 2 years' plumages are similar to that of immature, but head is paler, dark brown back and upperwing coverts are mottled whitish, and underparts are white, with dark brown streaking. Beak gradually lightens and begins to turn yellowish. Iris color lightens to light brown. Flight feathers are blackish, with only an occasional faint whitish mottling on inner secondaries. Tail is like that of immature but shorter. Leg feathers are solid dark brown.

Adult: This plumage is acquired at about 4 years of age. *Head and neck are creamy buff, without a sharp line of contrast with brown breast and back.* Beak and cere are yellow; iris color is pale whitish yellow. Back and upperwing coverts are grayish brown with pale feather edges, darker on lower back, rump, and outer upperwing coverts. Flight feathers are blackish. Underparts are brown and darker on belly. Leg feathers and *undertail coverts are dark brown. Short, wedge-shaped tail appears all white.* Leg color is yellow.

Similar species: (1) **Bald Eagle** adult (Pls. 18–20) has white head with sharp line of contrast with brown body, white undertail coverts, and longer, less wedge-shaped tail. (2) **Bald Eagle** immatures and subadults (Pls. 18–20) have tails of similar length with dark terminal band as if tail had been dipped in ink (in contrast to spiked appearance of tail tip on the immature or subadult White-tail); more pronounced white axillary spots (occasionally present on some White-tails); diagonal lines on underwing; and usually a sharp line of contrast between breast and belly. On whitish tails of immature Balds, only outer tail feathers have dark outer webs, whereas on similar White-tailed Eagle tails, every feather has a dark outer web. (3) **Steller's Sea Eagle** adult (Pl. 25) is unmistakable, with its huge yellow beak and white wing patch. (4) **Steller's Sea Eagle** immature and subadult (Pl. 25) have mostly white, extremely wedge-shaped tail and yellow beak.

Flight: Active flight is with slow, stiff, labored wingbeats. This eagle soars on flat to slightly upraised wings. It glides with its wings level or slightly arched.

Behavior: White-tailed Eagles are similar in habits to Bald Eagles, sharing their preference for fish and aquatic habitats. They too are superb fishermen and accomplished pirates.

Status and distribution: White-tailed Eagles are casual in the Aleutian Islands of Alaska and breed on Attu. They have also been recorded on Kodiak Island, Alaska, off the Massachusetts coast, and in the e. Canadian Arctic. Their primary range is most of n. Eurasia. The resident race in sw. Greenland is characterized by larger size.

Fine points: When White-tailed Eagles soar, 7 fingerlike emarginated primaries are visible on the wingtip; Bald Eagles show only 6.

Unusual plumages: Completely albino specimens exist and are overall grayish white with a yellow beak.

Subspecies: Eurasian race is *H. a. albicilla;* Greenland race is *H. a. groenlandicus.*

Etymology: *Albicilla* is from Latin *albus,* "white," and *illus,* a Latin diminutive suffix, used mistakenly to mean "tailed." The error probably originated from the name of the wagtail genus, *Motacilla.*

Measurements:
Length: 77–92 cm (84); 30–36 in. (33)
Wingspread: 208–247 cm (231); 82–97 in. (91)
Weight: 3.1–6.9 kg (4.8); 6.8–15.2 lb (10.6)

STELLER'S SEA EAGLE   Pl. 25
Haliaeetus pelagicus
Description: The accidental Steller's Sea Eagle is larger and
heavier-bodied than the Bald Eagle. It is unmistakable with its
*huge beak, white wing patches (in adults), and long, wedge-
shaped white tail.* Trailing edge of wing is more curved than
that of either Bald or White-tailed Eagle. Sexes are alike in
plumage, but females are noticeably larger.
Immature: In the first full plumage, head, body, and wing
coverts are dark blackish brown. *Huge beak, cere, and face
skin are yellow.* Iris color is dark brown. Neck and upper
breast have pale streaking. Upperwing and uppertail coverts
are mottled with white. Flight feathers are blackish. *Long, extremely wedge-shaped tail is white* and sometimes has dark
mottling. Leg color is yellow.
Subadult: The next 2 plumages are similar to that of the immature but with more whitish mottling on upperwing coverts,
legs, and tail coverts. Iris color gradually lightens.
Adult: Unmistakable. Black head has small white forehead
patch and fine white streaking on crown and neck. Iris color is
light brown. *Huge beak, cere, and face skin are orange-yellow.*
Body is black. White lesser and median upperwing and underwing coverts form *white patches on leading edge of upper and
lower wings* of flying birds and *white shoulder* of perched ones.
Flight feathers and greater coverts are black. Leg feathers, uppertail and undertail coverts, and wedge-shaped tail are white.
Leg color is yellow-orange. Adult plumage is acquired after 4
years.
Similar species: (1) **Bald Eagle** adult (Pls. 18–20) is smaller;
has white head, smaller beak, and square-tipped tail; and lacks
white patches on wings. (2) **Bald Eagle** immature (Pls. 18–20)
and subadult are smaller and have smaller beaks, white axillar
spot and white diagonal lines on underwing, dark tails or dark
border on whitish tails, and straighter trailing edge of wing. (3)
White-tailed Eagle adult (Pl. 25) is smaller, has pale head
and smaller beak, and lacks white patches on wing. (4) **White-
tailed Eagle** immatures and subadults (Pl. 25) are smaller and
have smaller beaks, dark tails or dark tip on whitish tails, and
straighter trailing edge of wing.
Flight: Active flight is with heavy, powerful wingbeats. Soars
and glides on flat wings.
Behavior: Steller's Sea Eagle is a typical sea eagle and eats
mainly fish and birds.

Status and distribution: Steller's Sea Eagle is accidental in the Aleutian and other Alaskan islands, with records from Attu, Unalaska, St. Paul, and Kodiak Island. There are approximately 2000 pairs in the main range along the n. Pacific coast of Asia from Bering Sea coast south to Kamchatka peninsula and n. coast of Sea of Okhotsk. They winter south to Korea and the Japanese island of Hokkaido.

Fine points: Steller's Sea Eagles have 14 tail feathers; other sea eagles have 12.

Unusual plumages: An adult color morph lacks the white patches on forehead and wing and white leg feathers.

Subspecies: Monotypic.

Etymology: Named after Georg Wilhelm Steller, a German naturalist, who accompanied Bering on his explorations of the n. Pacific. *Pelagicus* is from the Greek *pelagos,* "sea," and the Latin suffix *-icus,* "belonging to."

Measurements:

Length: 85–105 cm (95); 33–41 in. (37)
Wingspread: 220–245 cm (232); 87–96 in. (91)
Weight: 5–9 kg (7); 11–20 lb (15)

GOLDEN EAGLE   **Pls. 18–20; photos, pp. 151, 152**
Aquila chrysaetos

Description: The widespread but local Golden Eagle is a large, dark, long-winged soaring bird usually found in hilly and mountainous areas. The flight silhouette shows a short head and long tail; *head projection is less than half of tail length.* Goldens have a *golden nape and crown* in all plumages, varying in color from straw yellow to deep orange-brown. *Bill and cere are tricolored,* with beak tip dark, base horn-colored, and cere yellow. Sexes are similar in plumage (see **Fine points**). *Legs are feathered to the toes;* these feathers are usually paler in color than body feathers. Rufous undertail coverts are usually not noticeable in the field. Iris color varies from dark to light brown; older birds usually have paler eyes. Feet are yellow.

Immature: In the first plumage, head, body, and coverts are uniformly dark brown. Recently fledged birds may appear almost black. Upperwing coverts are uniformly dark brown, without a tawny bar. *White patches at base of inner primaries and outer secondaries* are usually visible on flying birds from below: these are sometimes visible from above as smaller patches. Some immatures have small white patches; some, especially eastern birds, lack them completely. Tail has white base (usually including *white edges,* but some individuals show grayish or dusky edges to this white area), wide dark brown subterminal band, and narrow white terminal band. White on tail is more easily seen from above.

Subadult: This plumage occurs in the next 2 or 3 years and is similar to that of the immature but with progressively smaller white patches on the flight feathers. *Tawny greater upperwing coverts form a diagonal bar on upperwing,* visible on both flying and perched birds. Tail has progressively less white on base (including *white edges*) and some wavy gray lines in the dark tip.

Note: Accurate determination of age of nonadult Golden Eagles using only the amount of white in the wings and tail is not possible because of individual variation and considerable overlap in these characters.

Adult: Head, body, and coverts are dark brown. Body plumage often appears mottled because new dark feathers contrast with old paler feathers. *Tawny upperwing coverts form a diagonal bar on upperwing.* Flight feathers are gray-brown below and appear somewhat lighter than underwing coverts when seen in good light. Faint wavy gray bars are visible in tail (see **Fine points**) and flight feathers in good light. Adult plumage is usually acquired by 4 years of age.

Similar species: (1) **Bald Eagle** (Pls. 18–20) in flight has head that protrudes more than half the tail length; head of Golden protrudes less than half the tail length. The trailing edge of wing is straighter on Balds. Immature and subadult Goldens have white on underwing restricted to base of flight feathers; white on Balds is on underwing coverts and axillars. White axillar spot on nonadult Balds can be seen from a great distance. White in Golden's tail almost always extends out to the edges, while nonadult Balds always have dark edges on whitish tails that are otherwise similar. Subadult and adult Goldens have tawny greater upperwing coverts that form a bar on each upperwing in flight and on folded wing when bird is perched; this bar is lacking on all Balds. Perched Goldens show the golden nape, yellow cere, and bicolored beak; Balds usually have cere and beak uniformly colored. Bald's tarsi are bare, while Golden's are covered completely with buffy feathers. Goldens never have extensive white areas on underparts or back. (2) **Dark-morph buteos** (Pls. 13–16) are much smaller and in flight show silvery flight feathers below, strongly contrasting with darker underwing coverts. (3) **Turkey Vulture** (Pl. 1) is smaller, flies with constant rocking or teetering, with wings in a strong dihedral, and has more contrasting two-toned underwing. (4) **Black Vulture** (Pl. 1) is black and smaller; has a short, squared-off tail; and has white patch on underwing restricted to the outer primaries.

Flight: Active flight is with slow wingbeats. The Golden Eagle soars with its wings usually in a slight dihedral but sometimes flat. It glides on flat to slightly upraised wings, with wrists above body, primaries level with wrists, and wingtips upswept.

This eagle is a masterful flyer and often hunts from the air, soaring or kiting where there are strong upcurrents. It stoops at high speeds, and Darling (1934) and others report that in a dive it flies faster than the Peregrine Falcon.

Behavior: Golden Eagles are very agile flyers for their size and are able to take mammalian prey much larger than they are, including adult coyotes, deer, pronghorn antelope, fox, and bighorn sheep. They also capture large birds, such as Sage Grouse, Canada Geese, and even Whooping Cranes. Their favorite prey, however, is jackrabbits and other small mammals. In winter Golden Eagles also feed on carrion and associate with Bald Eagles in waterfowl concentration areas. They hunt from perches and on the wing, when they glide slowly or kite on an updraft while searching the ground below. When prey is spotted, they stoop rapidly and directly. Mated adults often hunt as a pair. Most prey is captured on the ground, although Goldens also take birds in flight.

Golden Eagles usually nest on cliffs but will use trees. Unlike Bald Eagles, they readily perch and even nest on man-made structures such as power poles. In winter, a few roost communally at night with Bald Eagles.

Status and distribution: Golden Eagles are fairly common in summer in western and northern hilly and mountainous areas. They formerly bred sparsely in Appalachian Mts., and there

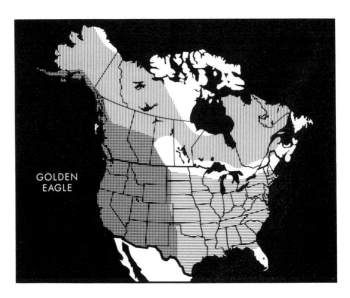

GOLDEN EAGLE

are recent reports of summering birds. In autumn, northern birds move southward, and many immatures move away from mountains. In winter they are found throughout the continent as far south as (rarely) Florida. Their worldwide range includes the mountainous areas of Asia, Europe, the Middle East, N. Africa, and N. America.

Golden Eagles have been persecuted by shooting, trapping, and poisoning, but population levels have nevertheless remained fairly stable. Local population declines have been reported, however, likely due to habitat modification, usually the encroachment of suburbia, and to shooting.

Fine points: Golden Eagle nape does not change color throughout the eagle's life; color varies among individuals (however, nape feathers are faded somewhat by sunlight). The tail of the adult male has fine wavy gray bands; that of the adult female has 1 wide and 1 narrow irregular wavy gray band.

Unusual plumages: A few cases of partial albinism have been reported.

Subspecies: The N. American race is *A. c. canadensis.*

Etymology: "Golden" refers to the color of crown and nape feathers. *Aquila* is Latin for "eagle," and *chrysaetos* is from the Greek *chrysos,* "golden," and *aetos,* "eagle."

Measurements:

Length: 70–84 cm (77); 27–33 in. (30)

Wingspread: 185–220 cm (200); 72–87 in. (79)

Weight: 3–6.4 kg (4.5); 6.6–14 lb (10)

Falcons

Family Falconidae

The family Falconidae is represented in N. America north of Mexico by 1 species in the genus *Polyborus* and 8 species of the genus *Falco*. Five of the latter are regular breeders; 2, the Northern Hobby and Eurasian Kestrel, are accidental; and the last, the Aplomado Falcon, is extirpated as a breeder and is now only a casual visitor. While the family Falconidae is not close taxonomically to Accipitridae, members of the 2 families nevertheless share many characteristics, including sharp, curved talons; hooked beaks; excellent eyesight; and both predatory and scavenging habits. The differences are mainly structural and behavioral.

The true falcons of *Falco* are characterized by long, pointed wings and medium to long tails. In all species the orbital skin (eye-ring) is bare and usually the same color as the cere. Falcons molt into adult plumage at approximately 1 year of age. All have notched beaks used to kill their vertebrate prey by severing the spinal column at the neck. They are all active predators, but most will, on occasion, eat carrion. Few accounts exist of piracy by falcons, but they often lose prey through piracy to other raptors. Falcons have 2 distinct behaviors when they are excited, bobbing their heads and pumping their tails up and down. Accipitrine raptors when excited wag their tails from side to side.

Falcons do not build their own nests. Instead they use tree cavities or cliff ledges or appropriate stick nests constructed by other raptors or corvids. Man-made structures, such as nest boxes, bridges, and building ledges and crevices, are also used.

Caracaras are quite different from true falcons. They have large heads and beaks; long necks; long legs; and wide, rounded wings. They are more piratical and vulturine and less predatory than falcons. They construct their own nests.

The terms *Falco* and "falcon" are derived from the Latin *falx,* meaning "sickle," in reference to the falcon's wing shape in flight or, according to another source, to the shape of their beaks and talons.

CRESTED CARACARA   Pl. 1; photos, p. 154
Polyborus plancus

Description: The Caracara of Florida, s. Texas, and Arizona is a large, unusual falconid. Its bold black-and-white plumage, *orange to pink to yellow face,* large horn-colored beak, large *crested head,* and *long neck in flight* are distinctive. Sexes are alike in plumage, but females are slightly larger. Iris color is medium brown.

Adult: Crown is black. Facial skin is orange to yellow. Upper back is black with fine white barring; lower back and upper wing coverts are dark blackish brown. Long neck and upper breast are white, with black barring on midbreast. Belly has wide, solid black band. Wings are dark except that mostly white outer primaries form a *large wing panel.* Underwing coverts are somewhat darker than secondaries. Undertail coverts are white. White tail has many narrow black bands and a wide dark terminal band. Long legs are yellow to yellow-orange.

Immature: Like adult except back and crown are brown, neck and throat are buffy, and midbreast and upper back are streaked with brown rather than barred with black. Facial skin is gray to pink; legs are pale yellowish gray.

Similar species: (1) **Black Vulture** (Pl. 1) has short neck and tail, and body is all dark. (2) **Common Black Hawk** immature (Pl. 16) has similar wing and tail pattern but lacks belly band and long neck.

Flight: Active flight is with medium slow, steady, almost mechanical wingbeats. The Caracara soars with its wings held flat, with leading and trailing edges straight. Caracaras appear eagle-like when soaring because of the long neck and straight wings. They glide with the wings crooked; wrists are cocked forward and above the body, and wingtips are pointed down.

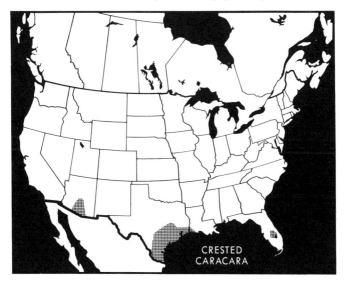

CRESTED CARACARA

When pursuing other raptors on the wing, Caracaras are agile and acrobatic.

Behavior: Caracaras are primarily scavengers but also pirate prey from other birds, especially vultures, forcing them to give up or disgorge food. They also prey on live birds, small mammals, reptiles and amphibians, and insects. They often harass other raptors and dominate Black and Turkey vultures at carcasses. Caracaras spend considerable time on the ground foraging for food and cruise highways searching for road-killed animals. Allopreening (mutual grooming) by the adults has been observed. Unlike falcons of the genus *Falco,* Caracaras build their own nest. Vocalizations include a low rattle and a single "wuck" note. When excited they throw their head back and snap it forward or roll the back of the head across the shoulders, at the same time giving the rattle call.

Status and distribution: Caracaras are fairly common on the prairies of cen. Florida and s. Texas, uncommon along the Gulf Coast into Louisiana, rare in s. Arizona, and casual in s. New Mexico. They are nonmigratory, but individuals wander into states adjacent to their breeding range.

Fine points: This species sometimes continues to flap when soaring. Facial skin changes color, depending on mood, ranging from orange on normal adult to bright yellow, indicating excitement.

Unusual plumages: A dilute-plumage specimen was collected in Argentina.

Subspecies: The N. American race is *P. p. auduboni.*

Etymology: "Caracara" probably comes from a S. American native onomatopoeic name. *Polyborus* derives from the Greek *poly,* "many" or "varied," and *boros,* "gluttonous," with reference to its voracious appetite. The Latin *plancus* means "flatfooted."

Note: "Audubon's Caracara" is another name for the N. American race. The former scientific name was *Caracara cheriway.*

Measurements:
Length: 54–60 cm (58); 21–24 in. (23)
Wingspread: 118–132 cm (125); 46–52 in. (49)
Weight: 800–1300 g (1006); 1.8–2.8 lb (2.2)

EURASIAN KESTREL
Pl. 21; photos, p. 155
Falco tinnunculus

Description: The Eurasian or Common Kestrel, accidental in North America, is similar to the American Kestrel but larger. *The two-toned pattern on upperwings in flight* is diagnostic; reddish brown or rufous back and upperwing coverts contrast with dark brown primaries, a feature lacking on the American Kestrel. Sexes have different plumages, but females are only slightly larger. Immature plumage of both sexes is similar to that of adult female. The *noticeably long tail* has a *wedge-shaped tip* when folded. Underwings appear pale in all plumages. Iris color is dark brown. Cere, eye-ring, and leg colors are orange-yellow to yellow, paler on immatures. On perched birds, wingtips fall short of tail tip.

Adult male: Head is gray, with pale cheeks, 1 thin dark mustache mark, and white throat. Back and upperwing coverts are rufous with small dark spots. Uppertail coverts are solid gray. Creamy to buffy underparts are finely streaked on breast, spotted on belly. Creamy undertail coverts and leg feathers are unstreaked. *Gray tail* is usually unbanded except for wide black subterminal band and narrow white terminal band.

Adult female: Head is reddish brown, with fine dark streaking, pale cheeks, 1 thin dark mustache mark, and white throat. Back and upperwing coverts are reddish brown and marked with short dark brown triangular bars. Uppertail coverts vary from reddish brown to gray, usually with faint dark barring. Buffy underparts have fine dark streaking. Creamy undertail coverts and leg feathers are unstreaked. Tail color varies from reddish brown, often with a grayish cast, to solid gray; tail has narrow dark brown banding and a wide dark brown subterminal band.

Immature: Similar to adult female but back and upperwing coverts are brown and have wide dark brown barring, tail has wider dark brown bands, and streaking on underparts is thicker. (Two-toned pattern on upperparts is not as noticeable on some immature females because heavy dark barring on back and coverts does not contrast as much with dark primaries.)

Similar species: American Kestrel (Pl. 21) is smaller, has 2 mustache marks, lacks two-toned upperwing in flight, and has noticeably shorter tail with a more rounded tip. American Kestrel males have rufous tails and grayish wing coverts; Eurasian Kestrel adult males have the opposite — grayish tails and rufous wing coverts. The females of these species are much more alike.

Flight: Active flight is with fast, shallow, loose, almost fluttery wingbeats. Eurasian Kestrels soar on flat wings with tail somewhat fanned and glide on flat wings or with wrists below body and tips upcurved. They regularly hover, searching for prey. Eurasian Kestrels have a heavier, more purposeful flight than the American Kestrel; they are more Merlin-like.

Behavior: Eurasian Kestrels act very much like American Kestrels. They take a variety of prey, but small mammals are their staple. Insects, reptiles, and birds, including nestlings, are also eaten. They hunt both from a high exposed perch and by hovering.

Status and distribution: Eurasian Kestrels are accidental;

there are single records from Massachusetts, New Jersey, and British Columbia and several from the Aleutian Islands. One individual was recorded from Martinique in the West Indies. **Fine points:** Adult males sometimes have many fine black tail bands. Immature females never have solid gray tails.

Unusual plumages: A dilute-plumage adult male specimen was taken in England. Albinism has been reported from the British Isles.

Subspecies: The most likely races to occur in N. America are the European race *F. t. tinnunculus* and the similar ne. Asian race *F. t. perpallidus.*

Etymology: "Kestrel" comes from the Old French *crecerelle,* a name for this species that derived from *crecelle,* meaning "to rattle," for the bird's call. *Tinnunculus* is Latin for "little bell-ringer," also for its call.

Measurements:

Length: 29–38 cm (34); 11–15 in. (13)
Wingspread: 68–82 cm (76); 27–32 in. (30)
Weight: Male 127–220 g (170); 4.5–7.8 oz (6)
         Female 142–280 g (190); 5–9.9 oz (6.7)

AMERICAN KESTREL   Pl. 21; photos, p. 156
Falco sparverius

Description: The widespread American Kestrel is the smallest N. American falcon and one of our most common and colorful raptors. Sexes have different adult and immature plumages, but all have gray heads with rufous crown patches and *white cheeks* with *2 black mustache marks.* In flight, *underwings appear pale.* Immature plumages are similar to those of adults. Females are slightly larger, but there is considerable overlap in size. On perched birds, wingtips do not reach tail tip. Iris color is dark brown. Cere, eye-ring, and leg colors are orange to yellow, paler on immatures.

Adult male: Crown is blue-gray, with a variably sized rufous crown patch, sometimes lacking. *Cheeks are white, with 2 black mustache marks,* 1 below the eye and 1 on the auriculars. Back is rufous, with black barring on lower half. *Upperwing coverts are blue-gray* with small black spots. Breast color varies from whitish to deep rufous; belly is white with black spots, heavier on flanks. *Pale underwings have a row of white circles on darker trailing edge,* visible when wing is backlighted. Leg feathers are white to rufous. *Typical tail is rufous* with thick black subterminal band and with terminal band that is white, rufous, or gray or some combination of these. Outer tail feathers are white with black bands. Tail patterns vary considerably, including some with little or no rufous.

Adult female: Head is like that of adult male but paler. Back and upperwing coverts are reddish brown with dark brown

Text continues on p. 98.

Plates

PLATE 1

Scavengers

TURKEY VULTURE *Cathartes aura*   **p. 15; photos, p. 120**
A large blackish brown raptor that flies with *wings in a strong dihedral.* In flight, note *two-toned underwing* and *long tail.* Perched birds show *brownish backs* and pinkish legs. *Head is red on adult*, pink on subadult, and dusky on immature. Subadult has two-toned beak; immature has dark beak. Wings are sometimes bowed under a "flex."
Similar species: Black Vulture, dark-morph buteos (Pls. 13–16 and 26), eagles.
Status and Distribution: Fairly common over most of N. America, ranging into s. Canada in summer. Western and northern populations move south in winter.

BLACK VULTURE *Coragyps atratus*   **p. 17; photos, p. 120**
A large, *short-tailed black* raptor that flies with wings held level or in a slight dihedral. Note *white primary patches* on black wings. Perched birds show *black backs* and whitish legs. Legs reach tip of tail on flying birds. Adult has *grayish wrinkled head* and ivory beak; immature has black, less wrinkled head and dark beak.
Similar species: Turkey Vulture, dark-morph buteos (Pls. 13–16 and 26).
Status and Distribution: Common in South and East. Uncommon to rare farther north and in Arizona. Nonmigratory.

CRESTED CARACARA   **p. 92; photos, p. 154**
Polyborus plancus
An unusual raptor with a *long neck; large, crested head;* and long legs. In flight, *long neck, bowed wings,* and *whitish wing patch* are diagnostic. Adult is black on back and wings; immature is brown. Face is orange to yellow on adult, pinkish to grayish on immature. Legs are yellow to yellow-orange on adult, pinkish to gray on immature. Upper back and breast are barred on adults and streaked on immatures. Edges of wings of soaring birds appear nearly straight and parallel.
Similar species: Black Vulture, Common Black Hawk immature (Pl. 16).
Status and Distribution: Common in cen. Florida and s. Texas, uncommon on Texas Gulf Coast, and rare in Arizona. Casual in New Mexico. Nonmigratory.

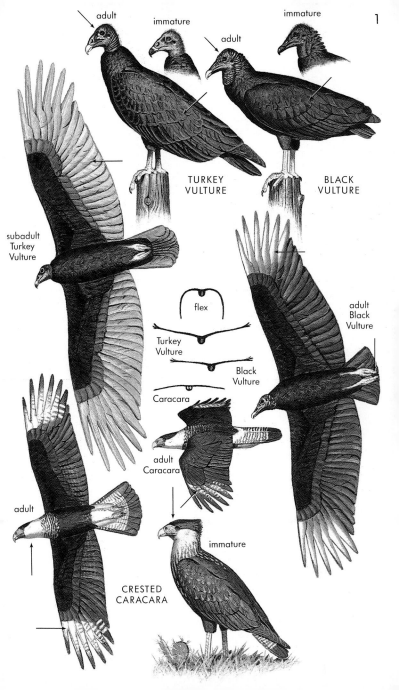

adult

immature

immature

1

adult

TURKEY VULTURE

BLACK VULTURE

subadult Turkey Vulture

flex

Turkey Vulture

Black Vulture

Caracara

adult Black Vulture

adult Caracara

adult

immature

CRESTED CARACARA

PLATE 2
California Condor

CALIFORNIA CONDOR   **p. 19; photos, p. 121**
Gymnogyps californianus
A *huge* black raptor with *large white triangles* on underside and *white bar* on upperside of long, broad wings. Adult has *orange-yellow head;* subadult's is orange-yellow with some black mottling; immature's is dusky. Adult and subadult *secondaries* are silvery above. Immature white triangle is mottled dusky. Condors soar with wings in a slight dihedral. Golden Eagle and Turkey Vulture are smaller and fly with more pronounced dihedrals.
Similar species: Turkey Vulture (Pl. 1), eagles (Pls. 18-20).
Status and Distribution: All wild condors have been taken into captivity.

CALIFORNIA CONDOR

Condor

Golden Eagle

Turkey Vulture

adult

immature

adult

immature

PLATE 3
Osprey and Northern Harrier

OSPREY *Pandion haliaetus*   **p. 21; photos, p. 121**
A large, long-winged raptor with a white body and *dark line through eye*. Wings are usually held in a *gull-like crook*. Note *dark carpal patches* on underwing. Female has short dark streaking on upper breast forming a necklace, sparser or absent on male. Adult eye is yellow, that of immature orange to red. **Immature** has pale feather edges on back and upperwing coverts and wider white terminal tail band.
Similar species: Eagles (Pls. 18–20), large gulls.
Status and Distribution: Common near water in Florida, also in areas of Atlantic Coast, Chesapeake Bay, and Great Lakes. Uncommon in parts of Montana, Idaho, and Wyoming and along Pacific Coast. Fairly common on lakes of boreal forest. In winter found only in s. Florida, along Gulf Coast, and in s. California.

NORTHERN HARRIER   p. 35; photos, p. 126
Circus cyaneus
A slender, long-winged, long-legged raptor that flies with *wings in a strong dihedral*. All plumages have distinctive *white uppertail coverts* and *dark head that appears hooded*. All also have an *owl-like facial disk*. **Adult male** is gray above and white below. Underwings are white except for mostly black outer primaries and *black* tips on secondaries that form a *bar on trailing edge*. **Adult female** is brown above, with tawny mottling, and is creamy below, heavily streaked with dark brown. **Immature** is similar to adult female but is rufous (fall) to creamy (spring) below and lacks streaking on belly. Adult females and immatures have noticeable *dark patch on underwing*, and central tail feathers that are darker than the others. Eye color of immature female is dark brown; that of immature male is gray-brown.
Similar species: Rough-legged Hawk (Pl. 10), Turkey Vulture (Pl. 1), Black-shouldered Kite (Pl. 5), Red-shouldered Hawk (Pl. 9).
Status and Distribution: Fairly common in n. United States and Canada, moving south for winter.

3

gliding

OSPREY

adult ♂

immature

adult ♀

Harrier

adult ♂

immature
♀ (fall)

NORTHERN
HARRIER

adult ♀

adult ♂

immature
♂ (spring)

PLATE 4

Florida Specialties

SNAIL KITE   p. 30; photos, pp. 122, 123
Rostrhamus sociabilis

A distinctive raptor with *paddle-shaped wings, a square tail,* and *a thin, hooked beak.* Flies on *bowed wings.* Dark *tail has white base; tail coverts are white. Wingtips extend beyond tail tip* on perched birds. **Adult male** is gray except for white tail coverts and tail base and has *red-orange legs and face skin.* **Adult female** is brown above and streaked below and has a distinctive face pattern. Legs and face skin are orange-yellow. **Immature** is almost identical to adult female but has yellow legs and face skin.

Similar species: Northern Harrier (Pl. 3).

Status and Distribution: Common but local in s. Florida.

SHORT-TAILED HAWK   p. 59; photos, p. 137
Buteo brachyurus

See Pl. 13 for dark morph.

A small aerial buteo that flies on flat wings with *wingtips upswept. Wingtips reach tail tip* on perched birds. Light morph told by *dark cheeks* and *secondaries that are darker than primaries on underwing.* Adult's white underparts are unmarked. **Immature** is similar but may have sparse streaking on sides and pale streaking on dark cheeks. Immature has *dark and light tail bands of equal width.*

Similar species: Broad-winged Hawk (Pl. 10), Swainson's Hawk (Pl. 12).

Status and Distribution: Rare and local in Florida. Dark morph is more common than light morph.

SWALLOW-TAILED KITE   p. 26; photos, p. 122
Elanoides forficatus

A distinctive raptor with bold *black-and-white plumage* and a *deeply forked tail.* This kite usually flies on flat wings. **Immature** is similar to adult but has shorter tail and white tips to wing and tail feathers.

Similar species: Swainson's Hawk (Pl. 12), Short-tailed Hawk, Magnificent Frigatebird.

Status and Distribution: Fairly common but local in Florida and uncommon along e. Gulf and Atlantic coasts to S. Carolina. Wanders far afield. Entire population migrates into S. America in early fall and returns the next spring.

gliding

adult ♂

immature

4

SNAIL KITE

adult ♂

Snail Kite adult ♀

SHORT-TAILED HAWK

adult

Short-tailed Hawk

Swallow-tailed Kite

Short-tail adult

Short-tail immature

Short-tail adult

immature

adult

SWALLOW-TAILED KITE

PLATE 5
Pointed-wing Kites

MISSISSIPPI KITE   p. 32; photos, pp. 124, 125
Ictinia mississippiensis
A graceful raptor that flies on flat wings. Note *short outer primary feathers. Wingtips extend beyond tail tip* on perched birds. **Adult** has *solid gray underparts, whitish head, and solid black tail that often appears flared.* It also shows *white trailing edge of inner upperwing* in flight (not shown; see photos) and *whitish bar on folded wings* when perched. **Subadult** has gray body like adult but often with *white spots* and has retained immature flight and tail feathers. **Immature** is brown above and streaked below, with 3 *narrow light bands in tail* and a *short creamy superciliary line.*
Status and Distribution: Fairly common but local within the breeding range in summer. Entire population migrates into S. America in early fall and returns the next spring.

BLACK-SHOULDERED KITE   p. 28; photos, p. 124
Elanus caeruleus
A whitish raptor with distinctive *black carpal patches* on underwings. It glides with wings in a *modified dihedral.* Wingtips reach tail tip on perched birds. **Adult** has *white tail,* head, and underparts and gray back. Black upperwing coverts form the *black shoulder.* **Immature** is similar but has brownish back with buffy feather edges, a dusky subterminal band to tail, white tips on primary feathers, and often a rufous wash on the breast.
Status and Distribution: Fairly common resident in w. California and s. Texas. Range is expanding into Oregon, Arizona, and Oklahoma and eastward along the Gulf Coast.

5

adult

subadult

immature

MISSISSIPPI KITE

soaring

adult

subadult

immature

Mississippi Kites

adult

immature

BLACK-SHOULDERED KITE

adult

soaring

immature

PLATE 6
Adult Accipiters

NORTHERN GOSHAWK   **p. 43; photos, pp. 127–129**
Accipiter gentilis
A large gray hawk, very buteo-like when soaring. Note the *relatively long, tapered wings* and wedge-shaped tail tip (when folded). *Head has dark hood* and *white superciliary line. Underparts are light blue-gray.*
Similar species: Cooper's Hawk, Red-shouldered Hawk (Pl. 9), Broad-winged Hawk (Pl. 10), Gyrfalcon (Pl. 24).
Status and Distribution: Fairly common but shy and retiring in northern woods and western mountains in summer. Uncommon elsewhere (rare in Southeast) during migration and in winter.

COOPER'S HAWK   **p. 41; photos, pp. 127–129**
Accipiter cooperii
A medium-sized hawk with relatively short wings. *On gliding birds, head projects beyond wrists. Large, squarish head has eye placed well forward. Crown is darker than nape.* Underparts appear rufous. *Long, rounded tail has wide white tip.* Female's back color is browner than male's. Always larger than Sharp-shinned Hawk.
Similar species: Sharp-shinned Hawk, Goshawk, Broad-winged Hawk (Pl. 10), Red-shouldered Hawk (Pl. 9).
Status and Distribution: Uncommon in East; fairly common in West in summer and in some locales during migration. More southern than other accipiters.

SHARP-SHINNED HAWK   **p. 38; photos, pp. 127–129**
Accipiter striatus
A small hawk with a *small, rounded head that barely projects beyond wrists on gliding birds. Eye is centrally placed on side of head. Crown and nape are same color.* Underparts appear rufous. *Tail tip is square with a narrow white terminal band* and often shows a notch when folded. Female's back color browner than male's.
Similar species: Cooper's Hawk, Merlin (Pl. 22).
Status and Distribution: Fairly common but shy and retiring in northern woods and western mountains in summer, uncommon to rare elsewhere. Abundant in some locales during migration.

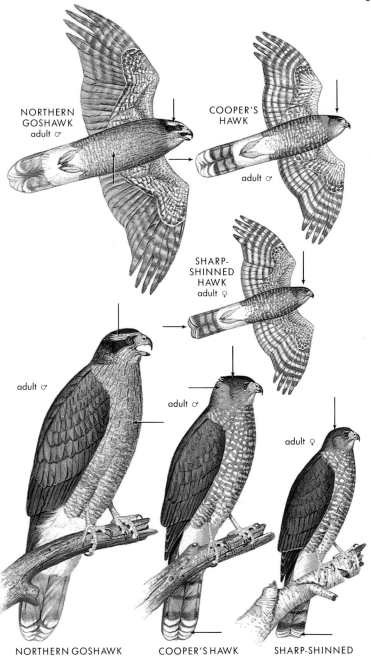

NORTHERN GOSHAWK
adult ♂

COOPER'S HAWK
adult ♂

SHARP-SHINNED HAWK
adult ♀

adult ♂

adult ♂

adult ♀

NORTHERN GOSHAWK   COOPER'S HAWK   SHARP-SHINNED

PLATE 7

Immature Accipiters

NORTHERN GOSHAWK
p. 43; photos, pp. 127–129

Accipiter gentilis

A large hawk, very buteo-like when soaring. Note *relatively long, tapered wings* and wedge-shaped tail tip (when folded). *Back is heavily mottled with tawny and buffy* and appears paler than on other accipiters. Tawny bar on upperwing coverts is noticeable on perched and flying birds. Underparts are heavily streaked, including belly and undertail coverts. *Tail has white "highlights"* (visible only at close range).

Similar species: Cooper's Hawk, Red-shouldered Hawk (Pl. 9), Broad-winged Hawk (Pl. 10), Gyrfalcon (Pl. 24).

Status and Distribution: Fairly common but shy and retiring in northern woods and western mountains in summer. Uncommon elsewhere (rare in Southeast) during migration and in winter.

COOPER'S HAWK
p. 41; photos, pp. 127–129

Accipiter cooperii

A medium-sized hawk with relatively short wings. This hawk soars with the leading edge of wing straighter than those of other accipiters. *Large head has a tawny neck and often appears hooded. Belly is less heavily streaked than breast. Long tail has a rounded tip with a wide white terminal band. Large, squarish head has eye placed well forward* and usually lacks superciliary line. *Back has some pale mottling.* Undertail coverts are unmarked. Often soars with wings in a slight dihedral. Always larger than Sharp-shinned Hawk.

Similar species: Sharp-shinned Hawk, Goshawk, Broad-winged Hawk (Pl. 10), Red-shouldered Hawk (Pl. 9).

Status and Distribution: Uncommon in East; fairly common in West in summer; and in some locales during migration. More southern than other accipiters.

SHARP-SHINNED HAWK
p. 38; photos, pp. 127–129

Accipiter striatus

A small hawk with a *small, rounded head. Eye is centrally placed on head. Underparts are heavily streaked with reddish brown, heaviest on belly. Dark brown back has little or no mottling. Tail tip is square,* with a *narrow white terminal band,* and often shows a notch when folded.

Similar species: Cooper's Hawk, Merlin (Pl. 22).

Status and Distribution: Fairly common but shy and retiring in northern woods and western mountains in summer; uncommon to rare elsewhere. Abundant in some locales during migration.

Note: Immature accipiters have equal-width light and dark tail bands, except on outer feathers.

COOPER'S
HAWK
immature ♂

NORTHERN
GOSHAWK
immature ♂

SHARP-
SHINNED
HAWK

immature
♀

immature ♂

immature ♀

immature ♀

NORTHERN GOSHAWK   COOPER'S HAWK   SHARP-SHINNED HAWK

PLATE 8
Mexican Border Specialties

GRAY HAWK *Buteo nitidus*   **p. 50; photos, p. 132**
A small accipiter-like buteo. *White greater uppertail coverts form a U above tail base.* **Adult** has gray back, gray barred underparts, *pale underwings,* and a *long black tail with 2 white bands, 1 wide and 1 narrow.* **Immature** has brown back, streaked underparts, and *distinctive bold face pattern.* Outer primary and leg feathers are barred. *Long tail* has more than 5 dark bands. On perched birds, wingtips reach only halfway down tail.
Similar species: Broad-winged Hawk (Pl. 10), accipiters (Pls. 6 and 7), Hook-billed Kite.
Status and Distribution: Uncommon and local in riparian areas of s. Arizona and in lower Rio Grande valley of Texas.

ROADSIDE HAWK   **p. 52; photos, p. 133**
Buteo magnirostris
A small chunky buteo with a *dark bib.* Northern Mexico race has little or no rufous in wing. *Long tail has dark and light bands of equal width.* Greater uppertail coverts form a *buffy U above tail base.* **Adult** has *yellow eye.* **Immature** has orangish eye, *pale superciliary line,* and *streaked bib and barred belly.*
Similar species: Gray Hawk, Broad-winged Hawk (Pl. 10), Red-shouldered Hawk (Pl. 9), accipiters (Pls. 6 and 7).
Status and Distribution: Accidental in lower Rio Grande valley of Texas.

HOOK-BILLED KITE   **p. 24; photos, p. 122**
Chondrohierax uncinatus
A distinctive raptor with *white eyes, paddle-shaped wings,* and *large hooked beak.* **Adult male** has gray barred underparts and contrasting dark gray head, *dark underwings with boldly barred outer primaries* and 2 white bands on undertail. **Adult female** is brown with a distinctive *rufous collar,* rufous on the primary feathers, and 2 pale tail bands. **Immature** is similar to adult female but has a *white collar,* less heavily barred underparts, and a brown eye.
Similar species: Gray Hawk, Red-shouldered Hawk (Pl. 9), Broad-winged Hawk (Pl. 10), Roadside Hawk, accipiters (Pls. 6 and 7), Common Black Hawk (Pl. 16).
Status and Distribution: 10 to 20 pairs in Rio Grande valley.

8

adult

adult

immature

adult

immature

GRAY
HAWK

Broad-
winged
Hawk
immature

Gray
Hawk
adult

Gray
Hawk
imm.

adult

adult

ROADSIDE
HAWK
immature

adult ♀

Hook-billed
Kite
adult ♂

adult ♂
Hook-billed
Kite

adult ♀

immature

HOOK-
BILLED
KITE

PLATE 9

Red-shouldered Hawk

RED-SHOULDERED HAWK   p. 53; photos, pp. 134, 135
Buteo lineatus
A medium to large buteo recognized in flight by the *crescent-shaped wing panels*, white on adults, tawny on immatures. (Wing panels are visible on backlighted wings.) *Glides on bowed wings.* Wingtips fall short of tail tip on perched birds.
Eastern adult: Brown head and back, rufous lesser upperwing coverts, and *black-and-white checkered flight feathers above.* Underparts are barred rufous and *black tail has 3 or 4 narrow white bands.* Upperwing coverts form *rufous (red) shoulder* on perched birds. *Underwing is two-toned;* coverts are rufous, and flight feathers are whitish.
Eastern immature: Brown head, back, and upperwing coverts and *dark brown tail with narrow light brown bands.* Underparts are streaked. Wings below are uniformly pale; wing panels are visible on backlighted wings. Note pale superciliary line and dark malar stripe on face.
Florida adult: *Pale gray head* and pale rufous underparts.
Florida immature: Heavily streaked and barred underparts and (usually) barred leg feathers.
California adult: Bright rufous underparts and shoulder patch.
California immature: Similar to adult, with barred, not streaked, underparts and white crescent-shaped wing panel, two-toned underwing, and brownish black tail with narrow white bands.
Texas adult: Not shown but similar to California adult.
Texas immature: Not shown but similar to Florida immature.
Similar species: Broad-winged Hawk (Pl. 10), Goshawk (Pls. 6 and 7), Cooper's Hawk (Pls. 6 and 7), Red-tailed Hawk (Pl. 11).
Status and Distribution: Eastern form is fairly common east of Great Plains. Northern birds are migratory, some moving into Florida and s. Texas. **Florida** form is common in peninsular Florida. **California** form is fairly common west of deserts and Sierras of California. Regularly recorded in sw. Oregon. Casual in Arizona, Nevada, and Utah. **Texas** form is fairly common and local in s. Texas.

adult

immature

adult

Eastern

immature

gliding

soaring

under-
wing of
adult

underwing
of
immature

immature

adult

Florida

immature

adult

California

immature

PLATE 10

Light-morph Broad-winged
and Rough-legged Hawks

BROAD-WINGED HAWK p. 56; photos, pp. 134, 136
Buteo platypterus
See Pls. 13 and 26 for dark morph.
A small, *pointed-wing buteo* that flies on flat wings. Wingtips do not reach tail tip on perched birds. **Adult** is uniformly dark brown above and barred rufous below. *Dark tail has a wide white band;* a narrower white band is sometimes visible near the base. *Underwing is unmarked except for dark border.* **Immature** has dark brown upperparts and lightly to heavily streaked underparts. Light brown tail has dark brown bands, subterminal band widest. *Underwing is uniformly pale* with a *dusky border.* Backlighted wing shows square wing panel. Face has pale superciliary line and dark malar stripe.
Similar species: Red-shouldered Hawk (Pl. 9), Cooper's Hawk, and Goshawk (Pls. 6 and 7).
Status and Distribution: In summer, common in eastern forests and in boreal forest west to Alberta. During migration, abundant at times in East, casual in West. Small numbers winter in subtropical areas of s. Florida, Gulf Coast, and s. California.

ROUGH-LEGGED HAWK p. 77; photos, pp. 148, 149
Buteo lagopus
See Pls. 15 and 26 for dark morph.
A large, long-winged buteo identified by *dark carpal patches* on underwings. Soars with wings in a medium dihedral; glides with wings in a modified dihedral. Wingtips reach tail tip on perched birds. Legs are feathered down to toes. **Adult** has dark eyes, more heavily marked underwing coverts, barred leg feathers, and a black band on the trailing edge of the underwing. **Adult male** type has grayish back and breast that is more heavily marked than creamy belly (which is sometimes unmarked), with a white U between, and *white tail* with a *wide dark subterminal band* and *1 or more narrower dark bands.* **Adult female** type has brownish back and creamy belly that is more heavily marked than creamy breast (sometimes a solid belly band), and *white tail* has a *wide dusky terminal band* with a *narrower black subterminal band* superimposed on it. **Immature** has a brownish back, unmarked underwing coverts, lightly spotted leg feathers, a *solid dark belly band,* and a *white tail* with a *wide dusky subterminal band.* Note white area on upper primaries, not present on adults.
Similar species: Northern Harrier (Pl. 3).
Status and Distribution: Fairly common but local on arctic tundra in summer. Common to uncommon but local throughout northern and central states in winter, reaching Mexico in West.

soaring

adult

immature

adult

immature

immature

BROAD-
WINGED
HAWK

immature

underwing of
immature

soaring

ROUGH-
LEGGED
HAWK

adult ♂

immature

undertail
of imm.

adult ♂

adult ♀

undertail
of adult ♀

gliding

10

PLATE 11
Light-morph Red-tailed Hawks

RED-TAILED HAWK p. 69; photos, pp. 142–145
Buteo jamaicensis
See Pls. 14 and 26 for dark morph.

A large, widespread, and common buteo that flies with its wings in a slight dihedral. Identified in flight by *dark patagial marks* on underwing. Wide pale edges of scapulars and upperwing coverts form a V on back and wings of perched and flying birds. Belly band is not always present on adults. Four forms are recognizable: Eastern, Krider's, Fuertes', and Western. Wingtips reach tail tip on perched adult Western and Fuertes' forms but not on Eastern and Krider's.

Eastern adult: *Rufous tail* and dark head that appears hooded. Underwing shows wide dark band on trailing edge.

Eastern immature: Light brown tail with numerous narrow dark bands of equal width, underwing with narrower and fainter dusky band on trailing edge than that on adult underwing, and primaries above paler than secondaries. Backlighted wings show square wing panels.

Krider's: *Whitish head and tail, back heavily mottled with white,* and patagial mark sometimes faint or absent. Adult has *pink tip of tail* with a *narrow dark subterminal band.* Immature has *3 or more narrow dark tail bands of equal width* and primaries and primary coverts that are white above.

Western: Generally darker and more richly colored rufous than Eastern. Adult rufous tail has a wider subterminal band and often has numerous narrow dark bands.

Fuertes': Usually darker and less mottled on the back than Eastern and lacks the belly band.

Partial albinos: Many white or partially white feathers; almost always adults with some rufous in tail.

Similar species: Ferruginous Hawk (Pl. 12), Red-shouldered Hawk (Pl. 9), Broad-winged Hawk (Pl. 10).

Status and Distribution: Eastern form is common east of and on Great Plains. **Western** form is common west of Great Plains. Common on Great Plains and casual in East in winter. **Krider's** form is rare on northern Great Plains, uncommon farther south in winter. **Fuertes'** form is common in Southwest. **Partial albino** is rare but regular and widespread.

RED-TAILED HAWKS

soaring

adult

Eastern

immature

immature

underwing of immature

Krider's immature

perched adults

partial albino

Eastern

Krider's

Fuertes'

Western

PLATE 12

Light-morph Swainson's and Ferruginous Hawks

SWAINSON'S HAWK   p. 61; photos, pp. 138, 139
Buteo swainsoni
See Pls. 13 and 26 for dark morph.
A large, slender, *pointed-wing buteo* that flies with its wings in a strong dihedral. Identified in flight by *two-toned underwing:* dark flight feathers and pale coverts. Wingtips reach tail tip on perched birds. Underparts vary from quite dark to almost white (extremes for both adult and immature are shown). **Adult** has *dark breast forming bib with large white throat patch,* barred belly (on darker birds), and small white forehead patch. **Immature** has underparts spotted and streaked, often with a hint of a necklace, and bold face pattern.
Similar species: Red-tailed Hawk (Pl. 11), Prairie Falcon (Pl. 22).
Status and Distribution: Fairly common in western grasslands in summer. Abundant during migration on southern Great Plains. Casual in East during migration. Small winter population in s. Florida.

FERRUGINOUS HAWK   p. 74; photos, pp. 146, 147
Buteo regalis
See Pls. 15 and 26 for dark morph.
A very large, long- and narrow-winged buteo that flies with its wings in a medium to strong dihedral. *Large head and gape* are noticeable at close range. Note combination of *white cheek, dark eye-line,* and *absence of malar stripe.* Pale area on upper primaries shared with immature Rough-legged Hawk. Wingtips almost reach tail tip on perched birds. Dark spots on underparts sometimes form breast or belly band. Legs are feathered to toes. **Adult** has *unbanded tail* that is rufous, white, gray, or a combination; *rufous back and upperwing coverts;* and (usually) *rufous patches on underwing coverts. Dark rufous leg feathers form a V on belly* of flying bird. **Immature** is whitish below with whitish, not rufous, leg feathers. Underwing lacks dark patagial mark. Tail above has white base and below is pale with a dusky subterminal band. White greater uppertail coverts have *large black spots.* Fledgling has a rufous bloom on breast that fades by fall.
Similar species: Red-tailed Hawk (Pl. 11), Rough-legged Hawk (Pl. 10).
Status and Distribution: Fairly common in arid areas of West from w. Great Plains to n. Texas and s. Oregon. Moves south and east in winter. Casual in East.

soaring

adult

immature

SWAINSON'S
HAWK

adult

immature

Ferruginous
adult

erruginous
immature

adult

FERRUGINOUS
HAWK

undertail
of
immature

immature
(recently
fledged)

soaring

PLATE 13
Dark-morph Pointed-wing Buteos

SWAINSON'S HAWK   **p. 61; photos, pp. 138, 139**
Buteo swainsoni
See Pl. 12 for light morph. See also Pl. 26.
A large, slender, *pointed-wing buteo* that flies with wings in a strong dihedral. Note *dark, not silvery, flight feathers*. Dark-morph adults have underparts that are solid dark rufous, solid dark brown, or solid black, and rufous-morph adults have a dark brown breast and dark rufous belly. Both always have *pale undertail coverts*. Underwing coverts vary from pale to solid dark brown. Note finely banded gray tail with subterminal band wider.
Similar species: Dark-morph buteos (Pls. 14, 15, and 26), White-tailed Hawk immature (Pls. 17 and 26).
Status and Distribution: Dark morph is uncommon to rare.

SHORT-TAILED HAWK   **p. 59; photos, p. 137**
Buteo brachyurus
See Pl. 4 for light morph.
A small aerial buteo that flies on flat wings with *upswept wingtips. Wingtips reach tail tip* on perched birds. Light morph told by *dark cheeks* and *secondaries that are darker than primaries on underwing*. **Adult's** white underparts are unmarked. **Immature** is similar but may have sparse streaking on sides and pale streaking on dark cheeks. Immature has *dark and light tail bands of equal width*.
Similar species: Broad-winged Hawk (Pl. 26), Swainson's Hawk.
Status and Distribution: Rare and local in Florida. Dark morph is more common than light.

BROAD-WINGED HAWK   **p. 56; photos, pp. 134, 136**
Buteo platypterus
See Pl. 10 for light morph. See also Pl. 26.
A small, *pointed-wing buteo* that flies on flat wings. *Primaries and secondaries are both silvery*. **Adult** has solid dark brown body and underwing coverts and *dark tail with 1 wide white band*. **Immature** has solid dark brown body and underwing coverts, sometimes mottled with rufous and white, and *light tail* with a *wide dark subterminal band* and *several narrow dark bands*.
Similar species: Dark-morph buteos (Pls. 14, 15, and 26).
Status and Distribution: Dark morph is rare and breeds only in Alberta.

SWAINSON'S HAWK

dark-morph
adult

SHORT-TAILED HAWK

dark-morph
adult

BROAD-WINGED HAWK

dark-morph
adult

SWAINSON'S
HAWK
rufous-morph
adult

SHORT-TAILED
HAWK
dark-morph
immature

BROAD-
WINGED
HAWK
dark-morph
immature

Swainson's Hawk

Short-tailed Hawk

Broad-winged Hawk

PLATE 14

Dark Red-tailed Hawks

RED-TAILED HAWK   **p. 69; photos, pp. 142–145**
Buteo jamaicensis
See Pl. 11 for light morph. See also Pl. 26.
A large, widespread, and common buteo that flies with its wings in a slight dihedral. The three types of dark Red-tails are dark morph, rufous morph, and Harlan's Hawk. Wingtips reach tail tip on perched birds.

Dark-morph adult
Solid dark brown (rarely jet black) body and undertail coverts. *Rufous tail* often has numerous narrow dark bands. Flight feathers below are heavily barred and have a wide dark band on tips.

Dark-morph immature
Dark brown body and underwing coverts, most often with breast and underwing coverts mottled with tawny or white. *Light brown tail has many dark bands of equal width,* wider than the bands on light-morph immature tail.

Rufous-morph adult
Rufous breast, leg feathers, and undertail coverts; wide belly band is dark brown. *Rufous tail* is banded like that of dark-morph adult.

Rufous-morph immature
Not rufous but like light-morph immature (Pl. 11). Note *heavily streaked breast and heavily mottled belly band* and underwing coverts, the latter obscuring the dark patagial mark.

Harlan's Hawk adult
Overall *coal black*, with a variable amount of *white breast streaking,* sometimes with white mottling on underwing coverts. Flight feathers below are darkly barred or mottled or both, with outer primaries having barred tips and dark tips of others forming a dark trailing edge of wing. *Tail is usually dirty white to dark gray, mottled lengthwise with black, almost always with a darker terminal or subterminal band but sometimes white with many dark bands, subterminal band widest.* Many characters, such as the tail, may intergrade with those of western Red-tailed Hawk.

Harlan's Hawk immature
Not shown. Similar to dark-morph immature but black; has wider, wavier dark tail bands; and has barring on underside of tips of outer primaries.
Similar species: Rough-legged Hawk (Pls. 15 and 26), Ferruginous Hawk (Pls. 15 and 26).
Status and Distribution: Dark- and **rufous-morph Red-tailed Hawks** are uncommon to rare in West. Uncommon in winter on Great Plains and farther south, casual in East. **Harlan's Hawk** is locally common in Alaska in summer, uncommon in Arkansas, Missouri, Kansas, Oklahoma, and Texas in winter. Widespread but rare in other areas in winter.

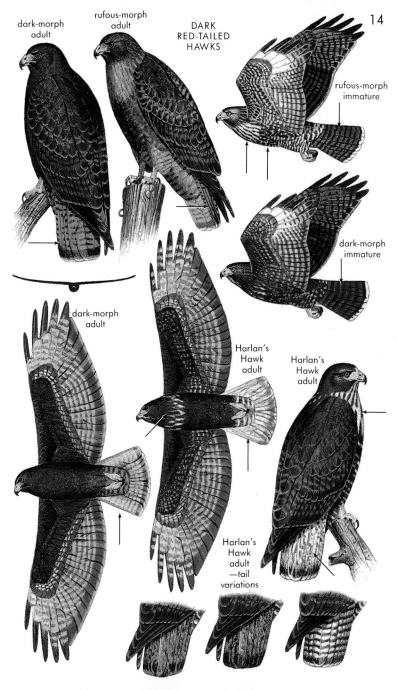

dark-morph adult

rufous-morph adult

DARK RED-TAILED HAWKS

14

rufous-morph immature

dark-morph immature

dark-morph adult

Harlan's Hawk adult

Harlan's Hawk adult

Harlan's Hawk adult —tail variations

PLATE 15

Dark-morph Rough-legged and Ferruginous Hawks

ROUGH-LEGGED HAWK p. 77; photos, p. 149
Buteo lagopus
See Pl. 10 for light morph. See also Pl. 26.
A large, long-winged buteo that soars with its wings in a medium dihedral and glides with its wings in a modified dihedral. Dark-morph birds are identified mainly by tail pattern, but *a small white area with central black spot on nape* is diagnostic. Wingtips reach tail tip on perched birds. A *black carpal patch* is sometimes notice-able on birds with brown underwing coverts. Legs are feathered to toes. **Adult** underwing shows heavily barred flight feathers with a wide band on trailing edge. **Adult male** type has jet black body and underwing coverts and *black tail* with *3 or 4 narrow white bands of equal width.* **Adult female** type has dark brown body and dark reddish brown underwing coverts and solid dark tail above but *silvery* with *wide dark terminal band below.* **Immature** has dark brown body and dark reddish brown underwing coverts and dark tail, often with faint pale bands above but silvery below with a wide dusky subterminal band. Note whitish primaries on upperwing. Flight feathers lack heavy barring and dark tips of adult's. Head and gape are smaller than those of Ferruginous Hawk.
Similar species: Ferruginous Hawk, Harlan's Hawk (Pls. 14 and 26), Turkey Vulture (Pl. 1).
Status and Distribution: Dark morph is fairly common in East and on Great Plains, less common in West.

FERRUGINOUS HAWK p. 74; photos, p. 147
Buteo regalis
See Pl. 12 for light morph. See also Pl. 26.
A very large, long- and narrow-winged buteo that flies with its wings in a medium to strong dihedral. Dark morph identified in flight by *white wrist commas on underwing.* Note the *large head and gape.* Light area on upper primaries shared by immature Rough-legged Hawk. Wingtips almost reach tail tip on perched birds. Legs are feathered to toes. **Adult** is solid dark brown to dark rufous on body and underwing coverts but may have some whitish or tawny mottling on breast. Flight feathers below are silvery and lightly marked. *Unbanded tail is gray above and white below.* **Immature** is solid dark brown on body and underwing coverts. Tail silvery below, with a wide dusky subterminal band, and appears solid dark above (but appears gray with dark bands when seen in good light).
Similar species: Rough-legged Hawk, dark-morph buteos (Pls. 13, 14, and 26).
Status and Distribution: Dark morph is uncommon to rare, usu-ally less than 10% of population.

ROUGH-LEGGED HAWK

15

dark-morph
adult ♂ type

undertail

undertail of
dark-morph
adult ♀ type

dark-morph
immature

Rough-leg
dark-morph
adult ♂ type

Rough-leg
dark-morph
immature

Ferruginous
dark-morph
immature

undertail

dark-morph
adult

Ferruginous
dark-morph
immature

dark-morph
adult

FERRUGINOUS
HAWK

PLATE 16
Black and Zone-tailed Hawks

COMMON BLACK HAWK   p. 46; photos, p. 130
Buteogallus anthracinus

A large, long-legged, *wide-winged* buteoine that flies on flat wings.
Adult is all black except for *small white patch at base of outer
primaries* and *wide white tail band.* On perched birds, wingtips
almost reach tail tip. Note *orange-yellow face skin* and cere. **Immature** is dark brown above with creamy underparts irregularly
streaked with black, forming black patches on flank and side of
upper breast. Flying birds show *tawny primary wing panels. White
tail has numerous irregular narrow dark bands.* Wingtips on
perched birds fall somewhat short of tail tip. *Bold face pattern* is
distinctive.
Similar species: Zone-tailed Hawk, dark-morph buteos (Pls.
13–15 and 26), Black Vulture (Pl. 1).
Status and Distribution: Uncommon and local in Arizona, w.
New Mexico, and w. Texas. Rare in s. Utah. Rare in winter in s.
Texas.

ZONE-TAILED HAWK   p. 67; photos, p. 141
Buteo albonotatus
See also Pl. 26.

A large, slender, long-winged buteo that *soars with its wings in a
strong dihedral, mimicking the Turkey Vulture.* Wingtips reach tail
tip on perched birds. **Adult** has black body and coverts; at close
range a grayish bloom is noticeable. Flight feathers are somewhat
silvery so that underwing is two-toned, like that of the Turkey
Vulture. *Black tail has 1 wide and 1 narrow white band (male) or
2 narrow white bands (female). Tail bands are dull gray above.*
Note that only 1 white band shows on underside of folded tail. Up
close, light gray face skin and yellow cere are noticeable. **Immature** is similar to adult but more brownish black and with distinctive *white spots on the body.* Tail is silvery below with numerous
narrow dark bands; subterminal band widest. Flight feathers on
underside are whiter than those of adults.
Similar species: Black Hawk, Turkey Vulture (Pl. 1), dark-morph
buteos (Pls. 13–15 and 26).
Status and Distribution: Fairly common in Arizona, uncommon
in New Mexico and w. Texas, casual in California. Migratory, rare
in winter in s. Texas.

16

Black Hawk

Zone-tailed
Hawk

BLACK
HAWK

immature

immature

adult

adult

adult

adult ♂

ZONE-
TAILED
HAWK

undertail
of immature

adult ♀

immature

closed tail
of adult

PLATE 17
White-tailed Hawk and Harris' Hawk

WHITE-TAILED HAWK   p. 64; photos, pp. 140, 141
Buteo albicaudatus
See also Pl. 26.
A very large, *pointed-wing buteo* that soars with its wings in a strong dihedral. *Trailing edge of wing is pinched in at body* on flying birds. Wingtips reach tail tip (immature) or extend beyond it (adult and subadult) on perched birds. **Adult** has gray head and back and white underparts, underwing and tail coverts, and *lower back. White tail has wide black subterminal band* and many faint narrow black bands. Lesser upperwing coverts form *rufous shoulder* of perched birds. *Primaries are darker than secondaries below. Dark gray cheek* of flying birds is noticeable. **Subadult** is similar to adult, but head and back are blackish, *white underparts have heavy rufous and black barring on belly,* and underwing coverts are dark. Tail is gray with dark subterminal band. **Immature** is quite different (see also Pl. 26)—almost entirely black except for *creamy breast patch* and *pale undertail coverts.* Tips of greater uppertail coverts form *a white U above base of tail.* Flight feathers are dark gray. *Tail is noticeably longer than that of adult or subadult and is medium gray with numerous narrow dark bands of equal width.* Note pale marks on side of head.
Similar species: Swainson's Hawk (Pls. 12, 13, and 26), Ferruginous Hawk (Pls. 12, 15, and 26), Harlan's Hawk (Pls. 14 and 26).
Status and Distribution: Fairly common on Texas coastal prairie. Nonmigratory.

HARRIS' HAWK   p. 48; photos, p. 131
Parabuteo unicinctus
A large, dark, long-legged, long-tailed buteoine that soars on flat wings and glides on bowed wings. *Chestnut underwing coverts* and *white tail coverts* and *white base and wide white tip to tail* are distinctive in flight. Note *chestnut shoulder patch and leg feathers* on perched birds. Wingtips reach only halfway to tail tip on perched birds. **Adult** has solid dark brown underparts, dark gray flight feathers below, and chestnut leg feathers. **Immature** is similar to adult but has creamy streaking on dark underparts, heavier on belly. Primaries are whitish and secondaries are pale grayish below. Creamy leg feathers are barred chestnut. Darkish tail has narrower white bands at base and tip than that of adult.
Similar species: Dark-morph buteos (Pls. 13–15 and 26).
Status and Distribution: Fairly common in deserts of Texas, New Mexico, and Arizona. Nonmigratory.

soaring

adult

immature

immature

WHITE-
TAILED
HAWK

adult

subadult

immature

adult

HARRIS'
HAWK

adult

immature

gliding

soaring

PLATE 18

Perched Eagles

GOLDEN EAGLE   p. 88; photos, pp. 151, 152
Aquila chrysaetos
See also Pls. 19 and 20.
A large dark eagle with *golden crown and nape* in all plumages.
Beak and cere are tricolored: cere yellow, base of beak horn-colored, and tip black. Legs are completely covered with buffy feathers. **Adult** (not shown) has dark brown body and coverts and appears somewhat mottled when viewed at close range because old faded feathers contrast with new dark ones. *Tawny bar on folded wing* of adult and subadult (not shown) noticeable at close range. Dark brown tail has faint wavy gray bands: 2 or 3 narrow ones (male) or 1 wide and 1 or more narrow ones (female, Pl. 20). Eye color is yellow. **Subadult** is like adult except that tail is white at base, usually including *white edges*. Eye color is light brown. **Immature** is dark brown except for golden nape and white patches, appearing darker than adult and subadult. Tail is white with *white edges* and wide dark brown terminal band. Eye color is dark brown.
Similar species: See Pl. 19.
Status and Distribution: See Pl. 19.

BALD EAGLE   p. 81; photos, pp. 150, 151
Haliaeetus leucocephalus
See also Pls. 19 and 20.
A large eagle with large head and beak and long neck. *Beak and cere are usually the same color.* Legs are not fully feathered. **Adult** has *white head, tail,* and tail coverts, with the rest of the body and wings dark brown. Eye is pale yellow and beak is orange-yellow. **Transition-plumage** birds look similar to adults but have black streaking on the white head, usually including a dark, Osprey-like eye-line, white mottling on the body and wing coverts, and an immature tail. **White-belly I and II** are similar and have head with *wide buffy superciliary line* and dark area behind eye, dark breast, *white belly* with short dark streaking, and an *upside-down white triangle* on the back. Eye color is light brown to white. Beak color is slate to horn-colored, with yellowish patches on older birds. The pattern and color of subadult and immature tails are variable and apparently not age related. **Immature** has dark head and eyes, dark back, and dark underparts consisting of dark brown breast and *dark to light tawny belly*.
Similar species: See Pl. 19.
Status and Distribution: See Pl. 19.

18

GOLDEN EAGLE

immature

BALD EAGLE

White-belly I

immature

tail of subadult Golden Eagle

tail of adult Golden Eagle

White-belly II

BALD EAGLE

transition

adult

PLATE 19

Soaring Eagles From Below

GOLDEN EAGLE   **p. 88; photos, pp. 151, 152**
Aquila chrysaetos
See also Pls. 18 and 20.
A large dark eagle with *golden crown and nape* in all plumages. *Head projects* beyond body *less than one-half the tail length.* Flies sometimes with wings in a slight dihedral but sometimes with wings flat (wing attitude is a useful clue but is not diagnostic). **Adult** is all dark, with coverts darker than flight feathers on underwing. Faint wavy gray bands are visible on flight feathers and tail at close range. **Subadult** is like adult but has some white in tail, including edges, and (though not always) *white patches at base of inner primaries and outer secondaries.* Tail has faint gray bands in dark area. **Immature** is solid dark except for white base of tail, usually *including edges,* and (though not always) *white patches at base of inner primaries and outer secondaries.* Wings are wider and tail is longer than in subsequent plumages.
Similar species: Bald Eagle, dark-morph buteos (Pls. 13–16 and 26), vultures (Pl. 1).
Status and Distribution: Fairly common in hilly and mountainous areas of West in summer, moving to plains and valleys in winter. Northern populations move south. Uncommon to rare in East in winter.

BALD EAGLE   **p. 81; photos, pp. 150, 151**
Haliaeetus leucocephalus
See also Pls. 18 and 20.
A large eagle that flies with wings flat. *Head projects more than one-half the tail length.* The trailing edge of wing is straighter and less pinched in at the body than that of the Golden Eagle. All nonadult plumages have *white axillary spots* and *white diagonal lines* on underwing. Note that white on flight feathers is not restricted to base of inner primaries and outer secondaries. If tail is white with a dark terminal band, then *outer edges are dark.* **White-belly I and II** have dark breast and *white belly.* **Immature** has dark breast and belly color that ranges from dark to light tawny. Wings are wider and tail longer than in subsequent plumages.
Similar species: Golden Eagle, Osprey (Pl. 3), Turkey Vulture (Pl. 1).
Status and Distribution: Locally common in breeding centers in summer. Northern population moves south or to coasts in winter. Locally common to abundant in winter concentration areas but also sparsely distributed over large areas covering most of the United States.

19

tail of
subadult
(underside)

wing of
subadult

GOLDEN
EAGLE

adult ♂

immature

White-
belly II

BALD
EAGLE

immature

Golden
Eagle

Bald
Eagle

PLATE 20
Soaring Eagles From Above

GOLDEN EAGLE   **p. 88; photos, pp. 151, 152**
Aquila chrysaetos
See also Pls. 18 and 19.
A large dark eagle with *golden crown and nape* in all plumages.
Head projects less than one-half the tail length. Usually flies with
wings in a slight dihedral but sometimes with wings flat. (Wing
attitude is a helpful clue but is not diagnostic.) **Adult** shows
tawny bars on upperwings. Note faint irregular grayish bands in
tail (female shown; see Pl. 18 for male pattern). **Subadult** is like
adult but with white at base of tail and (rarely) *white patches at
base of inner primaries and outer secondaries.* **Immature** lacks
tawny wingbar but has white at base of tail, usually *including the
outer edges,* and sometimes has *white patches at base of inner
primaries and outer secondaries.* Wings are wider and tail longer
than in subsequent plumages.
Similar species: Bald Eagle, dark-morph buteos (Pls. 13–16), vultures (Pl. 1).
Status and Distribution: Fairly common in mountainous areas of
West in summer, moving to plains and valleys in winter. Northern
populations move south. Uncommon to rare in East in winter.

BALD EAGLE   **p. 81; photos, pp. 150, 151**
Haliaeetus leucocephalus
See also Pls. 18 and 19.
A large eagle that flies with wings flat. *Head projects more than
one-half the tail length.* The trailing edge of wing is straighter and
less pinched in at the body than that of the Golden Eagle. The
dark tail of nonadult plumages may have a *whitish oval patch*
above. **White-belly II** (not shown) and **White-belly I** both have
upside-down white triangle on back. (The trailing edge of wing is
ragged; some new shorter secondary feathers have molted in.) **Immature** has *tawny back and upperwing coverts* that *contrast with
darker flight feathers.* Wings are wider and tail longer than in subsequent plumages.
Similar species: Golden Eagle, Osprey (Pl. 3), Turkey Vulture
(Pl. 1).
Status and Distribution: Locally common in breeding centers in
summer. Northern population moves south in winter. Locally common to abundant in winter concentration areas but also sparsely
distributed over large areas covering most of the United States.

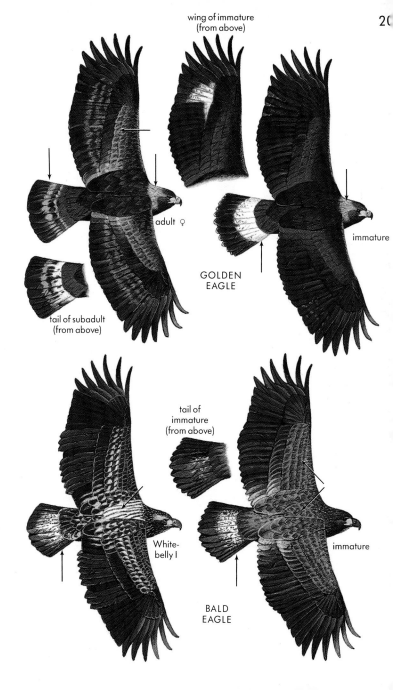

wing of immature
(from above)

adult ♀

tail of subadult
(from above)

GOLDEN
EAGLE

immature

tail of
immature
(from above)

White-
belly I

immature

BALD
EAGLE

PLATE 21
Small Colorful Falcons

AMERICAN KESTREL   p. 96; photos, p. 156
Falco sparverius
Our smallest, most colorful falcon. Identified by *2 black mustache marks. Underwings appear pale. Hovers regularly.* **Adult male** has rufous breast and back, *blue-gray upperwing coverts,* and *rufous tail* with *black subterminal band. A row of white spots on underside of trailing edge of backlighted wing* is distinctive. On many males tails also have black, white, and gray banding. **Immature male** is like adult except that rufous back is completely barred and breast is white and heavily streaked. **Female** has reddish brown back, upperwing coverts, and tail, all with dark brown bands. Creamy underparts are heavily streaked. **Immature female** is not always distinguishable from adult.
Similar species: Merlin (Pl. 22), Black-shouldered Kite (Pl. 5), Peregrine Falcon (Pl. 23).
Status and Distribution: Widespread and common.

EURASIAN KESTREL   p. 94; photos, p. 155
Falco tinnunculus
Much larger than the American Kestrel. Identified by *two-toned upperwings* (American Kestrel appears to be the same color throughout length of wing) and *single mustache mark.* Note also *wedge-shaped tip of folded tail.* **Adult male** has rufous back and upperwing coverts and *long blue-gray tail with black subterminal band.* **Adult female** is similar to American Kestrel female. **Immatures** are similar to adult female but have thicker dark barring on back and tail.
Similar species: American Kestrel.
Status and Distribution: Accidental.

APLOMADO FALCON   p. 103; photos, p. 158
Falco femoralis
A slender, long-winged, long-tailed falcon. Top of head, back, and upperwing coverts are lead gray. Note *bold face pattern;* lightly streaked, creamy breast; *dark belly band; narrow pale band on trailing edge of wing;* and *long, dark gray tail with numerous narrow white bands.* Underwing appears dark on flying birds. **Immature** is browner on the back, has buffy streaks on the belly band, and heavier streaking on the breast.
Similar species: American Kestrel, Merlin (Pl. 22), Peregrine Falcon (Pl. 23), Prairie Falcon (Pl. 22), Crested Caracara (Pl. 1), Mississippi Kite (Pl. 5).
Status and Distribution: Extirpated as a breeding bird in sw. United States; now accidental but being reintroduced in Texas.

Note: Falcons usually have a brightly colored ring of bare skin around the eye, called the orbital ring.

AMERICAN KESTREL

adult ♂

immature ♂

♂

adult ♂

♀

♂

EURASIAN KESTREL

adult ♂

adult ♀

American Kestrel ♀

immature

adult

APLOMADO FALCON

immature

adult

PLATE 22

Prairie Falcon and Merlin

PRAIRIE FALCON *Falco mexicanus*   **p. 114; photos, p. 160**
A large pale falcon identified in flight by *black center of underwing.*
Note narrow mustache mark; square, blockish head; and *white area between eye and dark ear patch.* Long tail has faint banding. Wingtips do not reach tail tip on perched birds. **Adult** back feathers are dark brown with light brown bars and edges. Whitish underparts are faintly spotted, with some short streaks as well. **Immature** back, lacking the light brown feather bars, appears darker. Whitish underparts are more heavily streaked.
Similar species: Peregrine Falcon (Pl. 23), Merlin (Prairie adult female or immature), Swainson's Hawk (Pl. 12).
Status and Distribution: Fairly common in hilly and mountainous areas of West. Some move eastward and southward for winter.

MERLIN *Falco columbarius*   **p. 100; photos, pp. 156, 157**
A small dashing falcon that *lacks bold mustache marks.* Three distinct forms are Taiga, Prairie, and Black. Wingtips do not reach tail tip on perched birds. Taiga and Black forms have *dark underwings;* Prairie form has paler underwing.
Taiga form has faint mustache mark, blue-gray back (adult male) or brown back (adult female or immature), heavily streaked creamy underparts, and *dark tail with blue-gray tail bands* (adult male) *or buffy bands* (adult female and immature). Adult females usually have a grayish cast to uppertail coverts that is lacking on immatures.
Prairie form is overall paler than Taiga, lacks mustache mark, and has wider, complete tail bands. Note large spots on flight feathers.
Black form is very dark overall, including cheeks, lacks the superciliary line, and has, at most, faint light tail bands. Blue-gray cast of adult male is seen only in good light.
Similar species: American Kestrel (Pl. 21), Peregrine Falcon (Pl. 23), Prairie Falcon, Sharp-shinned Hawk (Pls. 6 and 7).
Status and Distribution: Taiga—Boreal forest in summer, coasts and tropics in winter. **Prairie**—Northern prairies, moving somewhat farther south in winter. **Black**—Pacific humid forest of British Columbia, moving somewhat farther south and east in winter.

22

immature

adult

PRAIRIE
FALCON

adult

adult ♂

adult ♀
or
immature

Prairie
Merlin

MERLIN

adult ♂
Taiga Merlin

adult ♂

adult ♀
or
immature

Taiga
Merlin

adult ♂

adult ♀
or
immature

Black
Merlin

PLATE 23

Peregrine Falcon

PEREGRINE FALCON   **p. 107; photos, p. 159**
Falco peregrinus
See also Pl. 26.

A large, dark falcon with a *wide dark mustache mark* and dark underwing. In most plumages, *dark head appears hooded. White breast contrasting with darker marked belly* is noticeable on most adults. On perched birds, *wingtips almost reach tail tip (immature); wingtips reach tail tip (adult)*. Three forms are distinguishable in the field: Tundra, Continental, and Peale's. Adults have yellow legs, cere, and eye-ring; immatures, blue.

Tundra form is somewhat smaller than other forms. **Adult** has relatively unmarked white breast. **Immature** is quite different from other forms. The mustache mark is narrow and often broken; white auricular patch is large; crown is often whitish, especially forehead; and there is a pale superciliary line. The creamy breast is finely streaked, and there are wide buffy edges to brown back feathers.

Continental form has thickest mustache mark. **Adult** has rufous wash on underparts and small white auricular patch. **Immature** has thickly streaked underparts and little or no pale edges to back feathers.

Peale's is the largest and darkest form and usually has streaking on white auricular patch. **Adult** is usually heavily streaked on whitish breast. **Immature** is very dark, with back feathers having no pale edges; underparts appear almost solid dark.

Similar species: Prairie Falcon (Pl. 22), Gyrfalcon (Pls. 24 and 26), Merlin (Pl. 22), American Kestrel (Pl. 21).

Status and Distribution: Breeds in Arctic, migrates continent-wide in spring and fall, when it is common along coast. Rare and local breeder in w. United States, w. Canada and cen. Alaska. Northern birds migrate south into Cen. America, but many remain in N. America, especially along coasts. Sedentary along the coast from British Columbia to Alaska and on islands off British Columbia and Alaska, including the Aleutian chain.

PEREGRINE FALCONS

immature

adult

adult

immature

Tundra

adult

immature

adult

immature

Continental

Peale's

PLATE 24

Gyrfalcon

GYRFALCON *Falco rusticolus*   **p. 111; photos, pp. 160, 161**
See also Pl. 26.
A very large, long-tailed falcon. *Wide tail that tapers toward tip* is
distinctive. Wings are broader than those of other large falcons. On
perched birds, *wingtips reach only half to two-thirds of the way to
tail tip.* There are 3 color morphs: White, Gray, and Dark. Adult
has yellow to yellow-orange eye-ring, cere, and legs; immature has
blue ones.
White morph usually lacks faint mustache mark. **Adult** is white
overall with short black bars on back and tail and some faint spotting on underparts. **Immature** has brown back feathers with wide
white fringes and white underparts that are lightly to heavily
marked.
Gray morph has faint dark mustache mark and pale superciliary
line and *two-toned underwing;* light gray flight feathers contrast
with coverts that are usually (but not always) darker. **Adult** has
gray back and white underparts that are lightly to heavily spotted,
with barring on flanks. **Immature** (so-called brown morph) has
gray-brown back and heavily streaked creamy underparts. *Underwing appears two-toned.*
Dark morph is the dark extreme of variation in the gray morph
(however, there are few intermediate individuals). *Dark head appears hooded, and underwing is two-toned.* **Adult** is almost solid
dark but with some pale streaks on breast, pale bars on belly and
flanks, and pale spots on underwing coverts. Dark tail has faint
pale bands. **Immature** (see Pl. 26) is almost solid dark, but underparts have faint pale streaks. *Underwing appears two-toned.* Tail
appears solid above but may show 1 or 2 faint pale bands below.
Similar species: Peregrine Falcon (Pls. 23 and 26), Prairie Falcon
(Pl. 22), Goshawk (Pls. 6 and 7).
Status and Distribution: Uncommon to rare in the Arctic in
summer. Uncommon but local in s. Canada and northern border
states in winter. Casual farther south.

24

white-morph immature

gray-morph immature

white-morph adult

gray-morph adult

GYRFALCONS

gray-morph adult

dark-morph adult

PLATE 25
Alaska Accidentals

WHITE-TAILED EAGLE   **p. 85; photos, p. 153**
Haliaeetus albicilla
A large eagle similar in all plumages to the Bald Eagle. **Adult** has *creamy head; short, wedge-shaped white tail;* and *dark undertail coverts.* **Subadult** (not shown) is similar to same-age Bald Eagles (White-belly I and II) but usually lacks contrast between breast and belly. Underparts are generally more uniformly whitish, with some dark streaking or mottling. Tail is like that of immature. **Immature** has dark brown breast, usually with some white streaking, and dark tawny belly. On all non-adult plumages, white axillar spots and diagonal lines on underwing are not as distinct as those of Bald Eagles. White on tips of tail feathers form *white spikes on each feather.*
Similar species: Bald Eagle (Pls. 18–20), Steller's Sea Eagle.
Status and Distribution: Accidental.

STELLER'S SEA EAGLE   **p. 87**
Haliaeetus pelagicus
A very large eagle with a *huge beak. White tail is deeply wedge-shaped.* **Adult** has *huge orange beak* and *white shoulder patch.* **Subadult** is similar to immature but with more white on body and wings. **Immature** is all dark on the body and wings and has a *huge yellow beak* and *mostly white tail.*
Similar species: Bald Eagle (Pls. 18–20), White-tailed Eagle.
Status and Distribution: Accidental.

NORTHERN HOBBY *Falco subbuteo*   **p. 105; photos, p. 158**
(Not drawn to the same scale as eagles.)
A slender, long-winged falcon identified by its *narrow dark mustache mark, dark underwings,* and *thick streaks on underparts* that extend from throat to belly. *Wingtips extend beyond tail tip* on perched birds. **Adult** has gray back and *rufous leg feathers.* **Immature** has brown back feathers with buffy edges and streaked, creamy leg feathers. Breast streaking is wider than adult's.
Similar species: Peregrine Falcon (Pl. 23), Merlin (Pl. 22), American Kestrel (Pl. 21).
Status and Distribution: Accidental.

WHITE-
TAILED
EAGLE

adult

immature

adult
STELLER'S
SEA
EAGLE

immature

NORTHERN
HOBBY

adult

immature

PLATE 26
Dark Raptors—Summary

Top row
ZONE-TAILED HAWK   **p. 67; photos, p. 141**
Buteo albonotatus
Immature: White spots on body. **Adult:** See Pl. 16.

RED-TAILED HAWK   **p. 69; photos, pp. 142–145**
B. jamaicensis
Immature (dark morph): Narrow dark tail bands of equal width.
Adult: See Pl. 14.

HARLAN'S HAWK *B. j. harlani*   **p. 70; photos, pp. 143–145**
Adult: Whitish mottled (or banded) tail, streaked (usually) whitish breast, and flight feathers below either heavily mottled or barred or both.

ROUGH-LEGGED HAWK   **p. 77; photos, pp. 148, 149**
B. lagopus
Adult male type (dark morph): Jet black and dark tail with narrow white bands. **Adult female type:** See Pl. 15.

Middle row
ROUGH-LEGGED HAWK   **p. 77; photos, p. 149**
B. lagopus
Immature (dark morph): Tail silvery with dusky subterminal band; black carpal patch usually noticeable.

FERRUGINOUS HAWK *B. regalis*   **p. 74; photos, p. 147**
Immature (dark morph): White wrist comma but tail pattern like that of immature Rough-leg. **Adult:** See Pl. 15.

WHITE-TAILED HAWK   **p. 64; photos, pp. 140, 141**
B. albicaudatus
Immature: Creamy breast patch, dark flight feathers, white undertail coverts, and finely banded gray tail. Wings have pointed tips and are pinched in at body on trailing edge. **Adult:** See Pl. 17.

SWAINSON'S HAWK *B. swainsoni* **p. 61; photos, pp. 138, 139**
Adult (dark morph): White undertail coverts, pointed wingtips, and dark flight feathers.

Bottom row
GYRFALCON *Falco rusticolus*   **p. 111; photos, pp. 160, 161**
Immature (dark morph): Two-toned underwings; long, broad, tapered tail. **Adult:** See Pl. 24.

PEREGRINE FALCON *F. peregrinus*   **p. 107; photos, p. 159**
Immature (dark Peale's form): All-dark underwing. **Adult:** See Pl. 23.

BROAD-WINGED HAWK   **p. 56; photos, pp. 134, 136**
B. platypterus
Immature (dark morph): Light tail has dark bands, subterminal band widest. Pointed wingtips. **Adult:** See Pl. 13.

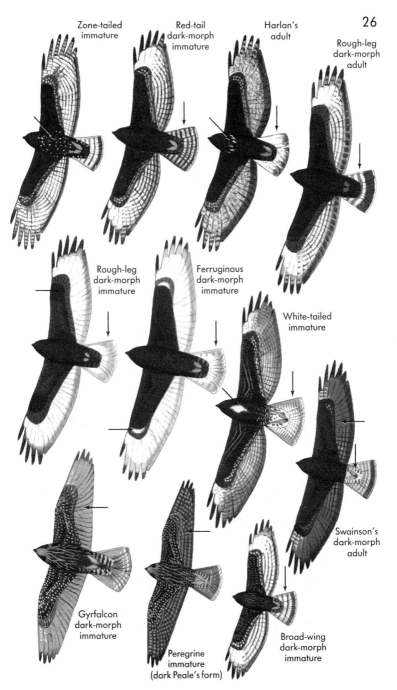

Zone-tailed
immature

Red-tail
dark-morph
immature

Harlan's
adult

Rough-leg
dark-morph
adult

Rough-leg
dark-morph
immature

Ferruginous
dark-morph
immature

White-tailed
immature

Swainson's
dark-morph
adult

Gyrfalcon
dark-morph
immature

Peregrine
immature
(dark Peale's form)

Broad-wing
dark-morph
immature

barring. Pale underwings have a row of paler circles on trailing edge of backlighted wing, less noticeable than those on wing of male. Creamy underparts are heavily streaked with reddish brown. Leg feathers are clear white to creamy. Tail is reddish brown with 8 or more dark brown bands and a noticeably wider subterminal band.

Immature male: Similar to adult male, but white breast is heavily streaked with black, back is completely barred, and crown patch has black shaft streaks. Usually molts into adult plumage during first fall, but some retain juvenal characteristics into next summer.

Immature female: Like adult female but often with dark subterminal tail band only as wide as or slightly wider than other dark bands.

Similar species: (1) **Merlin** (Pl. 22) is darker, lacks the 2 mustache marks, and is larger (female) or chunkier (male). In flight Merlins show darker underwings, broader wings, and larger head than Kestrels. (2) **Black-shouldered Kite** (Pl. 5) is larger, hovers more vertically like a kingfisher, and has an unbanded tail. (3) **Peregrine** (Pl. 23) is much larger and darker and has longer, broader wings and a much larger head.

Flight: Active flight is light and buoyant; however, Kestrels will chase birds in a direct, rapid, Merlin-like fashion. This Kestrel soars on flat wings, often with the tail fanned. It glides on flat wings or with wrists lower than body and wingtips

AMERICAN KESTREL

curved upward. The American Kestrel is the only N. American falcon to hunt regularly by hovering (wings flapping) or, in strong winds, by kiting (wings held steady).

Behavior: The often-encountered American Kestrel is usually seen hovering or sitting on exposed perches, such as poles, wires, or treetops, where it hunts for rodents, insects, birds, lizards, or snakes. Females tend to hunt in more open areas than males, especially during winter.

Kestrels nest in tree cavities but will readily use holes in cliffs and crevices in barns and buildings as well as nest boxes. They are fairly common in cities and towns. They can be vociferous, and their easily recognized "killy-killy" call carries some distance.

Status and distribution: American Kestrels are widespread and common throughout N. America south of the arctic treeline in most habitats and prefer more open country. Northern populations are migratory, with some birds moving as far south as Cen. America. They are abundant in s. United States in winter.

Fine points: Kestrels possess a pair of false eyes, or ocelli, on the nape, which are thought to be protective coloration, in that the watching "eyes" will deter potential predators.

Unusual plumages: Complete albinos and birds with some white feathers have been reported. A specimen exists of a gynandromorph, sexed internally as female but with many male feathers.

Subspecies: The race *F. s. sparverius* occupies most of N. America north of Mexico, except for the Florida peninsula, where it is replaced by the smaller race *F. s. paulus,* in which only males are distinguishable from *F. s. sparverius* (by having little or no spotting on underparts and generally a richer color).

Etymology: *Sparverius* in Latin means "pertaining to a sparrow," after the falcon's first common name, Sparrow Hawk. It had been misnamed after the European *Accipiter nisus,* the Sparrowhawk. "American Kestrel" comes from its Eurasian counterpart, the Eurasian Kestrel *Falco tinnunculus.* "Kestrel" is an Old English name for *F. tinnunculus.*

Measurements:
Length: Male 22–26 cm (24); 8–10 in. (9)
　　　　Female 23–27 cm (25); 9–11 in. (10)
Wingspread: Male 52–57 cm (55); 20–22 in. (21)
　　　　　　Female 54–61 cm (57); 21–24 in. (22)
Weight: Male 97–120 g (109); 3.4–4.5 oz (3.8)
　　　　Female 102–150 g (123); 3.6–5.3 oz (4.3)

MERLIN *Falco columbarius*   **Pl. 22; photos, pp. 156, 157**
Description: The Merlin of northern forests and prairies is a small, dashing falcon. There are 3 distinct forms: Taiga, Prairie, and Black merlins. All *lack the bold mustache mark* of other falcons, having at most only a faint one. Sexes are different in adult plumage and size, with females noticeably larger. Immature plumage is similar to that of adult female. On perched birds, wingtips do not reach tail tip. Iris color is dark brown. Cere and eye-ring colors are greenish yellow to yellow. Leg color is yellow.

Taiga Merlins are darkest in the East and become gradually paler westward. In all plumages *underwings are dark.* *Taiga adult male:* Head consists of slate blue crown with fine black streaking, buffy superciliary line, buffy cheek with darker marking behind eye, a faint dark mustache mark, faint whitish or rufous markings on hind neck, and white, unstreaked throat. Back and upperwing coverts are slate blue. Whitish underparts have reddish brown to dark brown streaking. Breast often has light rufous wash. Whitish leg feathers are lightly streaked and have a rufous wash. Whitish undertail coverts have light streaking. Black tail has 3 slate blue bands and a wide white terminal band. *Taiga adult female:* Head is like that of adult male except that crown is dark brown with thicker black streaking. Back and upperwing coverts are medium to dark brown, sometimes with a grayish cast, and brown uppertail coverts have a grayish cast. Creamy underparts have heavy dark brown streaking. Creamy leg feathers and undertail coverts are lightly streaked. Dark brown tail has 4 usually incomplete buffy bands and a wide white terminal band. *Taiga immature:* Similar to Taiga adult female, but back and upperwing and uppertail coverts are dark brown without a grayish cast. Dark brown tail has 4 buffy and gray bands (see **Fine points**) and a white terminal band.

Prairie Merlins are much paler and somewhat larger than other Merlins and their underwings do not appear dark. They have more and larger pale spots on dark primaries and secondaries. *Prairie adult male:* Overall pattern is like that of Taiga adult male but much paler. Mustache mark is faint or absent. Streaked crown, back, and upperwing coverts are light blue-gray. Pale areas on hind neck are larger and often have a rufous wash. Whitish underparts are streaked reddish brown. Pale rufous leg feathers have fine streaking. Black tail has 3 or 4 whitish to light gray bands and wide white terminal band. *Prairie adult female:* Overall pattern is like that of Taiga adult female but much paler. Crown, back, and upperwing and uppertail coverts are medium brown with a grayish cast. Creamy underparts are streaked reddish brown. Medium brown tail has 3 or 4 wider whitish bands and a white terminal band. *Prairie immature:* Similar to Prairie adult female, but back and upperwing and uppertail coverts lack the grayish cast. Tail is like that of Prairie adult female.

Black Merlins are much darker than the other forms. Cheeks are mostly dark, and throat is streaked. Superciliary line, hind neck markings, and tail bands are faint or absent. *Underwings are dark.* Characteristics of some individual Merlins are intermediate between those of Black and Taiga. **Black adult male:** Similar to Taiga adult male but overall color appears much darker. Back and upperwing coverts are dark black-brown, with grayish cast visible only in good light. Underparts are almost solidly dark. Leg feathers are almost solidly dark. Dark, usually unbanded tail has a narrow whitish terminal band. Tail bands, if present, are just spots and are visible only on spread tail. **Black adult female and immature:** Like Black adult male but without grayish cast.

Similar species: (1) **Kestrel** (Pl. 21) is smaller; has a lighter, more buoyant flight; and in flight shows smaller head and narrower wings with pale undersides. Perched Kestrels have rufous tails and backs and 2 distinct black mustache marks on each side of the face. (2) **Peregrine Falcon** (Pl. 23) is larger and has relatively longer wings, a distinct mustache mark, and larger head. Immature male Peale's Peregrine may appear similar to female Black Merlin, but when perched, the Peregrine's wingtips reach or almost reach the tail tip. (3) **Prairie Falcon** (Pl. 22) is much larger than Prairie Merlin, has distinct mustache mark, and in flight shows dark center of pale underwing. (4) **Sharp-shinned Hawk** (Pls. 6 and 7) has a smaller, rounded head; shorter, rounded wings; yellow or red eyes; and tail bands of equal width.

Flight: Active flight is direct, with strong, quick wingbeats. The Merlin soars on flat wings with the tail somewhat fanned. It glides on flat wings or with wrists lower than body and wingtips curved upward. The Merlin does not hover.

Behavior: Merlins are dashing falcons that hunt birds on the wing. Their rapid hunting flight is typically in a direct line over open forest (over grasslands for Prairie Merlins). They use speed to surprise a flock of birds and snatch one that is slow to react. They also hunt from exposed perches, making rapid forays after prey. Merlins fly fast enough to tail-chase swallows, swifts, and shorebirds. They are capable of very sudden changes in direction and can make spectacular aerial maneuvers. They often capture flying insects, especially dragonflies, in flight. Small birds are often forced to fly up to a great altitude and are captured when they try to drop back to earth. Merlins have an unusual flight mode when attacking a bird from a low altitude. They flap their wings in quick bursts interspersed with glides, producing an undulating but rapid flight that appears like that of passerines. This mode of attack may allow them to be mistaken for a passerine until it is too late for the prey to escape. Like many other raptors, they have been reported hunting cooperatively. They regularly harass larger birds, including gulls and other raptors. Their primary vocalization is a rapid, high-pitched "ki ki ki."

Status and distribution: Merlins are widely but sparsely distributed as a breeding bird in Canada and Alaska in open areas of boreal forests and in western mountains south to Oregon and Colorado, on the Great Plains south to the Dakotas, and in Pacific coastal rain forests.

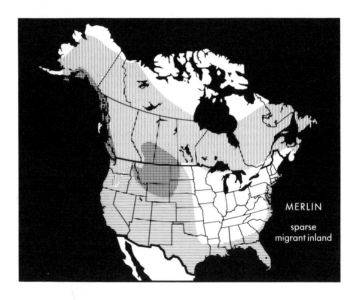

MERLIN

sparse
migrant inland

Taiga Merlin is an uncommon breeder in boreal forests from Newfoundland to w. Alaska and south into the United States in n. Maine, n. Great Lakes states, and the western mountains. Taigas are highly migratory, moving to coasts, the Caribbean, Cen. America, and S. America as far as Peru. Migration takes place throughout the contiguous states on a broad front. The birds are fairly common along the ocean coasts in migration, where some remain in winter.

Prairie Merlin is a fairly common but local breeder in prairie-parkland areas, especially along rivers and more recently in cities, of s.-cen. Canada and n. prairie states. Some birds move in fall and winter south to n. Mexico, east to Minnesota, and west to Pacific Coast. Some birds also winter throughout the breeding range, however, especially in cities, where they feed on sparrows and waxwings.

Black Merlin is an uncommon to rare resident in the Pacific coastal forest of British Columbia and se. Alaska. Some individuals move as far as s. California and New Mexico in fall and winter.

Fine points: Tail bands of Taiga immatures are buffy and often incomplete on females and buffy and grayish and more noticeable on males.

Unusual plumages: There is a report of a mostly white bird that also had some tan feathers. There are records of albinism in the European race.

Subspecies: The 3 N. American races correspond to the forms described. Taiga is *F. c. columbarius,* Prairie is *F. c. richardsoni,* and Black is *F. c. suckleyi.*

Etymology: *Columbarius* in Latin means "pertaining to a dove (pigeon)," a reference to the Merlin's original N. American common name of Pigeon Hawk, after its resemblance in flight to the Pigeon. "Merlin" derives from the Old French *esmerillon,* the name for this species.

Measurements: (Taiga Merlins; Prairie form is larger.)
Length: Male 24–27 cm (26); 9–11 in. (10)
　　　　Female 28–30 cm (29); 11–12 in. (11)
Wingspread: Male 53–58 cm (57); 21–23 in. (22)
　　　　Female 61–68 cm (64); 24–27 in. (25)
Weight: Male 129–187 g (155); 4.5–6.6 oz (5.5)
　　　　Female 182–236 g (210); 6.4–8.3 oz (7.4)

APLOMADO FALCON　　　　Pl. 21; photos, p. 158
Falco femoralis

Description: The Aplomado Falcon is a colorful, narrow-winged, long-tailed, medium-sized falcon. It formerly bred along the Mexican border from se. Arizona to s. Texas but now occurs only accidentally. *Silhouette and color pattern of face and underparts are distinctive.* Sexes are almost alike in plumage, but female is noticeably larger. Immature plumage is similar to that of adult. Iris color is dark brown. On perched birds, wingtips extend three-quarters of way down the tail.

Adult: Head has distinctive pattern of lead gray crown, black line behind eye, and thin black mustache mark; creamy to whitish superciliary lines, which join together to form a *V on hind neck;* and creamy to whitish cheek and throat. Back and upperwing coverts are lead gray. *Trailing edge of dark wing has noticeable light edge, extending from body to primaries.* Whitish to rufous breast usually has a few short dark streaks (heavier on females) and is separated from more rufous belly by *blackish cummerbund,* which is wider on sides. Underwings appear dark. Leg feathers and undertail coverts are rufous.

Long black tail has 7 or more thin white bands. Cere, eye-ring, and leg colors are yellow.

Immature: Similar to adult, but back has a brownish cast and rufous feather edges, breast is buffier and more heavily streaked, and dark cummerbund has buffy streaks. Dark tail has 9 or more thinner buffy bands. Cere, eye-ring, and leg colors are pale yellow to yellow.

Similar species: (1) **American Kestrel** (Pl. 21) is smaller, has rufous tail and back and 2 mustache marks, and lacks dark cummerbund. In flight, tail appears shorter and underwings paler than those of Aplomado. (2) **Merlin** (Pl. 22) is smaller, has completely streaked underparts, and lacks distinct facial pattern and dark cummerbund. In flight tail appears shorter than that of Aplomado. (3) **Peregrine Falcon** (Pl. 23) is larger, has broader wings and a single thick mustache mark, and lacks dark cummerbund. (4) **Prairie Falcon** (Pl. 22) is larger and paler, has broader wings with a black center on underwing, and lacks dark cummerbund. (5) **Crested Caracara** (Pl. 1) has similar pattern on body but is much larger and has different head pattern, much longer neck, and different wing shape. (6) **Mississippi Kite** (Pl. 5) is similar in size and silhouette and also has light line on trailing edge of wing but lacks strong face pattern and cummerbund.

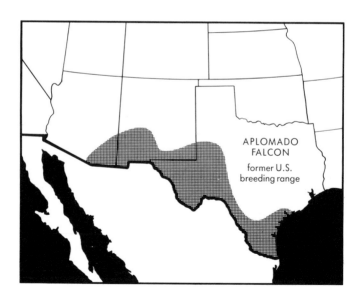

APLOMADO FALCON

former U.S. breeding range

Flight: Active flight is rapid and direct, with light, quick wingbeats, but when bird is not pursuing prey, flight is slower, buoyant, and kestrel-like. The Aplomado glides on flat wings or with wrists below body and wingtips curved upward. It soars on flat wings. This falcon hovers when its prey goes under cover.

Behavior: Aplomado Falcons feed primarily on birds, which are captured after a rapid direct flight from a perch, sometimes including a long tail-chase or pursuit in heavy brush on foot. They hunt from both exposed and inconspicuous perches. Insects, reptiles, rodents, and even bats are also taken, some of which are pirated from other raptors. Hunting from soar and cooperative hunting by pairs have also been reported. This species regularly gathers at grassfires to hunt displaced birds, insects, reptiles, and mammals. Breeding pairs remain together throughout the year and often perch close together.

Status and distribution: Aplomado Falcons formerly bred from s. Texas to se. Arizona in savanna grasslands with yucca, mesquite, and cacti. They are now reported only accidentally, mainly from s. and w. Texas but also from Arizona. Last breeding record was in 1952 from New Mexico. The reason for the population decline is most likely habitat loss and was probably not due to pesticides.

Note: Captive-bred birds are now being released within the former range in s. Texas.

Fine points: Adult's cummerbund has fine white barring, heavier on male, lacking on immature.

Unusual plumages: No unusual plumages have been reported.

Subspecies: The N. American race is *F. f. septentrionalis.*

Etymology: "Aplomado" in Spanish means "lead-colored," a reference to this species' back color. *Femoralis* is Latin, "referring to the thighs," for the rufous coloration of the leg feathers.

Measurements:
Length: Male 35–39 cm (37); 14–16 in. (15)
       Female 41–45 cm (43); 16–18 in. (17)
Wingspread: Male 78–84 cm (81); 31–33 in. (32)
       Female 93–102 cm (97); 37–40 in. (38)
Weight: Male 208–305 g (265); 8.4–10.7 oz (9.3)
       Female 310–460 g (391); 12.0–16.0 oz (13.8)

NORTHERN HOBBY   Pl. 25; photos, p. 158
Falco subbuteo

Description: The Northern Hobby, a medium-sized, long-winged falcon, is accidental in N. America. It is similar to the Peregrine Falcon but smaller, with a more slender body, narrower wings, and a thinner mustache mark. *Flight silhouette is particularly sickle-like,* with wingtips usually pulled back. Sexes are alike in plumage, with females only slightly larger. Immature plumage is similar to that of adult. Iris color is dark brown. Cere, eye-ring, and leg colors vary from yellowish green to bright yellow. On perched birds, *wingtips extend just past tail tips.*

Adult: Dark head has short white superciliary line, whitish cheek and throat, narrow dark mustache mark, and rufous marking on hind neck. Back and upperwing coverts are solid dark blue-gray. Whitish to buffy underparts have thick, well-defined dark streaking; *individual streaks extend from throat to lower belly. Leg feathers and undertail coverts are bright rufous.* Tail is solid dark above but appears lighter below, with 8 or more incomplete paler bands.

Immature: Like adult but back is browner, with rufous feather edges; underparts have thicker, heavier, and less well defined streaking. Creamy leg feathers and undertail feathers are darkly streaked.

Similar species: (1) **Peregrine Falcon** (Pl. 23) is larger and has broader wings and thicker mustache mark. Peregrines have a heavier, less buoyant flight. (2) **American Kestrel** (Pl. 21) has rufous back and tail and 2 mustache marks. In flight it shows pale underwings. (3) **Merlin** (Pl. 22) is smaller, has shorter wings, and lacks well-defined mustache mark.

Flight: Active flight when hunting is rapid, with fast, stiff wingbeats, but the Hobby also has a light, buoyant, more leisurely flight. It soars on flat wings, usually with wingtips pulled back and wings bent at wrist and with tail somewhat fanned. Glides with wrists lower than body and often with wingtips pointing downward 5 to 10 degrees below the horizontal. Leading edge of wing is somewhat convexly curved. Stoops after prey in rapid dives, with wings pulled in close to body. The Hobby hovers occasionally, usually when prey goes into cover.

Behavior: Hobbys are graceful, elegant, and aerobatic falcons that capture birds and insects on the wing. They hunt birds by making Peregrine-like lightning stoops, sometimes with a short upward swoop at end. They also eat bats and, less frequently, small mammals and reptiles. Hobbys are often active at dawn and dusk. In winter and on migration, they are social, forming feeding flocks and night roosts.

Status and distribution: Hobbys are accidental. There are a small number of sight records from the Pribilof and Aleutian islands and the adjacent seas and 1 from British Columbia. The Eurasian population is highly migratory.

Fine points: On folded tail, tip appears wedge-shaped because of shape of outer edge of feathers. Immature's tail has a wide buffy terminal band; adult's has a narrow one.

Unusual plumages: No unusual plumages have been reported.

Subspecies: The race in Europe and Asia is *F. s. subbuteo.*

Etymology: "Hobby" comes from the Old French *hobe,* meaning "to jump about," for the falcon's agility in capturing aerial insects. *Sub* in Latin means "somewhat," and *buteo* is "a kind of hawk or falcon."

Measurements:
Length: 29–32 cm (30); 11–13 in. (12)
Wingspread: 74–83 cm (78); 29–33 in. (31)
Weight: Male 131–223 g (193); 4.6–7.9 oz (6.8)
       Female 141–325 g (237); 5.0–11.5 oz (8.9)

PEREGRINE FALCON   **Pls. 23 and 26; photos, p. 159**
Falco peregrinus

Description: The far-ranging Peregrine Falcon is a large, dark falcon with *a thick dark mustache mark.* The 3 recognizable N. American forms differ in size and plumage. The highly migratory Tundra Peregrine is the smallest and lightest in color, the mainly western Continental Peregrine is larger and darker, and the sedentary Peale's Peregrine is largest and darkest. Females are noticeably larger than males. Sexes are almost alike in plumage (see **Fine points**). In most plumages, *dark head appears hooded.* Iris color is dark brown. Underwings in flight appear dark. This is the only N. American falcon whose *wingtips extend to, or almost to, tail tip on perched birds.* Immatures' tails are longer and wings are wider than those of adults. Adult eye-ring, cere, and leg colors are yellow to yellow-orange. Immature eye-ring and cere colors are light blue, occasionally yellowish; leg color varies from light blue to yellow.

Note: The forms described below do not relate strictly to races, but are general types that differ recognizably in the field. Birds of more than 1 type may occur within the range of a race.

Tundra adult: Blackish head has pale forehead, mustache mark narrower than those of other forms, large white area on cheek, and pale markings on hind neck. Slate back and upperwing coverts have blue-gray barring and fringes. White breast is unstreaked or lightly streaked and has, at most, a faint rufous wash. Bars on belly and undertail coverts are short and black. White leg feathers are finely barred black. Blackish tail has 8 or more gray bands and a wide white terminal band.

Tundra immature: Head has distinctive pattern: buffy forehead, sometimes buffy on entire normally dark brown crown; buffy superciliary line; thin dark eye-line; and buffy cheek and throat, separated by a dark mustache mark that is relatively narrow (for a Peregrine). Back and upperwing coverts are dark brown with wide buffy or rufous feather fringes. Dark streaks on creamy underparts are narrower than those of other forms. Creamy leg feathers have narrow vertical dark streaks. Creamy undertail coverts are barred dark brown. Dark brown tail has 10 or more usually incomplete buffy bands and a wide white terminal band.

Continental adult: Black head has white to buffy cheek and throat, setting off wide, dark mustache mark. Back and upperwing coverts are dark slate with blue-gray bars and feather fringing. Uppertail coverts are blue-gray with black barring. White breast is unstreaked or lightly streaked, and white belly is barred with black. Underparts of many birds have a noticeable rufous wash, heavier on breast and on females. White leg feathers have black barring. Blackish tail has 8 or more gray bands and thick white terminal band.

Continental immature: Head is dark blackish brown, with buffy throat and cheek and thick mustache mark. Hind neck has buffy markings. Back and upperwing coverts are dark brown, with narrow rufous feather fringes. Creamy underparts have thick dark brown streaking. Creamy leg feathers have dark, arrow-shaped barring. Creamy undertail coverts have dark brown bars. Dark brown tail has 10 or more buffy, usually incomplete bands and a wide white terminal band.

Peale's adult: Similar to Continental adult but overall darker. White area on cheek is larger and is streaked. White breast has heavier spotting and lacks rufous wash. Adults from Aleutian Islands are more heavily spotted on the breast than those from the eastern part of Peale's range.

Peale's immature: Similar to Continental immature, but head is almost completely dark except for faint pale mottling on forehead and nape and streaked throat and cheek. Mustache mark is not as noticeable as on other forms because of heavily marked cheeks and throat. Back is dark brown with little or no light feather edging. Back and upperwing coverts have a grayish powdery bloom visible at close range. Underparts and leg feathers are almost solidly dark but have some whitish streaking. Undertail coverts are creamy with thick dark brown bars. Dark brown tail usually has, at most, faint light bands.

Note: Peregrines reintroduced into e. N. America are similar to 1 of the above forms.

Similar species: (1) **Prairie Falcon** (Pl. 22) is paler and has much narrower mustache marks than Peregrine, but Tundra immature can be similar. Peregrines lack white area between eye and dark cheek found on all Prairies. In flight, Prairie shows dark patch in the center of pale underwing and, compared with Peregrine, flies with shallow wingbeats and with wings mostly below horizontal. When perched, Prairie's wingtips fall short of tail tip, but those of Peregrine reach or almost reach tail tip. (2) **Merlin** (Pl. 22) is much smaller, has a faint narrow mustache mark, and has relatively shorter wings. Merlins fly with quicker, shallower wingbeats. Dark immature Peale's form is similar to Black Merlin; wingtips reach only just over halfway down tail on perched Merlins but almost to tip on Peregrines. (3) **American Kestrel** (Pl. 21) is much smaller; has rufous back and tail, pale underwings, and narrower wings. Kestrel's head appears smaller in flight. (4) **Gyrfalcon** (Pls. 24 and 26) is larger; has longer, wider, more tapered tail, broader wings, and fainter, narrower mustache mark. Its two-toned underwing consists of dark coverts and pale flight feathers. On perched birds, wingtips extend less than two-thirds down tail. Dark immature Peale's form is similar to dark-morph immature Gyr, but Peregrines show dark underwing in flight, and wingtips extend to tail tip on perched birds.

Flight: Active flight is with shallow but stiff and powerful wingbeats, similar to that of a cormorant. When actively chasing prey, Peregrine may use deeper wingstrokes. It soars on flat wings and widely fanned tail; outer tail feathers almost touch trailing edge of wing, making tail appear diamond-shaped. Wingtips appear broad and rounded when soaring and narrow and pointed when gliding. A Peregrine glides with wings level or with wrists below body and wingtips up. Wingtips bow upward noticeably when falcon is executing a high-speed turn.

Behavior: Peregrine Falcons are awe-inspiring raptors to watch because of their power and grace in flight. Peregrines perform spectacular vertical dives (stoops) from great heights, with wings held tight against body, diving at and striking birds at high speeds. They eat birds almost exclusively, capturing them usually in the air but occasionally on the ground. This species nests primarily on cliffs but has used trees, buildings, and, recently, bridges. Fledglings often chase after and catch flying insects, such as dragonflies.

Water is no barrier to this falcon on migration, and individuals are frequently observed far at sea capturing birds, eating them on the wing, and perching on ships to eat and rest.

Status and distribution: Peregrine Falcons are worldwide in distribution, mainly in arctic to temperate areas. One or another of the 3 forms described above occurs in almost all parts of N. America sometime during the year.

Peregrines are uncommon to rare as breeding birds in the arctic areas of Canada and Alaska. Most of these birds migrate into S. America. Autumn concentrations are noted at coastal areas such as Cape May, New Jersey, Assateague Island, Maryland and Virginia, and Padre Island, Texas. This population now appears stable but was probably somewhat reduced by pesticide contamination. There is concern still because of increasing pesticide use in S. and Cen. America.

Peregrines were formerly widespread but local breeding birds throughout the rest of continental N. America, except the Southeast and Great Plains. The breeding population in e. N. America south of the Arctic was extirpated by DDT and other persistent pesticides. As a result of reintroduction efforts, Peregrines now breed along the cen. Atlantic Coast and in New York, New England, and e. Canada. Although numbers were seriously reduced by pesticides, breeding pairs still exist in most western states, the w. Canadian provinces, and cen. Alaska. These birds are also migratory, with more northern birds moving south as far as Cen. America. Some individuals remain in N. America, especially along the coasts.

A fairly common sedentary population exists of coastal and island birds from British Columbia north to the Aleutian chain. Some individuals, particularly immatures, move south along the coast in winter. This population is stable.

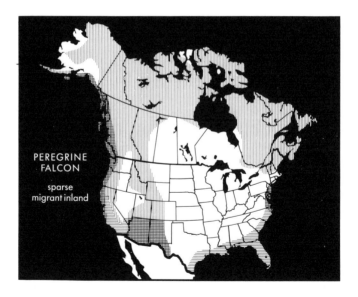

PEREGRINE
FALCON

sparse
migrant inland

Fine points: Peregrines have proportionally longer primaries than do other N. American falcons. As a result, the bend at wrist appears in flight relatively closer to body. In general, adult males are whiter on the breast and less heavily barred on the belly than adult females, which usually have a brownish cast on the back and upperwing coverts that is lacking on males.

Unusual plumages: Sight records exist of birds with a few white feathers. Two specimens of dilute-plumage immatures have many cream-colored (normally dark brown) feathers. Albinos have been reported from the British Isles.

Subspecies: There are 3 N. American subspecies, which correspond generally to the forms described: Tundra form with *F. p. tundrius,* Peale's form with *F. p. pealei,* and Continental form with *F. p. anatum.*

Etymology: *Peregrinus* in Latin means "wandering," for the falcon's long-distance migrations and dispersals. Formerly called "Duck Hawk" in N. America, for 1 type of prey.

Measurements: (Tundra Peregrine; other forms are larger.)
Length: Male 37–41 cm (39); 14–16 in. (15)
         Female 42–46 cm (44); 16–18 in. (17)
Wingspread: Male 94–100 cm (97); 37–39 in. (38)
         Female 102–116 cm (111); 40–46 in. (44)
Weight: Male 453–685 g (581); 1–1.5 lb (1.3)
         Female 719–952 g (817); 1.6–2.1 lb (1.8)

GYRFALCON   Pls. 24 and 26; photos, pp. 160, 161
Falco rusticolus

Description: The arctic Gyrfalcon, the largest falcon, is a rare winter visitor to s. Canada and n. United States. It occurs in 4 color morphs: white, gray, dark, and brown (immature of gray morph). Gyrfalcons are *heavier bodied, broader winged, and longer tailed* than other large falcons, with *wide, noticeably tapered tail.* Sexes are alike in plumage; females are noticeably larger. Immatures have different plumages than those of adults. *Wingtips reach only one-half to two-thirds down the tail* on perched birds. Iris color is dark brown. Adult cere, eye-ring, and legs are yellow to orange. Immature cere, eye-ring, and legs are dull blue-gray.

White-morph adult: *Unmistakable.* White head has fine dark streaking on crown, nape, and behind eye and sometimes a faint narrow mustache mark. White back and upperwing coverts have short black cross-barring. Underparts are white, with a few dark spots or bars on flanks or leg feathers. Underwing is white except for black outer primary tips, with at most sparse spotting on coverts. Tail is white, often with black bands.

White-morph immature: Similar to adult, but head is finely streaked dark brown, back is mostly dark brown with wide white feather edging, and white underparts and leg feathers have short dark brown streaks. Some individuals are whiter-looking; their back feathers are mostly white with dark brown center streaks and underparts have little or no streaking.

Gray-morph adult: **Head** has gray crown and nape, often with pale streaking, thin pale superciliary line, dark area behind eye, pale markings on hind neck, and pale cheek with fine dark streaking and white throat separated by a faint narrow dark mustache mark. Back and upperwing coverts are dark slate gray with many short pale gray cross-bars. Underparts are white, usually with some dark streaks on breast and heavier dark barring or spotting on belly. *Underwing is two-toned; dark coverts contrast with pale flight feathers.* Whitish leg feathers are darkly barred. Tail has light and dark gray bands of equal width.

Gray-morph immature (brown morph): Head has dark gray-brown crown and nape with pale streaking; short, thin pale superciliary line; dark area behind eye; pale markings on hind neck; and pale streaked cheek and white throat separated by a faint narrow dark mustache mark. (Some pale individuals have pale heads with fine dark streaking.) Back and upperwing coverts are medium to dark gray-brown. Underparts are creamy with heavy dark brown streaking. *Underwing is two-toned;* bird has dark coverts and pale flight feathers. Whitish leg feathers have dark streaking. Tail is dark brown with numerous narrow pale bands.

Dark-morph adult: Head, back, and upperwing coverts are dark blackish brown. (Some individuals show pale markings on hind neck and short pale barring on back.) Dark underparts have short whitish streaking on breast and short whitish barring on belly, leg feathers, and undertail tail feathers. *Underwing is two-toned;* bird has dark coverts and paler grayish flight feathers. Dark uppertail coverts have light gray barring. Dark tail has many narrow pale bands.

Dark-morph immature: Head, back, rump, and upperwing coverts are solid dark brown. (Sometimes there are faint marks on hind neck and crown.) Underparts are dark brown, with some whitish streaking. Leg feathers are solid dark brown. Dark undertail coverts have pale barring. *Underwing is two-toned.* Tail is usually solid dark brown without light bands but can have faint bands.

Note: Dark morph is most likely a dark variation of gray morph, as there is a clinal variation in color between these morphs. Dark birds are much less common than gray ones, and intergrades even less common.

Similar species: (1) **Peregrine Falcon** (Pls. 23 and 26) is smaller and has all-dark underwing; shorter, narrower tail; narrower wings; and thicker mustache mark. Wingtips reach tail tip on perched Peregrines. Adult Peregrine usually has unbarred breast (but see Peale's below). (2) **Peale's Peregrine**

(Pls. 23 and 26) can be similar to dark Gyr, but Gyr in flight has two-toned underwing, broader wings, and wider, more tapered tail. Perched Gyrs' wingtips do not reach tail tip. Adult Peale's may have heavily marked breast. (3) **Prairie Falcon** (Pl. 22) is smaller and paler and has dark central underwing patch. (4) **Goshawk** (Pls. 6 and 7) flies with wingbeats identical to those of Gyr. Its wingtips appear pointed and so can be difficult to distinguish from Gyr's, but Goshawks have pale, heavily barred underwings and broad tail bands of equal width. Adult Gos has a dark hood with thick white superciliary line. (5) **Red-tailed Hawk** albino or partial albino (Pl. 11) may appear similar to perched white-morph Gyr but usually has dark mark on nape or some rufous in tail, and wingtips almost reach tail tip.

Flight: Active flight is with slow, deep, powerful wingbeats. Resulting flight is rapid and, in level flight, is faster than that of Peregrine. Soars and glides on level wings. Gyrs hover occasionally, particularly when looking for prey that has taken cover.

Behavior: Gyrfalcons prey on mammals and birds, especially ptarmigan and ducks. They hunt from an exposed perch and, after sighting quarry, begin a tail chase, sometimes for a considerable distance. Hunting is also done by rapid contour flying (see **Behavior** under Prairie Falcon), occasionally while soaring higher. They seldom stoop from heights as Peregrines do.

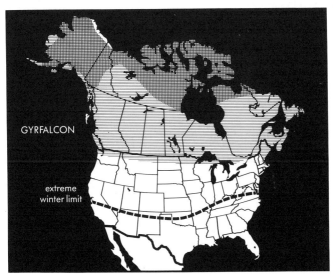

GYRFALCON

extreme winter limit

Nest is usually on a cliff, but tree nests have been reported. Wintering Gyrs are usually found near bird concentrations, often coastal dunes or airports.

Status and distribution: Gyrfalcons are uncommon to rare breeders in arctic tundra and subarctic mountain areas of Alaska and n. Canada. In winter they are uncommon and local but regular in s. Canada and n. border states and occasionally appear farther south to New Jersey, Pennsylvania, Nebraska, Oklahoma, Colorado, and California, but many adults remain throughout the winter on their breeding territories.

Fine points: Gyrfalcons have longer belly feathers than other falcons and, when perched, are able to cover their feet by spreading these feathers. Some gray-morph adults have no spotting on white underparts and look like white-morph adults. They are distinguished by light gray back and light and dark gray banded tail.

Unusual plumages: No unusual plumages have been reported.

Subspecies: The N. American race is *F. r. obsoletus.*

Etymology: Common name derives from Latin *gyrfalco* or *girofalco,* thought to be either a corruption of *hierofalco,* meaning "sacred falcon," for the bird's exalted place in falconry, or from the Old German *gir,* meaning "greedy," for its rapacity. *Rusticolus* in Latin means "living in the country," probably a reference to the tundra habitat.

Measurements:
Length: Male 50–54 cm (52); 19–21 in. (20)
       Female 57–61 cm (59); 22–24 in. (23)
Wingspread: Male 110–120 cm (115); 43–47 in. (45)
       Female 124–130 cm (127); 49–51 in. (50)
Weight: Male 1000–1300 g (1135); 2.2–2.9 lb (2.5)
       Female 1400–2100 g (1703); 3.1–4.6 lb (3.8)

PRAIRIE FALCON   Pl. 22; photos, p. 160
Falco mexicanus

Description: The Prairie Falcon of hilly and mountainous grasslands in the West is a large, pale, long-tailed falcon. Narrow mustache mark, *white area between eye and dark ear patch,* and *dark center of underwing* are best field marks. Large head appears blockish. Adult and immature plumages are similar. Sexes are almost alike in plumage. Females are noticeably larger than males. Iris color is dark brown. On perched birds, wingtips fall somewhat short of tail tip.

Adult: Brown head has pale superciliary line, large eyes, pale markings (ocelli) on hind neck, and whitish cheeks and throat separated by a narrow dark mustache mark. *Small white area between eye and dark ear patch* is unique. Back and upperwing coverts are medium brown, with pale bars and fringes on most feathers, and appear paler than on immatures. *Pale under-wings have a central dark brown area* that extends from flank to wrist and is composed of dark axillars and greater and median underwing coverts. Whitish underparts are marked with a few short streaks on breast and rows of spots on belly; spotting is heavier and appears barred on flanks. Whitish leg feathers have dark spots or bars. Brown tail shows incomplete pale bands from below. Cere, eye-ring, and leg colors are yellow-orange, brighter on males.

Immature: Similar to adult, but back appears darker because most back feathers have pale fringes and lack light barring. Buffy underparts are more heavily marked than those of adult, with more streaks and fewer spots. Creamy leg feathers have dark streaks. Cere, eye-ring, and leg colors are lead gray to yellow.

Similar species: (1) **Peregrine Falcon** (Pl. 23) is similar in size but is darker; has thicker mustache mark; appears darker-headed (but see immature Tundra Peregrine); and has uniformly dark underwing. Wingtips reach, or almost reach, tail tip on perched Peregrines, and they fly with deeper wingbeats and noticeably higher upstroke (see **Flight** below). (2) **Swainson's Hawk** (Pl. 12) has wingtips that reach tail tip when the bird is perched (surprisingly, some pale Swainson's Hawks have a similar face pattern and resemble Prairie Falcons when perched but lack white area between eye and dark ear patch). (3) **Prairie Merlin** (Pl. 22) is much smaller, has a faint mustache mark, and has noticeable light bands in tail and uniform underwing lacking dark patch in center.

Flight: Active flight is with shallow, stiff, powerful wingbeats, with wings mostly below the horizontal. The Prairie Falcon soars on flat wings, with tail somewhat fanned. It glides on flat wings or with wrists below body and wingtips curved upward. This falcon occasionally hovers (see **Behavior** below).

Behavior: Prairie Falcons hunt from either a high perch or a glide. Their favorite prey is small mammals, especially ground squirrels, and ground-dwelling birds, but they also take lizards and flying insects. They fly fast and low over open country and surprise prey, which they capture as it attempts to escape. From either perch or soar, Prairie Falcons stoop to pick up speed and then close rapidly on prey in a ground-hugging flight. Birds that flush are often tail-chased a considerable distance. Unlike Peregrines, this falcon readily takes prey on the ground. On occasion, Prairie Falcons hover, often for many seconds, looking for prey that was lost from sight. Prairies nest almost exclusively on cliffs, but tree nests and a building ledge nest have been reported. During winter they inhabit areas where birds concentrate; here they are often robbed of prey by buzzards (*Buteo*) and harriers (*Circus*).

Status and distribution: Prairie Falcons are fairly common breeders in hilly and mountainous grasslands of the West west of the Great Plains from s. Canada (British Columbia, Alberta, and Saskatchewan) south to n. Mexico. In late summer, after breeding, some falcons move up to the mountain tundra. Some birds disperse in winter south, east, and west to the coast, where they inhabit grasslands, deserts, and farmlands. Casual in e. United States, with records from Wisconsin, Illinois, Tennessee, both Carolinas, and Alabama, although some records could be of escaped falconry birds.

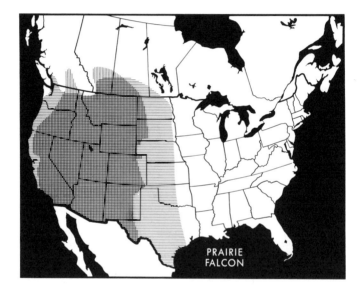

PRAIRIE
FALCON

Fine points: Prairie Falcon's eyes are larger and tail is longer than those of the Peregrine. First-plumage adults, especially males, have pale banding on central tail feathers (which are uniformly unbanded in other plumages) and may also have a grayish cast to upperparts, lacking in immatures and older adults.

Unusual plumages: Records exist of 2 partial albinos and a cream-colored individual with some normal feathers.

Subspecies: Monotypic.

Etymology: *Mexicanus* indicates where the first specimen was collected.

Measurements:
Length: Male 37–40 cm (38); 14–16 in. (15)
        Female 42–47 cm (44); 16–18 in. (17)
Wingspread: Male 91–97 cm (94); 36–38 in. (37)
        Female 105–113 cm (109); 41–44 in. (43)
Weight: Male 420–635 g (524); 0.9–1.4 lb (1.2)
        Female 675–975 g (848); 1.5–2.1 lb (1.9)

Photographs

References

Index to References
by Species and Topic

General Index

120 black head   gray wrinkled head

immatures   adult

▲ 1a. BLACK VULTURE—
adult and two immatures.

▲ 1b. BLACK VULTURE—immature sunning

▼ 1c. BLACK VULTURE—adult.

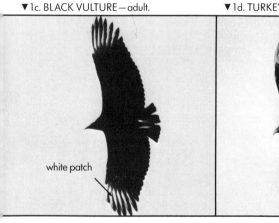

white patch

▼ 1d. TURKEY VULTURE—adult.

two-toned

▼ 1e. TURKEY VULTURE—adult.

red head

▼ 1f. TURKEY VULTURE—immature.

dusky head

white triangle

orange head

2a. CALIFORNIA CONDOR—adult.

▲ 2b. CALIFORNIA CONDOR—immature.

2c. OSPREY—adult female (note necklace on breast).

▼ 2d. OSPREY—adult male with fish.

dark carpal patch

dark eye-line

2e. OSPREY—adult male.

▼ 2f. OSPREY—immature (pale feather edges on back).

dark eye-line

white eye

2 pale bands

▲ 3a. HOOK-BILLED KITE — adult.

▲ 3b. HOOK-BILLED KITE — adult female.

▼ 3c. SWALLOW-TAILED KITE — adult.

▼ 3d. SWALLOW-TAILED KITE — immature.

deeply forked tail

deeply forked tail (shorter than adult's)

▼ 3e. SNAIL KITE — adult female.

▼ 3f. SNAIL KITE — adult male.

thin hooked beak

thin hooked beak

white tail coverts and tail base

white tail coverts and tail base

4a. SNAIL KITE—immature.

▲ 4b. SNAIL KITE—adult female.

4c. SNAIL KITE—subadult male.

▼ 4d. SNAIL KITE—adult female.

white tail coverts and tail base

4e. SNAIL KITE—adult female with snail.

▼ 4f. SNAIL KITE—adult male.

cupped wings

124

▲ 5a. BLACK-SHOULDERED KITE—adult.

▲ 5b. BLACK-SHOULDERED KITE—adult.

▼ 5c. MISSISSIPPI KITE—adult.

▼ 5d. MISSISSIPPI KITE—adult.

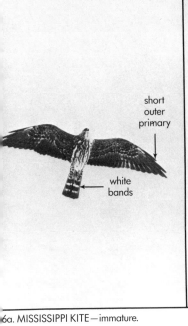

short
outer
primary

white
bands

white bands

gray
underparts

6a. MISSISSIPPI KITE—immature.

▲ 6b. MISSISSIPPI KITE—subadult.

6c. MISSISSIPPI KITE—adult.

▼ 6d. MISSISSIPPI KITE—immature.

whitish
head

wings
extend
beyond
tail

black bar

hooded effect

white uppertail coverts

2 central feathers are dark

▲ 7a. NORTHERN HARRIER—adult male.

▲ 7b. NORTHERN HARRIER—immature.

▼ 7c. NORTHERN HARRIER—immature.

▼ 7d. NORTHERN HARRIER—adult female

dark patch

hooded effect

dark patch

hooded effect

squarish tip and narrow white

rounded tip and wide white

heavily streaked

lightly streaked

8a. *Left:* SHARP-SHINNED—imm. female; *right:* COOPER'S HAWK—imm. male.

8c. *Left:* GOSHAWK—imm. male; *right:* COOPER'S HAWK—imm. female.

▲ 8b. *Left:* SHARP-SHINNED—imm. female; *right:* COOPER'S HAWK—imm. male.

▼ 8d. *Left:* COOPER'S HAWK—imm. female; *right:* GOSHAWK—imm. male.

squarish head

highlights

lightly streaked

heavily streaked

128

▲ 9a. SHARP-SHINNED HAWK — immature. ▲ 9b. COOPER'S HAWK — immature.

▼ 9c. GOSHAWK — adult. ▼ 9d. GOSHAWK — immature.

▼ 9e. COOPER'S HAWK — immature. ▼ 9f. SHARP-SHINNED HAWK — immature.

head barely projects beyond wrists

head projects beyond wrists

0a. SHARP-SHINNED HAWK— immature.

0c. GOSHAWK—adult (note tapered wings).

▲10b. COOPER'S HAWK—immature.

▼10d. GOSHAWK—immature.

light gray underparts

▼10g. GOSHAWK—immature.

0e. GOSHAWK—adult.

0f. SHARP-SHINNED HAWK—adult.

squarish tip

heavily streaked underparts

strongly marked
head pattern

▲ 11a. COMMON BLACK HAWK—
    immature.

▲ 11b. COMMON BLACK HAWK—
    immature.

▼ 11c. COMMON BLACK HAWK—
    immature.

▼ 11d. COMMON BLACK HAWK—adult.

tawny panel

white tail with
black wavy bands

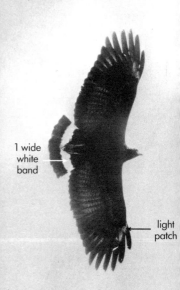

1 wide
white
band

light
patch

2a. HARRIS' HAWK—adult.

2c. HARRIS' HAWK—adult.

▲ 12b. HARRIS' HAWK—immature
(note streaked belly).

▼ 12d. HARRIS' HAWK—immature
(note streaked belly and light primaries).

132

▲ 13a. GRAY HAWK—adult.

gray
barred
underparts

▲ 13b. GRAY HAWK—adult.

▼ 13c. GRAY HAWK—immature.

▼ 13d. GRAY HAWK—immature.

strong
face
pattern

white
U-shaped
uppertail
coverts

▼ 13e. GRAY HAWK—adult.

▼ 13f. GRAY HAWK—
Left: immature; right: adult.

2 white bands
(1 wide,
1 narrow)

buffy
uppertail
coverts

133

light and dark
bands of
equal width

14a. ROADSIDE HAWK—adult.　　　　▲14b. ROADSIDE HAWK—adult.

14c. ROADSIDE HAWK—adult.　　　　▼14d. ROADSIDE HAWK—adult.

dark
bib

14e. ROADSIDE HAWK—adult.　　　　▼14f. ROADSIDE HAWK—immature.

yellow
eye

pale
superciliary
line

streaked
breast

tawny crescent-shaped panel

narrow light bands

▲ 15a. RED-SHOULDERED HAWK — immature.

pale head

checkered black and white

▲ 15b. RED-SHOULDERED HAWK — Florida adult.

▼ 15d. RED-SHOULDERED HAWK — immature.

▲ 15c. RED-SHOULDERED HAWK — California immature.

▼ 15e. BROAD-WINGED HAWK — immature (for comparison).

narrow light bands

wide light bands

white crescent-shaped panel

rufous coverts

narrow white bands

16a. RED-SHOULDERED HAWK—adult.

▲16b. RED-SHOULDERED HAWK— Florida adult.

16c. RED-SHOULDERED HAWK— Florida immature.

▼16d. RED-SHOULDERED HAWK— immature.

tawny crescent-shaped panel

narrow light bands

16e. RED-SHOULDERED HAWK— immature.

▼16f. RED-SHOULDERED HAWK— immature.

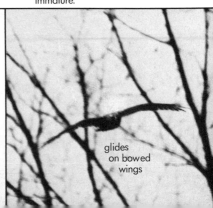

tawny crescent-shaped panel

glides on bowed wings

136

pointed tips

2 white bands

▲ 17a. BROAD-WINGED HAWK — adult.

narrow dark band
subterminal wides

▲ 17b. BROAD-WINGED HAWK — immatur

▼ 17c. BROAD-WINGED HAWK — immature.

▼ 17d. BROAD-WINGED HAWK — immatur
(variant — no streaking on underparts)

square panel

pointed tips

▼ 17e. BROAD-WINGED HAWK —
dark-morph adult.

▼ 17f. BROAD-WINGED HAWK —
dark-morph immature.

2 white bands

pointed tips

narrow dark bands
subterminal widest

137

18a. SHORT-TAILED HAWK—adult.

▲ 18b. SHORT-TAILED HAWK—adult.

18c. SHORT-TAILED HAWK—
dark-morph adult.

▼ 18d. SHORT-TAILED HAWK—
dark-morph immature.

dark
flight
feathers

dark bib

▲ 19a. SWAINSON'S HAWK — adult.

▲ 19b. SWAINSON'S HAWK — adult.

▲ 19c. SWAINSON'S HAW adult.

▼ 19d. SWAINSON'S HAWK — immature.

▼ 19e. SWAINSON'S HAWK — immature.

▼ 19f. SWAINSON'S HAW immature.

dark
flight
feathers

▼ 19g. SWAINSON'S HAWK — dark-morph immature.

▼ 19h. SWAINSON'S HAWK — rufous-morph adult.

▼ 19i. SWAINSON'S HAWK dark-morph adult.

dark
flight
feathers

dark
flight
feathers

light
undertail
coverts

dark
flight
feathers

light
undertail
coverts

20a. SWAINSON'S HAWK—adult.   ▲20b. SWAINSON'S HAWK—adult.

20c. SWAINSON'S HAWK—immature.   ▼20d. SWAINSON'S HAWK—immature.

20e. SWAINSON'S HAWK—immature.   ▼20f. SWAINSON'S HAWK—dark-morph
                                        adult.

wide
black band
on white tail

creamy
patch

▲ 21a. WHITE-TAILED HAWK — adult.

▲ 21b. WHITE-TAILED HAWK — immature.

black band
on grayish
tail

belly band

▲ 21c. WHITE-TAILED HAWK — adult.

▲ 21d. WHITE-TAILED HAWK — subadult.

▼ 21e. WHITE-TAILED HAWK — immature.

▼ 21f. WHITE-TAILED HAWK — immature.

fous shoulder patch

gray upperparts

wingtips extend beyond tail

barred belly

22a. WHITE-TAILED HAWK—adult.

▲ 22b. WHITE-TAILED HAWK—subadult.

22c. ZONE-TAILED HAWK—adult female.

▼ 22d. ZONE-TAILED HAWK—immature.

white bands

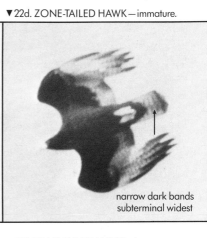

narrow dark bands subterminal widest

22e. ZONE-TAILED HAWK—adult.

▼ 22f. ZONE-TAILED HAWK—immature.

(only 1 white band shows on closed tail)

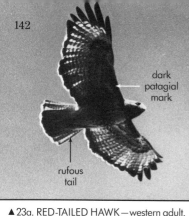

dark patagial mark

rufous tail

▲ 23a. RED-TAILED HAWK—western adult.

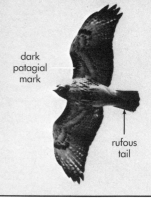

dark patagial mark

rufous tail

▲ 23b. RED-TAILED HAWK—eastern adult.

▼ 23c. RED-TAILED HAWK—Fuertes' adult.

▼ 23d. RED-TAILED HAWK—immature.

narrow dark bands of equal width

dark patagial mark

▼ 23e. RED-TAILED HAWK—partial albino adult.

▼ 23f. RED-TAILED HAWK—immature.

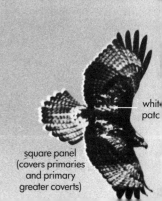

white patch

square panel (covers primaries and primary greater coverts)

148

dark bib

1 or more
dark tail bands,
subterminal
widest

black
carpal
patch

▲ 29a. ROUGH-LEGGED HAWK—
adult male.

▼ 29c. ROUGH-LEGGED HAWK—
adult female.

▲ 29b. ROUGH-LEGGED HAWK—
adult male.

▼ 29d. ROUGH-LEGGED HAWK—
immature.

black
subterminal
band

black
carpal
patch

b
cc
p

solid
belly
band

▼ 29e. ROUGH-LEGGED HAWK—
immature.

▼ 29f. ROUGH-LEGGED HAWK—
dark-morph adult male.

solid
belly
band

black spot

149

dark
tail
has
white
bands

broad
dark
subterminal
band

30a. ROUGH-LEGGED HAWK —
   dark-morph adult male.
30c. ROUGH-LEGGED HAWK —
   dark-morph immature.

▲ 30b. ROUGH-LEGGED HAWK —
   dark-morph adult female.
▼ 30d. ROUGH-LEGGED HAWK —
   dark-morph immature.

dusky
subterminal
band

ack
rpal
tch

30e. ROUGH-LEGGED HAWK —
   adult male.

▼ 30f. ROUGH-LEGGED HAWK —
   dark-morph immature.

dark bib

more dark tail bands,
subterminal widest

rectangular panels
(covers primaries)

dusky tail

white mottling

tawny belly

black borders 151

32a. BALD EAGLE— immature.
32d. BALD EAGLE— White-belly I.

▲32b. BALD EAGLE— immature.
▼32e. BALD EAGLE— White-belly I.

▲32c. BALD EAGLE— immature.
▼32f. BALD EAGLE— White-belly II.

white mottling

white belly

32g. BALD EAGLE— transition.

▼32h. BALD EAGLE— first adult plumage.

▼32i. BALD EAGLE— adult.

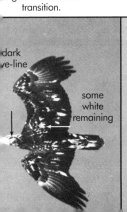

dark eye-line

some white remaining

white tail (and under-tail coverts)

white head

153

white spikes

34a. WHITE-TAILED EAGLE—immature. ▲34b. WHITE-TAILED EAGLE—immature.

34c. WHITE-TAILED EAGLE—adult. ▼34d. WHITE-TAILED EAGLE—adult.

short
white
tail

dark
undertail
coverts

154

dark crested head →

dark crested head →

▲ 35a. CRESTED CARACARA—immature (streaked on breast).

▲ 35b. CRESTED CARACARA—adult (barred on breast).

▼ 35c. CRESTED CARACARA—adult.

▼ 35d. CRESTED CARACARA—adult.

▼ 35e. CRESTED CARACARA—adult.

▼ 35f. CRESTED CARACARA—adult.

long white neck →

← white patch

white patch →

two-toned wing

long gray tail with wide subterminal black band

155

36a. EURASIAN KESTREL—adult male.

▲ 36b. EURASIAN KESTREL—adult male.

36c. EURASIAN KESTREL—immature.

▼ 36d. EURASIAN KESTREL—adult female.

1 mustache mark

36e. EURASIAN KESTREL—adult male.

▼ 36f. EURASIAN KESTREL—immatures.

1 mustache mark

Left: female; right: male.

156

rufous with dark subterminal band

white spots

rufous with narrow dark bands

▲ 37a. AMERICAN KESTREL—immature male (underparts white and streaked).

▲ 37b. AMERICAN KESTREL—female.

▼ 37c. AMERICAN KESTREL—adult male (orangish underparts).

▼ 37d. AMERICAN KESTREL—female.

2 mustache marks

2 mustache marks

▼ 37e. MERLIN—immature.

▼ 37f. MERLIN—immature.

narrow light bands

narrow light bands

faint
mustache
mark

narrow
light
bands

38a. MERLIN—immature.

▲38b. MERLIN—immature.

38c. MERLIN—Prairie adult male.

▼38d. MERLIN—Prairie immature.

pale blue back

no
mustache
mark

no mustache
mark

pale brown back

38e. MERLIN—Black immature.

▼38f. MERLIN—Black immature.

lacks pale bands

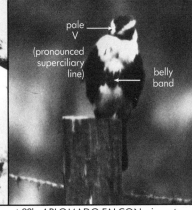

pale
V
(pronounced
superciliary
line)

belly
band

bold
face
pattern

▲ 39a. APLOMADO FALCON—adult.

▲ 39b. APLOMADO FALCON—immature.

▼ 39c. APLOMADO FALCON—adult.

▼ 39d. APLOMADO FALCON—adult.

numerous narrow
light bands
on long tail

▼ 39e. NORTHERN HOBBY—adult.

▼ 39f. NORTHERN HOBBY—adult.

sickle-
shaped
wings

mustache

wingtip
extend
beyond
tail

References

General

Beebe, F. L. 1974. *Field studies of the Falconiformes of British Columbia.* B.C. Prov. Mus., Occ. Paper No. 17. Victoria.

Bent, A. C. 1961. *Life histories of North American birds of prey.* Vols. I and II. Reprint. Dover, New York.

Brown. L., and D. Amadon. 1968. *Eagles, hawks, and falcons of the world.* McGraw-Hill, New York.

Cade, T. J. 1982. *The falcons of the world.* Cornell Univ. Press, Ithaca.

Craighead, J. J., and F. C. Craighead, Jr. 1969. *Hawks, owls, and wildlife.* Reprint. Dover, New York.

Cramp, S., and K. E. L. Simmons (eds.). 1980. *Handbook of the birds of the Palearctic.* Vol. II. Oxford Univ. Press, Oxford.

Friedmann, H. 1950. *The birds of North and Middle America.* Vol. XI. Smithson. Inst. USNM Bull. 50.

Grossman, M. L., and J. Hamlet. 1964. *Birds of prey of the world.* Clarkson N. Potter, New York.

Heintzelman, D. S. 1975. *Autumn hawk flights.* Rutgers Univ. Press, New Brunswick, N.J.

Heintzelman, D. S. 1982. *A guide to hawk watching in North America.* Keystone Books, Univ. Park, Pa.

Newton, I. 1979. *Population ecology of raptors.* Buteo Books, Vermillion, S.D.

Specific

Abramson, I. J. 1976. The Black Hawk *(Buteogallus anthracinus)* in South Florida. Am. Birds 30:661–662.

Allaire, P. N. 1977. Aberrant pigmentation in Kentucky birds. Ky. Warb. 53:13–16.

Amadon, D. 1975. Variation in the Everglade Kite. Auk 92:380–382.

Amadon, D. 1977. Notes on the taxonomy of vultures. Condor 79:413–416.

Amadon, D. 1982. A revision of the sub-buteoine hawks (Accipitidae, Aves). Am. Mus. Novitates. No. 2741.

Amadon, D., and A. R. Phillips. 1939. Notes on the Mexican Goshawk. Auk 56:183–184.

Ames, P. L. 1964. Notes on the breeding behavior of the Osprey. Atl. Nat. 19:15–27.

Angell, T. 1969. A study of the Ferruginous Hawk: Adult and brood behavior. Living Bird 8:225–241.

Appleberry, E. L. 1957. White-tailed Kite at Wilmington. Chat 21:70–71.

Ault, J. W., III. 1975. Harris's Hawk in southwestern Oklahoma. Bull. Okla. Ornith. Soc. 8:34–36.

Austing, G. R. 1964. *The world of the Red-tailed Hawk.* J. B. Lippincott, New York.

Bailey, B. H. 1917. Description of a new subspecies of the Broad-winged Hawk. Auk 34:73–75.

Balch, L. 1982. An Attu diary. Birding 14:114–128.

Balgooyen, T. G. 1975. Another possible function of the American Kestrel deflection face. Jack Pine Warbler 53:115–116.

Balgooyen, T. G. 1976. *Behavior and ecology of the American Kestrel* (Falco sparverius L.) *in the Sierra Nevada of California.* Univ. Calif. Pub. Zool. 106. Univ. Calif. Press, Berkeley.

Bartolotti, G. R. 1984a. Sexual size dimorphism and age-related size variation in Bald Eagles. J. Wildl. Manage. 48:72–81.

Bartolotti, G. R. 1984b. Age and sex variation in Golden Eagles. J. Field Ornith. 55:54–66.

Bednarz, J. C., and J. J. Dinsmore. 1982. Status, habitat use, and management of Red-shouldered Hawks in Iowa. J. Wildl. Manage. 45:236–241.

Beebe, F. L. 1960. The marine Peregrines of the northwest Pacific coast. Condor 62:145–189.

Beissinger, S. R. 1983. Hunting behavior, prey selection, and energetics of Snail Kites in Guyana: Consumer choice by a specialist. Auk 100:84–92.

Beissinger, S. R., and J. E. Takekawa. 1983. Habitat use by and dispersal of Snail Kites in Florida during drought conditions. Fla. Field Nat. 11:89–106.

Berger, D. D. 1971. A Mississippi Kite at Cedar Grove. Pass. Pigeon 33:155.

Berger, D. D. 1982. A Black Vulture in Wisconsin. Pass. Pigeon 44:125.

Bildstein, K. L. 1979. Fluctuations in the number of Northern Harriers *(Circus cyaneus hudsonius)* at communal roosts in south central Ohio. Raptor Res. 13:40–46.

Bildstein, K. L., W. S. Clark, D. L. Evans, M. Field, L. Soucy, and E. Henckel. 1984. Sex and age differences in fall migration of Northern Harriers. J. Field Ornith. 55:143–150.

Birkenholz, D. E. 1977. Nesting trends and habits of Northern Harriers at Goose Lake Prairie, Grundy County. Ill. Aud. Bull. No. 179:31–33.

Black, C. T. 1941. Gyrfalcon in Wisconsin. Auk 58:254.

Blair, C. L., and F. Schitoskey, Jr. 1982. Breeding biology and diet of the Ferruginous Hawk in South Dakota. Wilson Bull. 94:46–54.

Blake, E. R. 1949. *Ictinia misisippiensis* collected in Paraguay. Auk 66:82.

Bloom, P. H. 1980. *The status of the Swainson's Hawk in California, 1979.* BLM Report, Sacramento.

Bock, C. E., and L. W. Lepthien. 1977. Geographic ecology of the common species of *Buteo* and *Parabuteo* wintering in North America. Condor 78:554–557.

Boeker, E. L. 1974. Status of Golden Eagle surveys in the Western states. Wildl. Soc. Bull. 2:46–49.

Bohl, W. H., and E. Traylor. 1958. A correction of the Zone-tailed Hawk as a Mexican Black Hawk. Condor 60:139.

Bond, R. M., and R. M. Stabler. 1941. Second-year plumage of the Goshawk. Auk 58:346–349.

Borneman, J. 1978. To see a Condor. Birding 10:1–5.

Brandt, H. W. 1924. The nesting of the Short-tailed Hawk. Auk 41:59–64.

Brodkorb, P. 1935. A Sparrow Hawk gynandromorph. Auk 52:183–184.

Broley, C. L. 1947. Migration and nesting of Florida Bald Eagles. Wilson Bull. 59:3–20.

Brooks, A. 1933. Some notes on the birds of Brownsville, Texas. Auk 5:59–63.

Brown, W. H. 1971. Winter population trends in the Red-shouldered Hawk. Am. Birds. 25:813–817.

Browning, M. R. 1973. Bendire's records of Red-shouldered Hawk *(Buteo lineatus)* and Yellow-bellied Sapsucker *(Sphyrapicus varius nuchalis)* in Oregon. Murrelet 54:34–35.

Browning, M. R. 1974. Comments on the winter distribution of the Swainson's Hawk *(Buteo swainsoni)* in North America. Am. Birds 28:865–867.

Burford, F. C. 1963. Mississippi Kite in Norfolk. Raven 39:24.

Burns, F. L. 1911. A monograph of the Broad-winged Hawk *(Buteo platypterus)*. Wilson Bull. 23:139–320.

Burr, B. M., and D. M. Current. 1975. Status of the Gyrfalcon in Illinois. Wilson Bull. 87:280–281.

Buskirk, W. H., and M. Lechner. 1978. Frugivory by Swallow-tailed Kites in Costa Rica. Auk 95:767–768.

Cade, T. J. 1953. Behavior of a young Gyrfalcon. Wilson Bull. 65:26–31.

Cade, T. J. 1955. Variation of the common Rough-legged Hawk in North America. Condor 57:313–346.

Cade, T. J. 1960. Ecology of the Peregrine and Gyrfalcon populations in Alaska. Univ. Calif. Publ. Zoo. 63:151–290.

Cade, T. J. 1982. *The falcons of the world.* Cornell Univ. Press, Ithaca.

Cameron, E. S. 1913. Notes on Swainson's Hawk *(Buteo swainsoni)* in Montana. Auk 30:381–394.

Campbell, C. A. 1975. Ecology and reproduction of Red-shouldered Hawks in the Waterloo region, southern Ontario. Raptor Res. 9:12–17.

Campbell, R. W. 1985. First record of the Eurasian Kestrel for Canada. Condor 87:294.

Campbell, R. W., M. A. Paul, and M. S. Rodway. 1978. Tree-nesting Peregrine Falcons in British Columbia. Condor 80:500–501.

Carter, D. L., and R. H. Wauer. 1965. Black Hawk nesting in Utah. Condor 67:82–83.

Carter, W. A., and C. L. Fowler. 1983. Black-shouldered Kite in Oklahoma, 1860 and 1982. Bull. Okla. Ornith. Soc. 16:9–11.

Cely, J. E. 1979. An albinistic Red-tailed Hawk near Greenwood, S. C. Chat 43:21–22.

Clark, R. J. 1972. Observations of nesting Marsh Hawks in Manitoba. Blue Jay 30:42–48.

Clark, W. S. 1967. Partial albino Red-tailed Hawk. Md. Birdlife 23:21.

Clark, W. S. 1974a. Second record of the Kestrel *(Falco tinnunculus)* for North America. Auk 91:172.

Clark, W. S. 1974b. Occurrence of Swainson's Hawk substantiated in New Jersey. Wilson Bull. 86:284–285.

Clark, W. S. 1981. Flight identification of common North American *Buteos.* Cont. Birdl. 2:129–143.

Clark, W. S. 1983. Field identification of North American eagles. Am. Birds 37:822–826.

Clark, W. S. 1984a. Field identification of *Accipiters* in North America. Birding 16:251–263.

Clark, W. S. 1984b. Agonistic "whirling" by Zone-tailed Hawks. Condor 86:488.

Clark, W. S. 1985a. Migration of the Merlin along the coast of New Jersey. Raptor Res. 19:85–94.

Clark, W. S. 1985b. The migrating Sharp-shinned Hawks at Cape May Point: Banding and recovery results. In Harwood, M. (ed.), *Proc. N. Am. Hawk Conf. IV, Rochester, N.Y. March 1983.* Hawk Migr. Assn. of N. Amer.

Clark, W. S., and C. M. Anderson. 1984. First record of the

Broad-winged Hawk for Washington. Murrelet 5:93–94.

Clay, W. H. 1953. Protective coloration in the American Sparrow Hawk. Wilson Bull. 65:129–134.

Clermont, R. 1979. Photographs of New York State rarities, 33. Mississippi Kite, Kingbird 29:178–180.

Collopy, M. W. 1983. Foraging behavior and success in Golden Eagles. Auk 100:747–749.

Collopy, M. W. 1984. Parental care and feeding ecology of Golden Eagle nestlings. Auk 101:753–760.

Conner, R. N. 1974. Note on aerial courtship of Red-tailed Hawks. Bird Band. 45:269.

Craddock, D. R., and R. D. Carlson. 1970. Peregrine Falcon observed feeding far at sea. Condor 72:375–376.

Craig, G. R. 1971. Gyrfalcon trapped in Colorado. Colo. Field Ornith. 9:20.

Craig, T. H., and E. H. Craig. 1984. A large concentration of roosting Golden Eagles in southeastern Idaho. Auk 101:610–613.

Craighead, J., and F. Craighead. 1940. Nesting Pigeon Hawks. Wilson Bull 52:241–248.

Cramp, S., and K. E. L. Simmons (eds.). 1980. *Handbook of the birds of Europe, the Middle East, and North Africa*. Vol. II. Oxford Univ. Press, Oxford.

Cranson, B. F. 1972. Mississippi Kite nesting in Colorado. Colo. Field Ornith. 11:5–11.

Cruickshank, A. D. 1937. A Swainson's Hawk migration. Auk 54:385.

Darling, F. F. 1934. Speed of Golden Eagle's flight. Nature 134:325–326.

Davis, R. S. 1970. Another white one. IBBA News 42:206–207.

Dekker, D. 1979. Characteristics of Peregrine Falcons migrating through central Alberta, 1969–1978. Can. Field-Nat. 93:296–302.

Delnicki, D. 1978. Second occurrence and first successful nesting record of the Hook-billed Kite in the United States. Condor 90:427.

Dementiev, G. P., N. A. Gladov, E. S. Ptushenko, E. P. Spangenberg, and A. M. Sudilovskaya. 1966. *Birds of the Soviet Union*. Vol I. Transl. from Russian. Israel Prog. for Sci. Transl., Jerusalem.

Dillon, O. W., Jr. 1963. Notes on the nesting of the Caracara. Wilson Bull. 73:387.

Dixon, J. B. 1928. Life history of the Red-bellied Hawk. Condor 30:228–236.

Dixon, J. B., R. E. Dixon, and J. E. Dixon. 1957. Natural History of the White-tailed Kite in San Diego County, California. Condor 59:156–165.

Dunkle, S. W. 1977. Swainson's Hawks on the Laramie plains, Wyoming. Auk 94:65–71.

Dunn, J., and K. Garrett. 1982. Field notes on the Red-tailed Hawk. Birding News Survey, 1982–1983 Annual:44–45.

Eckert, K. R. 1982. Ferruginous Hawk identification. Loon 54:161.

Eisenmann, E. 1963a. Mississippi Kite in Argentina, with comments on migration and plumages in the genus *Ictinia*. Auk 80:74–77.

Eisenmann, E. 1963b. Is the Black Vulture migratory? Wilson Bull. 75:244–249.

Eisenmann, E. 1971. Range expansion and population increase in North and Middle America of the White-tailed Kite. Am. Birds 25:529–536.

Elias, D. J., and D. Valencia. 1982. Unusual feeding behavior by a population of Black Vultures. Wilson Bull. 94:214.

Elliot, B. G. 1981. Defensive behavior of an immature California Condor. West. Birds 12:139–140.

Ellis, D. H., and G. Monson. 1979. White-tailed Kite records for Arizona. West. Birds 10:165.

Ellis, D. H., and W. H. Whaley. 1979. Two winter breeding records for the Harris' Hawk. Auk 96:413.

Elwell, L., J. Mathisen, and A. Mathisen. 1978. Black Hawk found in Bemidji. Loon 50:31–34.

Enderson, J. H. 1962. Three unusual raptor records from Wyoming. Auk 79:714.

Enderson, J. H. 1964. A study of the Prairie Falcon in the central Rocky Mountain region. Auk 81:332–352.

Enderson, J. H., and J. Craig. 1974. Status of the Peregrine Falcon in the Rocky Mountains in 1973. Auk 91:727–736.

Engle, M. C. 1980. Mississippi Kite strikes human being. Bull. Okla. Ornith. Soc. 13:21–22.

Errington, P. L. 1930. Territory disputes of three pairs of nesting Marsh Hawks. Wilson Bull. 42:237–239.

Evans, D. L. 1975. A Gyrfalcon at Hawk Ridge. Loon 47:45–46.

Evans, D. L. 1978. Partial albinism: Saw-whet Owl and Goshawk. Loon 50:52–53.

Evans, D. L. 1982. *Status report on twelve raptors.* USDI Fish and Wildl. Ser. Spec. Sci. Rep.–Wildl. No. 238. Washington, D.C.

Evans, D. L., and R. N. Rosenfield. 1984. Migration and mortality of Sharp-shinned Hawks ringed at Duluth, Minnesota, Univ. S. A. In Newton, I., and R. D. Chancellor (eds.), *Proc. World Conf. on Birds of Prey, Thessalonika, 1982.* ICBP, London.

Fatora, J. R. 1968. Early summer records of the American
    Rough-legged Hawk in South Carolina. Chat 30:50–51.
Feldsine, J. W., and L. W. Oliphant. 1985. Breeding behavior
    of the Merlin: The courtship period. Raptor Res.
    19:60–67.
Fingerhood, E., and S. Lipschutz. 1980. Gyrfalcon *(Falco
    rusticolus)* records in Pennsylvania. Cassinia 59:68–76.
Fischer, D. L. 1985. Piracy behavior in wintering Bald Eagles.
    Condor 87:246–251.
Fischer, W. 1982. *Die Seeadler.* (In German.) Die Neue
    Brehm-Bücherei, Wittenberg, Lutherstadt.
Fitch, H. S. 1963. Observations on the Mississippi Kite in
    southwestern Kansas. Univ. of Kan. Pub. Mus. Nat.
    Hist. 12:503–519.
Fitch, H. S. 1974. Observations on the food and nesting of
    the Broad-winged Hawk *(Buteo platypterus)* in
    northeastern Kansas. Condor 76:331–333.
Fitzner, R. E. 1980. *Behavioral ecology of the Swainson's
    Hawk* (Buteo swainsoni) *in Washington.* Pac. NW Lab.,
    Battelle, Richland, Wash.
Fitzner, R. E., D. Berry, L. L. Boyd, and C. A. Reick. 1977.
    Nesting of Ferruginous Hawks *(Buteo regalis)* in
    Washington 1974–75. Condor 79:245–249.
Fitzpatrick, M. D. 1979. Marsh Hawk takes prey in water.
    Ont. Field Biol. 32:79.
Fleetwood, R. J., and J. L. Hamilton. 1967. Occurrence and
    nesting of the Hook-billed Kite *(Chondrohierax
    uncinatus)* in Texas. Auk 84:598–601.
Flieg, G. M. 1972. Northern range extension and breeding
    behavior of the Mississippi Kite and Black Vulture in S.
    Illinois. Aud. Bull. 163:20.
Forsman, D. 1981. (Moult sequence and ageing in the White-
    tailed Eagle). (In Swedish with an English summary.)
    Luonnonvarainhoitotoimiston julkaisuja 3:165–193.
Fox, R. P. 1956. Large Swainson's Hawk flight in south
    Texas. Auk 73:281–282.
Freeman, F. J. 1952. Communal roosting of American Rough-
    legged Hawks. Auk 69:85–86.
Friedmann, H. 1925. Notes on the birds observed in the lower
    Rio Grande valley of Texas during May, 1924. Auk
    62:537–545.
Fyfe, R. W., S. A. Temple, and T. J. Cade. 1976. The 1975
    North American Peregrine Falcon survey. Can. Field-
    Nat. 90:228–273.

Ganier, A. F. 1902. The Mississippi Kite *(Ictinia
    mississippiensis).* Osprey 1:85–90.
Gerrard, J. M., D. W. A. Whitfield, and W. J. Maher. 1976.

Osprey–Bald Eagle relationships in Saskatchewan. Blue Jay 34:240–246.

Gerrard, J. M., D. W. A. Whitfield, P. Gerrard, N. Gerrard, and W. J. Maher. 1978. Migratory movements and plumages of subadult Saskatchewan Bald Eagles. Can. Field-Nat. 92:375–382.

Gilmer, D. S., D. L. Evans, P. M. Konrad, and R. E. Stewart. 1985. Recoveries of Ferruginous Hawks banded in south-central North Dakota. J. Field Ornith. 56:184–187.

Gilmer, D. S., and R. E. Stewart. 1983. Ferruginous Hawk populations and habitat use in North Dakota. J. Wildl. Manage. 47:146–157.

Glazener, W. C. 1964. Note on the feeding habits of the Caracara in south Texas. Condor 66:162.

Glinski, R. L. 1982. The Red-shouldered Hawk *(Buteo lineatus)* in Arizona. Am. Birds. 36:801–803.

Glinski, R. L., and R. D. Ohmart. 1983. Breeding ecology of the Mississippi Kite in Arizona. Condor 85:200–207.

Green, J. C. 1967. The identification of Harlan's Hawk. Loon 39:4–7.

Green, R. C. 1982. White-tailed Kite in Garden County. Neb. Bird Rev. 50:10–11.

Green, R. O., Jr., N. D. Reed, and M. H. Wright, Jr. 1972. Swallow-tailed Kite. Nat. Geogr. 142:496–505.

Greider, M., and E. S. Wagner. 1960. Black Vulture extends breeding range northward. Wilson Bull. 72:291.

Grey, H. 1917. Zone-tailed Hawk at San Diego, California. Condor 19:103.

Grier, J. W. 1982. Ban of DDT and subsequent recovery of reproduction in Bald Eagles. Science 218:1232–1235.

Groskin, H. 1952. Observations on Duck Hawks nesting on man-made structures. Auk 69:246–253.

Grubb, T. C., Jr. 1977. Why Ospreys hover. Wilson Bull. 89:149–150.

Grube, G. E. 1953. Black Vulture breeding in Pennsylvania. Wilson Bull. 65:119.

Grzybowski, J. A. 1983. Gyrfalcon in Oklahoma City: Southernmost record for North America. Bull. Okla. Ornith. Soc. 16:27–29.

Hamerstrom, F. 1965. A White-tailed Kite in Wisconsin. Pass. Pigeon 27:3–8.

Hamerstrom, F. 1968. Ageing and sexing Harriers. IBBA News 40:43–44.

Hamerstrom, F. 1969. A Harrier population study. In Hickey, J. J. (ed.), *Peregrine Falcon Populations.* Univ. of Wis. Press, Madison.

Hamerstrom, F., and F. Hamerstrom. 1978. External sex

characteristics of Harris's Hawks in winter. Raptor Res. 12:1–14.

Hamerstrom, F., and J. D. Weaver. 1968. Ageing and sexing Rough-legged Hawk in Wisconsin and Illinois. Ont. Bird Band. 4:133–138.

Hansen, K. 1979. (Population status of the Greenland White-tailed Eagle, *Haliaeetus albicilla groenlandicus* Brehm, covering the years 1972–74.) (In Danish with an English summary.) Dansk. orn. foren. tidsshi. 73:106–131.

Hardin, M. E., J. W. Hardin, and W. D. Klimstra. 1977. Observations on nesting Mississippi Kites in southern Illinois. Trans. Ill. State Acad. Sci. 70:341–348.

Hardin, M. E., and W. D. Klimstra. 1976. *An annotated bibliography of the Mississippi Kite* (Ictinia misisippiensis). Coop. Wildl. Res. Lab., S. Ill. Univ., Carbondale.

Harmata, A. R. 1981. Recoveries of Ferruginous Hawks banded in Colorado. N. Am. Bird Band. 6:144–147.

Harmata, A. R. 1982. What is the function of undulating flight display in Golden Eagle? Raptor Res. 16:103–109.

Harmata, A. R., J. E. Toepfer, and J. M. Gerrard. 1985. Fall migration of Bald Eagles produced in northern Saskatchewan. Blue Jay 43:232–237.

Hatch, D. R. 1968. Golden Eagle hunting tactics. Blue Jay 26:78–80.

Haverschmidt, F. 1962. Notes on the feeding habits and food of some hawks of Suriname. Condor 64:154–158.

Haverschmidt, F. 1977. Allopreening in the Black Vulture. Auk 94:392.

Hecht, W. R. 1951. Nesting of the Marsh Hawk at Delta, Manitoba. Wilson Bull. 63:167–176.

Hector, D. P. 1980. Our rare falcon of the desert grassland. Birding 12:92–102.

Hector, D. P. 1985. The diet of the Aplomado Falcon *(Falco femoralis)* in eastern Mexico. Condor 87:336–342.

Heinzmann, G. 1970. The Caracara survey: A four year report. Fla. Nat. 43:149.

Henckel, E. 1981. Ageing the Turkey Vulture. N. Am. Bird Band. 6:106–107.

Henny, C. J., and J. E. Cornely. 1985. Recent Red-shouldered Hawk range expansion north into Oregon, including first specimen record. Murrelet 66:29–31.

Henny, C. J., and A. P. Noltemeier. 1975. Osprey nesting populations in the coastal Carolinas. Am. Birds 29:1073–1079.

Henny, C. J., R. A. Olson, and T. L. Fleming. 1985. Breeding chronology, molt, and measurements of accipiter hawks in northeastern Oregon. J. Field Ornith. 56:97–112.

Henny, C. J., F. C. Schmid, E. M. Martin, and L. L. Hood. 1973. Territorial behavior, pesticides, and the population ecology of Red-shouldered Hawks in central Maryland, 1943-1971. Ecology 54:545–554.

Henny, C. J., and H. M. Wight. 1969. An endangered Osprey population: Estimates of mortality and production. Auk 86:188–198.

Herbert, R. A., and K. G. Skelton. 1953. Another American Rough-legged Hawk in Florida. Wilson Bull. 65:199–200.

Herman, S. G. 1971. The Peregrine Falcon decline in California. Am. Birds 25:818–820.

Herndon, L. R. 1973. Sight record of a Ferruginous Hawk in southwest Virginia. Raven 44:70–71.

Herndon, L. R. 1974. Sight record of Ferruginous Hawk in Sullivan County, Tennessee. Migrant 43:48–49.

Hickey, J. J. (ed.). 1969. *Peregrine Falcon populations: Their biology and decline.* Univ. Wis. Press, Madison.

Hicks, T. W. 1955. An early seasonal record of the Swallow-tailed Kite in Florida. Wilson Bull. 67:63.

Hogg, R. 1976. Osprey nests in Wayne County, West Virginia. Redstart 43:110.

Hope, C. E. 1949. First occurrence of the Black Vulture in Ontario. Auk 66:81–82.

Hopkins, M., Jr. 1953. The Black Vulture as a predator in southern Georgia. Oriole 18:15–17.

Houston, C. S. 1968. Recoveries of Marsh Hawks banded in Saskatchewan. Blue Jay 26:12–13.

Houston, C. S. 1974. South American recoveries of Franklin's Gulls and Swainson's Hawks banded in Saskatchewan. Blue Jay 32:156–157.

Houston, C. S., and M. J. Bechard. 1984. Decline of the Ferruginous Hawk in Saskatchewan. Am. Birds. 38:166–170.

Hubbard, J. P. 1974a. Flight displays in two American species of *Buteo.* Condor 76:214–215.

Hubbard, J. P. 1974b. The status of Gray Hawk in New Mexico. Auk 91:163–165.

Huber, W. 1929. Zone-tailed Hawk in Lincoln Co., New Mexico. Auk 66:544

Husain, K. Z. 1959. Notes on the taxonomy and zoogeography of the genus *Elanus.* Condor 61:153–154.

Jackson, J. J., I. D. Prather, and R. N. Conner. 1978. Fishing behavior of Black and Turkey vultures. Wilson Bull. 90:141–143.

Jacot, E. C. 1934. An Arizona nest of the Ferruginous Hawk. Condor 36:84–85.

Janik, C., and J. A. Mosher. 1982. Raptor breeding biology in the central Appalachians. Raptor Res. 16:18–24.

Jenkins, J. 1979. White Kestrel of Eastend, Saskatchewan. Blue Jay 37:227.

Jenkins, M. A. 1978. Gyrfalcon nesting behavior from hatching to fledging. Auk 95:122–127.

Johnson, E. V., D. L. Aulman, D. A. Clendenen, G. Guliasi, L. M. Morton, P. I. Principe, and G. M. Wegener. 1983. California Condor: Activity patterns and age composition in a foraging area. Am. Birds 17:941–945.

Johnson, N. K., and H. J. Peeters. 1963. The systematic position of certain hawks in the genus *Buteo*. Auk 80:417–446.

Jollie, M. 1947. Plumage changes in the Golden Eagle. Auk 64:549–576.

Jones, S. 1979. *The accipiters—Goshawk, Coopers Hawk, Sharp-shinned Hawk.* Habitat Management Series of Unique or Endangered Species, Report No. 17. USDI–BLM, Denver.

Julian, P. R. 1967. Harlan's Hawk—A challenging taxonomic and field problem. Colo. Field Ornith., Winter 1967, No. 1:1–6.

Kale, H. W., II. 1978. White-tailed Kite. In Kale, H. W., II (ed.), *Rare and endangered biota of Florida,* Vol. II, *Birds.* Univ. Presses of Fla., Gainesville.

Kalla, P. I., and F. J. Alsop, III. 1983. The distribution, habitat preference, and status of the Mississippi Kite in Tennessee. Am. Birds. 37:146–149.

Keating, P. 1975. Caracara sighted in northern Texas. Bull. Okla. Ornith. Soc. 8:27–28.

Keir, J. R., and D. R. Wilde. 1976. Observations of Swainson's Hawk nesting in northeastern Illinois. Wilson Bull. 88:658–659.

Kemper, J. B., and D. S. Eastman, 1970. Osprey nesting survey in British Columbia, Canada. Auk 87:814.

Kennedy, R. S. 1973. Notes on the migration of juvenile Ospreys from Maryland and Virginia. Bird Band. 44:180–186.

Kenyon, K. W. 1947. Breeding populations of the Osprey in lower California. Condor 49:152–158.

Kern, P. A. 1976. Osprey with muskrat. Blue Jay 34:55.

Kilham, L. 1964. Interspecific relationships of Crows and Red-shouldered Hawks in mobbing behavior. Condor 66:247–248.

Kilham, L. 1979. Courtship of Common Caracaras in Costa Rica. Raptor Res. 13:17–19.

Kilham, L. 1980. Pre-nesting behavior of the Swallow-tailed Kite *(Elanoides forficatus),* including interference by an unmated male with a breeding pair. Raptor Res. 14:29–31.

Kleiman, P. 1966. Migration of Rough-legged Hawks over Lake Erie. Wilson Bull. 78:122.

Koford, C. B. 1953. *The California Condor.* Nat. Aud. Soc. Res. Rep. 4.

Koplin, J. R. 1973. Differential habitat use by sexes of American Kestrels wintering in northern California. Raptor Res. 7:39–42.

Kushlan, J. A. 1973. Spread-wing posturing in Cathartid Vultures. Auk 90:889–890.

Kuyt, E. 1962. A record of a tree-nesting Gyrfalcon. Condor 64:508–510.

Larrison, E. J. 1977. A sighting of the Broad-winged Hawk in Washington. Murrelet 58:18.

Larson, D. 1980. Increase in the White-tailed Kite populations of California and Texas—1944–1978. Am. Birds 34:689–690.

Lavers, N. 1975. Status of the Harlan's Hawk in Washington and notes on its identification in the field. West. Birds 6:55–62.

Lawrence, L. deL. 1949. Notes on nesting Pigeon Hawks at Pimisi Bay, Ontario. Wilson Bull. 61:15–25.

Layne, J. N. 1978. Audubon's Caracara. In Kale, H. W. (ed.), *Rare and endangered biota of Florida,* Vol. II, *Birds.* Univ. Presses of Fla., Gainesville.

Lee, J. A., and W. Brown, Jr. 1980. Red-tailed Hawk capturing fish. Chat 44:16.

LeFranc, M. N., Jr., and W. S. Clark. 1983. *Working bibliography of the Golden Eagle and the genus* Aquila. Sci. and Tech. Series No. 7. Nat. Wildl. Fed., Washington, D.C.

LeGrand, H. L., Jr., and J. M. Lynch. 1973. Mississippi Kites in northeastern North Carolina. Chat 37:105–106.

Lemke, T. O. 1979. Fruit-eating behavior of Swallow-tailed Kites *(Elanoides forficatus)* in Columbia. Condor 81:207–208.

Levy, S. H. 1971. The Mississippi Kite in Arizona. Condor 73:476.

Lewis, B. 1980. White-tailed Kite in South Carolina piedmont. Chat 44:15–16.

Ligon, J. S. 1961. *New Mexico birds and where to find them.* Univ. New Mex. Press, Albuquerque.

Lincer, J. L., W. S. Clark, and M. N. LeFranc, Jr. 1979. *Working bibliography of the Bald Eagle.* Sci. and Tech. Series No. 2. Nat. Wildl. Fed., Washington, D.C.

Lish, J. W., and W. G. Voelker. 1986. Flight identification aspects of some Red-tailed Hawk subspecies. Am. Birds 40:197–202.

Litkey, W. R. 1973. First state record of the Mississippi Kite. Loon 45:131.

Littlefield, C. D. 1970. A Marsh Hawk roost in Texas. Condor 72:245.

Littlefield, C. D., S. T. Thompson, and B. D. Ehlers. 1984. History and present status of Swainson's Hawks in southeast Oregon. Raptor Res. 18:1–5.

Lobkov, E. G. 1985. Raptor populations monitoring programme in Kamchatka. In Chancellor, R. D., and B. U. Meyburg (eds.), *Bull. World Work, Group Birds of Prey, No. 2*. Berlin.

Loftin, H., and E. L. Tyson. 1965. Stylized behavior in the Turkey Vulture's courtship dance. Wilson Bull. 77:193.

Lohrer, F. E., and C. E. Winegarner. 1980. Swallow-tailed Kite predation on nestling Mockingbird and Loggerhead Shrike. Fla. Field Nat. 8:47–48.

Lokemoen, J. T., and H. F. Duebbert. 1976. Ferruginous Hawk nesting ecology and raptor populations in northern South Dakota. Condor 78:464–470.

Love, J. A. 1983. *The return of the Sea Eagle*. Cambridge Univ. Press, Cambridge.

Lovell, H. B. 1947. Black Vultures kill young pigs in Kentucky. Auk 64:131–132.

Lynch, J. M. 1981. Status of the Mississippi Kite in North Carolina. Chat 45:42–43.

Lyons, D. L., and J. A. Mosher. 1982. Food caching and cannibalism by the Broad-winged Hawks. Ardea 70:217–219.

McCaskie, R. G. 1968. A Broad-winged Hawk in California. Condor 70:93

McClelland, B. R., L. S. Young, D. S. Shea, P. T. McClelland, H. L. Allen, and E. B. Spettigue. 1980. The Bald Eagle concentration in Glacier National Park, Montana: Origin, growth, and variation in numbers. Living Bird 19:133–155.

McCoy, J. 1966. Unusual prey for Osprey. Chat 30:108–109.

McGahan, J. 1968. Ecology of the Golden Eagle. Auk 85:1–12.

McIlhenny, E. A. 1937. Hybrid between Turkey Vulture and Black Vulture. Auk 54:384.

McIlhenny, E. A. 1939. Feeding habits of Black Vulture. Auk 56:472–474.

MacLaren, P. A., D. E. Runde, and S. N. Anderson. 1984. A record of tree-nesting Prairie Falcon in Wyoming. Condor 86:487–488.

Mader, W. J. 1975a. Extra adults at Harris's Hawk nests. Condor 77:482–485.

Mader, W. J. 1975b. Biology of the Harris's Hawk in

southern Arizona. Living Bird 14:59–85.

Mader, W. J. 1978. A comparative nesting study of Red-tailed Hawks and Harris' Hawks in southern Arizona. Auk 95:327–337.

Mader, W. J. 1979. Breeding behavior of a polyandrous trio of Harris's Hawks in southern Arizona. Auk 96:776–788.

Mader, W. J. 1981. Notes on nesting raptors in the llanos of Venezuela. Condor 83:48–51.

Marti, C. D., and C. T. Braun. 1975. Use of tundra habitats by Prairie Falcons in Colorado. Condor 77:213–214.

Mathisen, J. 1976. Osprey feeds at night. Loon 48:188.

Matray, P. F. 1974. Broad-winged Hawk nesting and ecology. Auk 91:307–324.

Matteson, S. W., and J. O. Riley. 1981. Distribution and reproductive success of Zone-tailed Hawks in west Texas. Wilson Bull. 93:282–284.

Mattox, W. G. 1969. The white falcon: Field studies of *Falco rusticolus* L. in Greenland. Polar Notes 9:46–62.

Melquist, W. E., D. R. Johnson, and W. D. Carrier. 1978. Migration patterns of northern Idaho and eastern Washington Ospreys. Bird Band. 49:234–236.

Melquist, W. E., and G. J. Schroeder. 1974. Sub-albinistic Red-tailed Hawk sighted in Idaho. Murrelet 55:8–9.

Meng, H. 1959. Food habits of nesting Coopers Hawks and Goshawks in New York and Pennsylvania. Wilson Bull. 71:169–174.

Miles, M. L. 1964. First records of the white-tailed Kite for El Salvador and Alabama. Auk 81:229.

Miller, L. 1930. Further notes on the Harris Hawk. Condor 32:210–211.

Mills, G. S. 1976. American Kestrel sex ratios and habitat separation. Auk 93:740–748.

Millsap, B. A. 1981. *Distributional status of falconiformes in west-central Arizona . . . , with notes on ecology, reproductive success, and management.* BLM Tech. Note 355. BLM, Phoenix, Ariz.

Millsap, B. A., and S. L. Vana. 1984. Distribution of wintering Golden Eagles in eastern United States. Wilson Bull. 96:692–701.

Mindell. D. P. 1983. Harlan's Hawk *(Buteo jamaicensis harlani)*: A valid subspecies. Auk 100:161–169.

Mindell, D. P. 1985. Plumage variation and winter range of the Harlan's Hawk *(Buteo jamaicensis harlani).* Am. Birds 39:127–133.

Moore, J. C., L. A. Stimson, and W. B. Robertson. 1953. Observations of the Short-tailed Hawk in Florida. Auk 70:470–478.

Moore, R. T., and A. Barr. 1941. Habits of the White-tailed Kite. Auk 58:453–462.

Morris, M. M. J., and R. E. Lemon. 1983. Characteristics of vegetation and topography near Red-shouldered Hawk nests in southwestern Quebec. J. Wildl. Manage. 47:138–145.

Morrison, M. L. 1978. Breeding characteristics, eggshell thinning, and population trends of White-tailed Hawks in Texas. Bull. Texas Ornith. Soc. 11:35–40.

Mosher, J. A., and P. F. Matray. 1974. Size dimorphism: A factor in energy savings for the Broad-winged Hawk. Auk 91:325–341.

Mote, W. R. 1969. Turkey Vultures land on vessel in fog. Auk 86:766–767.

Mowbray, M. V. 1979. An albinistic Kestrel. Cont. Birdl. 1:16.

Mrosovsky, N. 1971. Black Vultures attack live turtle hatchlings. Auk 88:672–673.

Mueller, H. C. 1972. Zone-tailed Hawk and Turkey Vulture: Mimicry or aerodynamics? Condor 74:221–222.

Mueller, H. C., D. D. Berger, and G. Allez. 1976. Age and sex variation in the size of Goshawks. Bird Band. 47:310–318.

Mueller, H. C., D. D. Berger, and G. Allez. 1981a. Age and sex differences in wing loading and other aerodynamic characteristics of Sharp-shinned Hawks. Wilson Bull. 93:491–499.

Mueller, H. C., D. D. Berger, and G. Allez. 1981b. Age, sex, and seasonal differences in size of Cooper's Hawks. J. Field Ornith. 52:112–126.

Mueller, H. C., N. S. Mueller, and R. W. Mueller. 1966. Rough-legged Hawk catches fish. Wilson Bull. 78:470.

Nicholsen, D. J. 1928. The Swallow-tailed Kite of southwest Florida. Oologist 45:158–160.

Nicholsen, D. J. 1930. Habits of the Florida Red-shouldered Hawk. Wilson Bull. 42:32–35.

Oakley, S. M., and M. S. Eltzroth. 1980. The nesting of an albinistic Red-tailed Hawk *(Buteo jamaicensis)* in Oregon. Raptor Res. 14:68–70.

Oberholser, H. C. 1974. *The bird life of Texas.* Vol. I. Univ. Texas Press, Austin.

Ofnes, G. L. 1976. White-tailed Kite in Wilkin County. Loon 48:180–182.

Ogden, J. C. 1973. Field identification of difficult birds: I, Short-tailed Hawk. Fla. Field Nat. 1:30–33.

Ogden, J. C. 1974. The Short-tailed Hawk in Florida, I: Migration, habitat, hunting techniques, and food habits. Auk 91:95–110.

Ogden, J. C. (ed.). 1977. *Trans. North American Osprey*

Conference, Williamsburg, 1972. Trans. & Proc. Ser. No. 2.
USDI-Park Service, Washington, D.C.

Ogden, J.C. 1978. Short-tailed Hawk. In Kale, H. W., II (ed.).,
Rare and endangered biota of Florida, Vol. II, Birds. Univ.
Presses of Fla., Gainesville.

Ogden, V., and M.G. Hornocker. 1977. Nesting density and
success of Prairie Falcons in southwestern Idaho. J. Wildl.
Manage. 41:1–10.

Ohlander, B. G. 1976. Gyrfalcon taken in Nebraska. Nebr. Bird
Rev. 44:3.

Olendorff, R. R. 1974. A courtship flight of the Swainson's Hawk.
Condor 76:215.

Oliphant, L. W. 1985. North American Merlin breeding survey.
Raptor Res. 1937–41.

Oliphant, L. W., and W. J. P. Thompson, 1978. Recent breeding
success of Richardson's Merlins in Saskatchewan. Raptor
Res. 12:35–39.

Oliphant, L. W., W. J. P. Thompson, T. Donald, and R. Rafuse.
1975. Present status of the Prairie Falcon in Saskatchewan.
Can. Field-Nat. 90:365–368.

Over, W. H. 1946. Gyrfalcon in South Dakota. Auk 63:446.

Owre, T. O., and P. O. Northington. 1961. Indication of the sense
of smell in the Turkey Vulture, Cathartes aura (Linnaeus),
from feeding tests. Am. Mid. Nat. 66:200–205.

Pache, P. H. 1974. Notes on prey and reproductive biology of
Harris' Hawk in southeastern New Mexico. Wilson Bull.
86:72–74.

Parker, J. W. 1985. Albinism and maladaptive feather wear in
American Kestrels. Kingbird 35:159–162.

Parker, J. W., and J. C. Ogden. 1979. The recent history and
status of the Mississippi Kite. Am. Birds. 33:119–129.

Parker, J. W., and M. Ports. 1982. Helping at the nest by
yearling Mississippi Kites. Raptor Res. 16:14–17.

Parkes, K. C. 1955. Notes on the molts and plumages of the
Sparrow Hawk. Wilson Bull. 67:194–199.

Parkes, K. C. 1958. Specific relationships in the genus Elanus.
Condor 60:139–140.

Parmalee, D. F., and H. A. Stephans. 1954. Status of the Harris
Hawk in Kansas. Condor 66:443–445.

Parmalee, P. W. 1954. The vultures: Their movements, economic
status, and control in Texas. Auk 71:443–453.

Parmalee, P. W., and B. G. Parmalee. 1967. Results of banding
studies of the Black Vulture in eastern North America.
Condor 69:146–153.

Paulson, D. R. 1983. Flocking in the Hook-billed Kite. Auk
100:749.

Pearson, D. 1960. Red-shouldered Hawk comes to feeding station. Flicker 32:65.

Peters, J. L. 1927. The North American races of *Falco columbarius*. Bull. Essex County Ornith. Club for 1926:20–24.

Petrovic, C. A. 1972. Osprey preys on Cardinal. Redstart 39:86.

Platt, J. B. 1976. Bald Eagles wintering in a Utah desert. Am. Birds 30:783–788.

Porter, Richard D., M. Alan Jenkins, and Andrea Gasky; M. N. Le Franc, Jr. (ed.). 1987. *Working bibliography of the Peregrine Falcon*. Sci. and Tech. Series No. 9. Natl. Wildl. Fed., Washington, D.C.

Porter, R. F. 1981. Ageing and sexing Rough-legged Buzzards. Dutch Birding 3:79–80.

Porter, R. F., I. Willis, S. Christensen, and B. P. Neilsen. 1981. Flight identification of European raptors. 3d ed. T. and A. D. Poyser, Calton.

Portnoy, J. W., and W. E. Dodge. 1979. Red-shouldered Hawk nesting ecology and behavior. Wilson Bull. 91:104–117.

Prather, I. D., R. N. Conner, and C. S. Adkisson. 1976. Unusually large vulture roost in Virginia. Wilson Bull. 82:667–668.

Preston, C. R. 1981. Environmental influence on soaring in wintering Red-tailed Hawks. Wilson Bull. 93:350–356.

Prevost, Y. 1979. Osprey-Bald Eagle interactions at a common foraging site. Auk 96:413.

Pruett-Jones, S. G., M. A. Pruett-Jones, and R. L. Knight. 1980. The White-tailed Kite in North and Middle America: Current status and recent population changes. Am. Birds 43:682–688.

Rand, A. L. 1960. Races of the Short-tailed Hawk, *Buteo brachyurus*. Auk 77:448–459.

Reynolds, R. T., and H. M. Wight. 1978. Distribution, density, and productivity of accipiter hawks breeding in Oregon. Wilson Bull. 90:182-196.

Rice, W. R. 1982. Acoustical location of prey by the Marsh Hawk: Adaptation to concealed prey. Auk 99:403-413.

Richards, B. 1962. Hunting behavior of a Swainson's Hawk. Blue Jay 20:15.

Richmond, A. R. 1976. Feeding of nestlings by the Caracara in Costa Rica. Wilson Bull. 88:667.

Ridgway, R. 1881. On a tropical American hawk to be added to the North American fauna. Bull. Nuttal Ornith. Club 6:207–214.

Ridgway, R. 1896. Harlan's Hawk, a race of the Red-tail and not a distinct species. Auk 7:205.

Roberson, D. 1980. *Rare birds of the West Coast.* Woodcock, Pacific Grove, Calif.

Roberts, J. O. L. 1967. Iris colour and age of Sharp-shinned Hawks. Ont. Bird Band. 3:95–106.

Robinson, T. S. 1957. Notes on the development of a brood of Mississippi Kites in Barber County, Kansas. Trans. Kan. Acad. Sci. 60:174–180.

Roest, A. I. 1957. Notes on the American Sparrow Hawk. Auk 74:1–19.

Rogers, D. T., and M. A. Dauber. 1977. Status of the Red-shouldered Hawk in Alabama. Ala. Birdlife 25:19.

Rogers, W., and S. Leatherwood. 1981. Observations of feeding at sea by a Peregrine Falcon and an Osprey. Condor 83:89–90.

Rosenfield, R. N. 1978. Attacks by nesting Broad-winged Hawks. Pass. Pigeon 40:419.

Rosenfield, R. N. 1984. Nesting ecology of Broad-winged Hawks in Wisconsin. Raptor Res. 18:6–9.

Rosenfield, R. N., M. W. Gratson, and L. B. Carson. 1984. Food brought by Broad-winged Hawks to a Wisconsin nest. J. Field Ornith. 55:246–247.

Ross, C. C. 1963. Albinism among North American birds. Cassinia 47:2–21.

Rudebeck, G. 1951. The choice of prey and modes of hunting of predatory birds, with special reference to the selective effect. Oikos 3:200–230.

Rusch, D. H., and P. D. Doerr. 1972. Broad-winged Hawk nesting and food habits. Auk 89:139–145.

Rust, H. J. 1914. Some notes on the nesting of the Sharp-shinned Hawk. Condor 16:14–24.

Sage, B. L. 1962. Albinism and melanism in birds. Brit. Birds 55:201–225.

Sallee, G. W. 1977. A Turkey Vulture roost on a sandbar. Bull. Okla. Ornith. Soc. 3:17–19.

Salt, W. R. 1939. Notes on recoveries of banded Ferruginous Rough-legged Hawks *(Buteo regalis).* Bird Band. 50:80–84.

Schmutz, S. M., and J. K. Schmutz. 1981. Inheritance of color phases of Ferruginous Hawks. Condor 83:187–189.

Schnell, G. D. 1967a. Population fluctuations, spatial distribution, and food habits of Rough-legged Hawks in Illinois. Bull. Kan. Ornith. Soc 18:21–28.

Schnell, G. D. 1967b. Environmental influence on the incidence of flight in the Rough-legged Hawk. Auk 84:173–182.

Schnell, J. H. 1979. *Black hawk* (Buteogallus anthracinus). Habitat Management Series for Unique or Endangered Species. USDI BLM Tech. Note 329.

Servheen, C. 1985. Notes on wintering Merlins in western Montana. Raptor Res. 19:97–99.

Sharp, W. M. 1951. Observations on predator-prey relationships between wild ducks, Trumpeter Swans, and Golden Eagles. J. Wildl. Manage. 15:224–226.

Sherrod, S. K., C. M. White, and F. S. L. Williamson. 1976. Biology of the Bald Eagle on Amchitka Island. Living Bird 15:42–45.

Shuster, W. C. 1977. *A bibliography of the Northern Goshawk* (Accipiter gentilis). USDI BLM Tech. Note 308.

Skinner, R. W. 1962. Feeding habits of the Mississippi Kite. Auk 79:273–274.

Skinner, R. W. 1968. First specimen of the Rough-legged Hawk from Alabama. Auk 85:501.

Skutch, A. F. 1945. The migration of Swainson's and Broad-winged Hawks through Costa Rica. Northwest Sci. 19:80–89.

Skutch, A. F. 1965. Life history notes on two tropical American kites. Condor 67:235–246.

Slud, P. 1964. *Birds of Costa Rica.* Bull. Am. Mus. Nat. Hist. 128. New York.

Smith, B. 1982. White Hawk: Glimpses into the nest of a rare albino Redtail. Tex. Parks & Wildlife 40(5): 33–36.

Smith, D. G., and J. R. Murphy. 1973. Breeding ecology of raptors in the eastern great basin of Utah. BYU Sci. Bull., Vol. 18, No. 3.

Smith, D. G., and J. R. Murphy. 1978. Biology of the Ferruginous Hawk. Sociobiology 3:79–95.

Smith, D. G., J. R. Murphy, and N. D. Woffinden. 1981. Relationships between jackrabbit abundance and Ferruginous Hawk reproduction. Condor 83:52–56.

Smith, N. G. 1980. Hawk and Vulture migrations in the neotropics. In Keast, A., and E. U. Morton (eds.), *Migrant birds in the neotropics: Ecology, behavior, distribution, and conservation.* Smithsonian Press, Washington, D.C.

Smith, T. A., and S. A. Temple. 1982. Feeding habits and bill polymorphism in Hook-billed Kites. Auk 99:197–207.

Smithe, F. B. 1966. *The birds of Tikal.* Natural History Press, New York.

Snow, C. 1972. *Peregrine Falcon.* Habitat Management Series for Unique or Endangered Species, Report No. 1. USDI BLM Tech. Note 167.

Snow, C. 1973a. *Golden Eagle.* Habitat Management Series for Unique or Endangered Species, Report No. 7. USDI BLM Tech. Note 239.

Snow, C. 1973b. *Bald Eagle.* Habitat Management Series for Unique or Endangered Species, Report No. 5. USDI BLM Tech. Note 171.

Snow, C. 1974a. *Prairie Falcon.* Habitat Management Series for Unique or Endangered Species, Report No. 8. USDI BLM Tech. Note 240.

Snow, C. 1974b. *Ferruginous Hawk*. Habitat Management Series for Unique or Endangered Species, Report No. 13. USDI BLM Tech. Note 255.

Snow, C. 1974c. *Gyrfalcon*. Habitat Management Series for Unique or Endangered Species, Report No. 9, USDI BLM Tech. Note 241.

Snyder, L. L. 1938. *The northwest coast Sharp-shinned Hawk*. Occ. Papers Royal Ont. Mus. Zool., No. 4. Toronto.

Snyder, N. F. R. 1974a. Breeding biology of Swallow-tailed Kites in Florida. Living Bird 13:73–97.

Snyder, N. F. R. 1974b. Can the Cooper's Hawk survive? Natl. Geog. 145:433–442.

Snyder, N. F. R., and E. V. Johnson. 1985. Photographic censusing of the 1982-1983 California Condor population. Condor 87:1–13.

Snyder, N. F. R., and H. A. Snyder. 1969. A comparative study of mollusc predation by Limpkins, Everglade Kites, and Boat-tailed Grackles. Living Bird 6:77–223.

Snyder, N. F. R., and H. A. Snyder. 1970. Feeding territories in the Everglade Kite. Condor 72:492–493.

Spitzer, P., and A. Poole. 1980. Coastal Ospreys between New York City and Boston: A decade of reproductive recovery, 1969–1979. Am. Birds 34:234–241.

Spofford, W. R. 1971. The breeding status of the Golden Eagle in the Appalachians. Am. Birds 25:3–7.

Sprunt, A., Jr. 1946. Predation of living prey by the Black Vulture, Auk 63:260–261.

Sprunt, A., Jr. 1954. Audubon's Caracara. Fla. Nat. 27:99–101, 119.

Stager, K. E. 1958. An Osprey in mideastern Pacific Ocean. Condor 60:257–258.

Stager, K. E. 1964. *The role of olfaction in food location by the Turkey Vulture* (Cathartes aura). L. A. County Mus. Contrib. Sci., No. 81.

Steenhof, K. 1983. Activity patterns of Bald Eagles wintering in South Dakota. Raptor Res. 17:57–62.

Steenhof, K. 1984. Use of an interspecific communal roost by wintering Ferruginous Hawks. Wilson Bull. 90:137–138.

Steenhof, K., M. N. Kochert, and M. Q. Moritsch. 1984. Dispersal and migration of southwestern Idaho raptors. J. Field Ornith. 55:357–368.

Steirly, C. C. 1966. Black Vultures attacking pigs. Raven 37:65.

Stendell, R. C., and P. Myers. 1973. White-tailed Kite predation on a fluctuating vole population. Condor 75:359–360.

Stensrude, C. 1965. Observations on a pair of Gray Hawks in southern Arizona. Condor 67:319–321.

Stevenson, J. O., and L. H. Meitzen. 1946. Behavior and food habits of Senett's White-tailed Hawk in Texas. Wilson Bull. 58:198–205.

Stewart, P. A. 1977. Migratory movements and mortality rate of Turkey Vultures. Bird Band. 48:122–124.

Stewart, P. A. 1978. Behavioral interactions and niche separation in Black and Turkey vultures. Living Bird 17:79–84.

Stewart, R. E. 1949. Ecology of a nesting Red-shouldered Hawk population. Wilson Bull. 61:26–35.

Storer, R. W. 1952. Variation in the resident Sharp-shinned Hawks of Mexico. Condor 54:283–287.

Storer, R. W. 1966. Sexual dimorphism and food habits in three North American accipiters. Auk 83:423–436.

Struthers, D. R. 1955. Great Blue Heron robs Osprey of fish. Flicker 27:129.

Sutton, G. M. 1939. The Mississippi Kite in spring. Condor 41:41–53.

Sutton, G. M. 1944. The Kites of the genus *Ictinia*. Wilson Bull. 56:3–8.

Sutton, G. M. 1953. Gray Hawk. Wilson Bull. 65:5–7.

Sutton, G. M., and D. F. Parmalee, 1956. The Rough-legged Hawk in the American Arctic. Arctic 9:202–207.

Sutton, G. M., and J. Van Tyne. 1935. *A new Red-tailed Hawk from Texas*. Occ. Papers Mus. Zool., Univ. Mich., No. 321. Ann Arbor.

Swarth, H. S. 1926. Birds and mammals from the Atlin region. Calif. Pub. Zool. 30:105–111.

Swenson, J. E. 1981. Status of the Osprey in southeast Montana before and after the construction of reservoirs. West. Birds 12:47–51.

Sykes, P. W., Jr. 1964. Pigeon Hawks hunting as a team. Raven 35:47–51.

Sykes, P. W., Jr. 1979. Status of the Everglade Kite in Florida 1968-1978. Wilson Bull. 91:495-511.

Sykes, P. W., Jr. 1983a. Recent population trend of the Snail Kite in Florida and its relationship to water levels. J. Field Ornith. 54:237–246.

Sykes, P. W., Jr. 1983b. Snail Kite use of the freshwater marshes of south Florida. Fla. Field Natur. 11:73–88.

Sykes, P. W., Jr. 1984. The range of the Snail Kite and its history in Florida. Bull. Fla. State Mus. 29:210–264.

Sykes, P. W., Jr. 1985. Evening roosts of the Snail Kite in Florida. Wilson Bull. 97:57–70.

Sykes, P. W., Jr., and H. A. Kale II. 1974. Everglade Kites feed on nonsnail prey. Auk 91:818–820.

Tait, W. W., H. M. Johnson, and W. D. Courser, 1972. Osprey carring a mammal. Wilson Bull. 84:341.

Taverner, P. A. 1927. *A study of* Buteo borealis, *the Red-tailed*

Hawk, and its varieties in Canada. Vic. Mem. Mus. Bull. No. 48.

Taverner, P. A. 1934. Birds of the Eastern Arctic. In *Canada's Western Arctic.* J. O. Patenaude, Ottawa.

Taverner, P. A. 1936. Taxonomic comments on Red-tailed Hawks. Condor 38:66–71.

Taverner, P. A. 1940. Variation in the American Goshawk. Condor 42:157–160.

Taylor, J. 1964. Noteworthy predation on the guano bat. J. Mammal. 45:300–301.

Temple, S. A. 1969. A case of Turkey Vulture piracy on Great Blue Herons. Wilson Bull. 81:94.

Temple, S. A. 1972a. Systematics and evolution of North American Merlins. Auk 89:325–338.

Temple, S. A. 1972b. Sex and age characteristics of North American Merlins. Bird Band. 43:191–196.

Thompson, B. C. 1975. A new prey-pursuit behavior by White-tailed Kites. Wilson Bull. 92:395.

Thompson, M. C. 1983. Nesting records of the Northern Harrier from Kansas. Kan. Ornith. Soc. Bull 34:25.

Thurber, W. A. 1981. Aerial "play" of Black Vultures. Wilson Bull. 93:97.

Titus, K., and J. A. Mosher. 1981. Nest site habitat selected by raptors in the central Appalachians. Auk 98:270–281.

Todd, W. E. C., and H. Friedmann. 1947. A study of the Gyrfalcons with particular reference to North America. Wilson Bull. 59:139–150.

Tomback, D. F., and J. R. Murphy. 1981. Food deprivation and temperature regulation in nestling Ferruginous Hawks. Wilson Bull. 93:92–97.

Trautman, M. B. 1964. A specimen of the Roadside Hawk, *Buteo magnirostris griseocauda,* from Texas. Auk 81:435.

Trimble, S. A. 1975. *Merlin.* Habitat Management Series for Unique or Endangered Species, Report No. 15. USDI BLM Tech. Note 271.

Van Vuren, D. 1980. A Harris' Hawk in Utah. Western Birds 11:111.

Village, A., M. Marquiss, and D. C. Cook. 1980. Moult, ageing, and sexing of Kestrels. Ringing and Migration 3:53–59.

Voelker, W. G. 1976. Albinistic Turkey Vulture in Harmon County, Oklahoma. Bull. Okla. Ornith. Soc. 9:32–33.

Voous, K. H. 1968. Distribution and geographic variation of the White-tailed Hawk *(Buteo albicaudatus).* Beaufortia 15:195–208.

Voous, K. H., and T. J. Van Dijk. 1973. How do Snail Kites extract snails from their shells? Ardea 61:179–185.

Waian, L. B., and R. C. Stendell. 1970. The White-tailed Kite in

California, with observations of the Santa Barbara population. Cal. Fish and Game 56:188–198.

Wakeley, J. S. 1978. Hunting methods and factors affecting their use by Ferruginous Hawks. Condor 80:327–333.

Wander, W. 1978. Fine points: Red-shouldered versus Red-tailed Hawks. N.J. Aud. Suppl. 4:57.

Warner, J. S., and R. I. Rudd. 1975. Hunting by the White-tailed Kite. Condor 77:226–230.

Waterston, G. 1964. Studies of less familiar birds, 130. White-tailed Eagle. Brit. Birds 57:458–466.

Watson, D. 1977. *The Hen Harrier*. T. and A. D. Poyser, Berkhamsted.

Wattel, J. 1973. *Geographic differentiation in the genus* Accipiter. Publ. Nuttall Ornith. Club, No. 13. Cambridge.

Webb, B. 1978. The occurrences of the Red-shouldered Hawk in Colorado. Colo. Field Ornith. J. 32:19–21.

Weber, J. W. 1976. Harlan's race of the Red-tailed Hawk in southeastern Washington and adjacent Idaho. Murrelet 57:70–71.

Weller, M. W., I. C. Adams, and B. J. Rose. 1955. Winter roosts of Marsh Hawks and Short-eared Owls in central Missouri. Wilson Bull. 67:189–193.

Westcott, P. W. 1964. Unusual feeding behavior of a Goshawk. Condor 66:163.

Weston, J. B., and D. H. Ellis. 1968. Ground nesting of the Ferruginous Hawk in west-central Utah. Great Basin Nat. 28:111.

Wetmore, A. 1964. A revision of the American vultures of the genus *Cathartes*. Smithson. Misc. Coll. 146 No. 6:15–17.

Wetmore, A. 1965. *The birds of the Republic of Panama*. Part 1. Smiths. Inst., Washington, D.C.

Whitacre, D., D. Ukrain, and G. Faxla. 1982. Notes on the hunting behavior and diet of the Crested Caracara in northeastern Chiapas and Tabasco, Mexico. Wilson Bull. 94:565–566.

White, C. M. 1962. Prairie Falcon displays accipitrine and circine hunting methods. Condor 64:439–440.

White, C. M. 1968. Diagnosis and relationships of the North American tundra-inhabiting Peregrine Falcons. Auk 85:179–191.

White, C. M., and T. J. Cade. 1971. Cliff-nesting raptors and Ravens along the Colville river in arctic Alaska. Living Bird 10:107–150.

White, C. M., and R. B. Weeden. 1966. Hunting methods of Gyrfalcons and behavior of their prey (Ptarmigan). Condor 68:517–519.

Wierenga, H. 1981. Northern Harrier nest in Dorchester County, 1981. Md. Birdlife 37:104.

Wilbur, S. R. 1973. The Red-shouldered Hawk in the western United States. West. Birds 4:15–22.

Wilbur, S. R. 1975. California Condor plumage and molt as field study aids. Calif. Fish and Game 61:144–148.

Wilbur, S. R. 1976. Status of the California Condor, 1972-1975. Am. Birds 30:789–790.

Wilbur, S. R. 1978. The California Condor, 1966-76: A look at its past and future. USDI N. Am Fauna, no. 78.

Wiley, J. E. 1975. The nesting and reproductive success of Red-tailed Hawks and Red-shouldered Hawks in Orange County, California, 1973. Condor 77:133–139.

Wiley, J. W., and F. E. Lohrer. 1973. Additional records of non-fish prey taken by Ospreys. Wilson Bull. 85:468–470.

Wilhelm, E. J. 1960. Marsh Hawk breeding in northwestern Arkansas. Wilson Bull. 72:401-402.

Wille, F., and K. Kampp. 1983. Food of the White-tailed Eagle, *Haliaeetus albicilla,* in Greenland, Holarctic Ecology 6:81–88.

Williams, E. A. 1962. Sight record of White-tailed Kite in Georgia. Oriole 27:52–53.

Willis, E. O. 1963. Is the Zone-tailed Hawk a mimic of the Turkey Vulture? Condor 65:313–317.

Willis, E. O. 1966. A prey capture by the Zone-tailed Hawk. Condor 68:104–108.

Willoughby, E. J., and T. J. Cade. 1964. Breeding behavior of the American Kestrel. Living Bird 3:75–96.

Willoughby, H. 1976. A Massachusetts record of a dark-phase Gyrfalcon. Bird Obs. of E. Mass. 4:141.

Woffinden, N. D., and J. R. Murphy. 1983. Feruginous Hawk nest site selection. J. Wildl. Manage. 47:216–219.

Wood, N. A. 1932. Harlan's Hawk. Wilson Bull. 44:78–87.

Yocum, C. F. 1944. Evidence of polygamy among Marsh Hawks. Wilson Bull. 56:116–117.

Zarn, M. 1974. Osprey. *Habitat Management Series for Unique or Endangered Species.* Report No. 12. USDI BLM Tech. Note 254.

Zarn, M. 1976, *Rough-legged Hawk.* Habitat Management Series for Unique or Endangered Species. Report No. 14. USDI BLM Tech. Note 270.

Zimmermann, D. A. 1965. The Gray Hawk in the southwest. Aud. Field Notes 19:475–477.

Zimmermann, D. A. 1976a. Comments on feeding habits and vulture-mimicry in the Zone-tailed Hawk. Condor 78:420–421.

Zimmermann, D. A. 1976b. On the Status of *Buteo nitidus* in New Mexico. Auk 93:650–655.

Index to References
by Species and Topic

American Kestrel

Natural History: Cade 1982, Balgooyen 1976, Willoughby and Cade 1964, Roest 1957.
Behavior: Mills 1976, Koplin 1973.
Plumage: Balgooyen 1975, Parkes 1955, Clay 1953, Brodkorb 1935.
Migration: Roest 1957.
Albinism: Parker 1985, Jenkins 1979, Mowbray 1979, Ross 1963.

Aplomado Falcon

Natural History: Hector 1985, Cade 1982.
Behavior: Mader 1981, Hector 1980, Brooks 1933.
Status and Distribution: Evans 1982, Hector 1980, Ligon 1961.
Plumage: Hector 1980.

Bald Eagle

Natural History: Sherrod et al. 1976, Snow 1973b.
Behavior: Fischer 1985, Steenhof 1983, McClelland et al. 1980, Platt 1976.
Status and Distribution: Grier 1982.
Plumage: Bartolotti 1984a, Clark 1983.
Identification: Clark 1983.
Bibliography: Lincer et al. 1979.
Migration: Harmata et al. 1985, Gerrard et al. 1978, Broley 1947.
Albinism: Clark 1983.

Black-shouldered Kite

Natural History: Stendell and Myers 1973, Dixon et al. 1957, Moore and Barr 1941.
Behavior: Ofnes 1976, Thompson 1975, Warner and Rudd 1975, Waian and Stendell 1970.
Distribution: Carter and Fowler 1983, Green 1982, Larson

1980, Lewis 1980, Pruett-Jones et al. 1980, Ellis and Monson 1979, Kale 1978, Eisenmann 1971, Waian and Stendell 1970, Hamerstrom 1965, Miles 1964, Williams 1962, Appleberry 1957.
Plumage: Kale 1978.
Taxonomy: Husain 1959, Parkes 1958.

Black Vulture

Behavior: Elias and Valencia 1982, Thurber 1981, Jackson et al. 1978, Stewart 1978, Haverschmidt 1977, Prather et al. 1976, Kushlan 1973, Mrosovsky 1971, Steirly 1966, Parmalee 1954, Hopkins 1953, Lovell 1947, Sprunt 1946, McIlhenny 1939.
Distribution: Proctor 1985, Berger 1982, Flieg 1972, Parmalee and Parmalee 1967, Eisenmann 1963b, Greider and Wagner 1960, Grube 1953, Hope 1949.
Plumage: McIlhenny 1937.
Albinism: Ross 1963.

Broad-winged Hawk

Natural History: Rosenfield 1984, Rosenfield et al. 1984, Janik and Mosher 1982, Fitch 1974, Matray 1974, Rusch and Doerr 1972, Burns 1911.
Behavior: Lyons and Mosher 1982, Titus and Mosher 1981, Rosenfield 1978.
Distribution: Clark and Anderson 1984, Larrison 1977, McCaskie 1968, Enderson 1962, Burns 1911.
Plumage: Mosher and Matray 1974, Johnson and Peeters 1963, Bailey 1917.
Identification: Clark 1981.
Migration: Smith 1980, Skutch 1945.

California Condor

Natural History: Koford 1953.
Behavior: Johnson et al. 1983, Elliot 1981.
Status and Distribution: Snyder and Johnson 1985, Wilbur 1978, Wilbur 1976.
Plumage: Wilbur 1975.
Identification: Borneman 1978.

Common Black Hawk

Natural History: Millsap 1981, Schnell 1979.
Behavior: Wetmore 1965.
Distribution: Schnell 1979, Elwell et al. 1978, Abramson 1976, Carter and Wauer 1965, Bohl and Traylor 1958.
Plumage: Schnell 1979, Wetmore 1965.

Cooper's Hawk

Natural History: Henny et al. 1985, Janik and Mosher 1982, Jones 1979, Reynolds and Wight 1978, Snyder 1974b, Storer 1966, Meng 1959.
Behavior: Titus and Mosher 1981.
Distribution: Evans 1982, Jones 1979.
Plumage: Mueller et al. 1981b, Wattel 1973.
Identification: Clark 1984a.
Albinism: Ross 1963.

Crested Caracara

Natural History: Layne 1978.
Behavior: Whitacre et al. 1982, Mader 1981, Kilham 1979, Richmond 1976, Glazener 1964, Dillon 1963, Sprunt 1954.
Distribution: Evans 1982, Keating 1975, Heinzmann 1970, Sprunt 1954.
Taxonomy: Wetmore 1965.

Eurasian Kestrel

Natural History: Cade 1982, Cramp and Simmons 1980.
Status and Distribution: Campbell 1985, Roberson 1980, Clark 1974a.
Plumage: Cramp and Simmons 1980, Village et al. 1980.
Identification: Porter et al. 1981.
Albinism: Sage 1962.

Ferruginous Hawk

Natural History: Gilmer and Stewart 1983, Blair and Schitoskey 1982, Evans 1982, Smith et al. 1981, Smith and Murphy 1978, Fitzner et al. 1977, Lokemoen and Duebbert 1976, Snow 1974b, Angell 1969.
Behavior: Steenhof 1984, Woffinden and Murphy 1983, Tomback and Murphy 1981, Wakeley 1978, Weston and Ellis 1968.
Distribution: Houston and Bechard 1984, Evans 1982, Bock and Lepthien 1977, Herndon 1974, Snow 1974b, Herndon 1973, Jacot 1934.
Plumage: Schmutz and Schmutz 1981, Lokemoen and Duebbert 1976.
Identification: Eckert 1982, Clark 1981.
Migration: Gilmer et al. 1985, Harmata 1981, Salt 1939.

Golden Eagle

Natural History: Snow 1973a, McGahan 1968.
Behavior: Collopy 1984, Craig and Craig 1984, Collopy

1983, Harmata 1982, Hatch 1968, Sharp 1951, Darling 1934.
Distribution: Millsap and Vana 1984, Boeker 1974, Snow 1973a, Spofford 1971.
Plumage: Bartolotti 1984b, Jollie 1947.
Identification: Clark 1983.
Bibliography: LeFranc and Clark 1983.
Migration: Steenhof et al. 1984.

Gray Hawk

Natural History: Stensrude 1965, Zimmermann 1965, Sutton 1953, Amadon and Phillips 1939.
Distribution: Zimmermann 1976b, Hubbard 1974b, Zimmermann 1965.
Plumage: Smithe 1966, Johnson and Peeters 1963.
Identification: Smithe 1966.
Taxonomy: Amadon 1982, Johnson and Peeters 1963.

Gyrfalcon

Natural History: Cade 1982, Snow 1974c, White and Cade 1971, Cade 1960.
Behavior: Jenkins 1978, White and Weeden 1966, Kuyt 1962, Cade 1953.
Distribution: Grzybowski 1983, Fingerhood and Lipschutz 1980, Ohlander 1976, Willoughby 1976, Burr and Current 1975, Evans 1975, Craig 1971, Cade 1960, Over 1946, Black 1941.
Plumage: Mattox 1969, Todd and Friedmann 1947.

Harris' Hawk

Natural History: Ellis and Whaley 1979, Mader 1979, Mader 1978, Mader 1975a, Mader 1975b, Pache 1974.
Distribution: Van Vuren 1980, Bock and Lepthien 1977, Ault 1975, Parmalee and Stephans 1964, Miller 1930.
Plumage: Hamerstrom and Hamerstrom 1978.

Hook-billed Kite

Behavior: Paulson 1983, Smith and Temple 1982.
Distribution: Delnicki 1978, Fleetwood and Hamilton 1967.
Plumage: Smith and Temple 1982, Wetmore 1965.

Merlin

Natural History: Cade 1982, Evans 1982, Trimble 1975, Lawrence 1949, Craighead and Craighead 1940.
Behavior: Feldsine and Oliphant 1985, Sykes 1964, Rudebeck 1951.
Status and Distribution: Oliphant 1985, Servheen 1985,

Evans 1982, Oliphant and Thompson 1978, Temple 1972a.
Migration: Clark 1985a
Taxonomy: Temple 1972a, Peters 1927.
Plumages: Clark 1985a, Temple 1972b.
Albinism: Ross 1963, Sage 1962.

Mississippi Kite

Natural History: Glinski and Ohmart 1983, Cranson 1972, Robinson 1957, Sutton 1939, Ganier 1902.
Behavior: Parker and Ports 1982, Engle 1980, Taylor 1964, Fitch 1963, Skinner 1962.
Distribution: Kalla and Alsop 1983, Lynch 1981, Clermont 1979, Parker and Ogden 1979, Hardin et al. 1977, LeGrand and Lynch 1973, Litkey 1973, Cranson 1972, Flieg 1972, Berger 1971, Levy 1971, Burford 1963.
Plumage: Eisenmann 1963a, Sutton 1944.
Taxonomy: Sutton 1944.
Bibliography: Hardin and Klimstra 1976.
Migration: Eisenmann 1963a, Blake 1949.

Northern Goshawk

Natural History: Jones 1979, Reynolds and Wight 1978, Storer 1966, Meng 1959.
Behavior: Westcott 1964.
Distribution: Jones 1979.
Plumage: Mueller et al. 1976, Wattel 1973, Bond and Stabler 1941, Taverner 1940.
Identification: Clark 1984a.
Bibliography: Shuster 1977.
Albinism: Evans 1978.

Northern Harrier

Natural History: Watson 1977, Clark 1972, Hamerstrom 1969, Hecht 1951.
Behavior: Rice 1982, Bildstein 1979, Fitzpatrick 1979, Littlefield 1970, Weller et al. 1955, Yocum 1944, Errington 1930.
Status: Evans 1982.
Distribution: Thompson 1983, Evans 1982, Wierenga 1981, Birkenholz 1977, Wilhelm 1960.
Plumage: Hamerstrom 1968.
Migration: Bildstein et al. 1984, Houston 1968.
Albinism: Watson 1977.

Northern Hobby

Natual History: Cade 1982, Cramp and Simmons 1980.
Status and Distribution: Cramp and Simmons 1980.

Plumages: Cramp and Simmons 1980.
Identification: Porter et al. 1981.

Osprey

Natural History: Spitzer and Poole 1980, Ogden 1977, Gerrard et al. 1976, Zarn 1974, Henny and Wight 1969, Ames 1964.
Behavior: Prevost 1979, Grubb 1977, Mathisen 1976, Stager 1958.
Status and Distribution: Evans 1982, Rogers and Leatherwood 1981, Swenson 1981, Spitzer and Poole 1980, Melquist et al. 1978, Ogden 1977, Hogg 1976, Henny and Noltemeier 1975, Zarn 1974, Kemper and Eastman 1970, Kenyon 1947.
Prey: Kern 1976, Wiley and Lohrer 1973, Petrovic 1972, Tait et al. 1972, McCoy 1966, Struthers 1955.
Plumage: Ogden 1977.
Migration: Melquist et al. 1978, Ogden 1977, Kennedy 1973.

Peregrine Falcon

Natural History: Cade 1982, Snow 1972, White and Cade 1971, Beebe 1960, Cade 1960.
Behavior: Rogers and Leatherwood 1981, Campbell et al. 1978, Craddock and Carlson 1970, Groskin 1952, Rudebeck 1951.
Status and Distribution: Evans 1982, Fyfe et al. 1976, Enderson and Craig 1974, Herman 1971, Hickey 1969.
Plumage: White 1968, Beebe 1960.
Taxonomy: White 1968.
Bibliography: Jenkins et al. 1986.
Migration: Dekker 1979.
Albinism: Ross 1963, Sage 1962.

Prairie Falcon

Natural History: Cade 1982, Ogden and Hornocker 1977, Snow 1974a, Enderson 1964.
Behavior: MacLaren et al. 1984, Cade 1982, Marti and Braun 1975, White 1962.
Status and Distribution: Evans 1982, Oliphant et al. 1975, Snow 1974a, Enderson 1964.
Plumages: Enderson 1964.
Migration: Steenhof et al. 1984, Enderson 1964.
Albinism: Ross 1963.

Red-shouldered Hawk

Natural History: Morris and Lemon 1983, Bednarz and

Dinsmore 1982, Janik and Mosher 1982, Portnoy and Dodge 1979, Campbell 1975, Wiley 1975, Henny et al. 1973, Stewart 1949, Nicholson 1930, Dixon 1928.
Behavior: Titus and Mosher 1981, Kilham 1964, Pearson 1960.
Distribution: Henny and Cornely 1985, Glinski 1982, Webb 1978, Bock and Lepthien 1977, Rogers and Dauber 1977, Browning 1973, Wilbur 1973, Brown 1971.
Plumage: Johnson and Peeters 1963.
Identification: Clark 1981, Wander 1978.
Albinism: Allaire 1977, Austing 1964, Ross 1963.

Red-tailed Hawk

Natural History: Janik and Mosher 1982, Mader 1978, Austing 1964.
Behavior: Preston 1981, Titus and Mosher 1981, Lee and Brown 1980, Conner 1974, Hubbard 1974a.
Distribution: Mindell 1985, Mindell 1983, Bock and Lepthien 1977, Weber 1976, Lavers 1975, Swarth 1926.
Plumage: Mindell 1985, Lavers 1975, Taverner 1936, Wood 1932, Taverner 1927.
Identification: Lish and Voelker 1986, Dunn and Garrett 1982, Clark 1981, Green 1967, Julian 1967.
Taxonomy: Mindell 1983, Taverner 1936, Sutton and Van Tyne 1935, Ridgway 1896.
Migration: Steenhof et al. 1984.
Albinism: Lish and Voelker 1986, Smith 1982, Oakley and Eltzroth 1980, Cely 1979, Allaire 1977, Melquist and Schroeder 1974, Clark 1967, Austing 1964, Ross 1963.

Roadside Hawk

Behavior: Slud 1964, Haverschmidt 1962.
Distribution: Trautman 1964.
Plumage: Smithe 1966.

Rough-legged Hawk

Natural History: Zarn 1976, White and Cade 1971, Sutton and Parmalee 1956.
Behavior: Schnell 1967a, Schnell 1967b, Kleiman 1966, Mueller *et al.* 1966, Freeman 1952.
Distribution: Bock and Lepthien 1977, Zarn 1976, Fatora 1968, Skinner 1968, Herbert and Skelton 1953.
Plumage: Cade 1955.
Identification: Clark 1981, Porter 1981, Hamerstrom and Weaver 1968.
Taxonomy: Cade 1955.

Sharp-shinned Hawk

Natural History: Jones 1979, Reynolds and Wight 1978, Storer 1966, Rust 1914.
Distribution: Evans 1982, Jones 1979.
Plumage: Mueller et al. 1981a, Wattel 1973, Roberts 1967.
Identification: Clark 1984a.
Taxonomy: Storer 1952, Snyder 1938.
Migration: Clark 1985b, Evans and Rosenfield 1984.
Albinism: Ross 1963.

Short-tailed Hawk

Natural History: Ogden 1978, Ogden 1974, Brandt 1924.
Behavior: Ogden 1978.
Distribution: Ogden 1978, Oberholser 1974, Ogden 1974, Moore et al. 1953.
Plumage: Ogden 1973, Ridgway 1881.
Taxonomy: Rand 1960.

Snail Kite

Behavior: Sykes 1985, Beissinger 1983, Mader 1981, Sykes and Kale 1974, Voous and Van Dijk 1973, Snyder and Snyder 1970, Snyder and Snyder 1969.
Status and Distribution: Sykes 1984, Beissinger and Takekawa 1983, Sykes 1983a, Sykes 1983b, Sykes 1979.
Plumage: Sykes 1979, Amadon 1975.
Taxonomy: Amadon 1975.

Steller's Sea Eagle

Natural History: Fischer 1982, Dementiev et al. 1966.
Status and Distribution: Lobkov 1985, Roberson 1980.
Plumage: Dementiev et al. 1966.

Swainson's Hawk

Natural History: Fitzner 1980, Smith and Murphy 1973.
Behavior: Dunkle 1977, Olendorff 1974, Richards 1962.
Distribution: Littlefield et al. 1984, Bloom 1980, Keir and Wilde 1976, Browning 1974, Clark 1974b.
Plumage: Cameron 1913.
Identification: Clark 1981.
Migration: Smith 1980, Houston 1974, Fox 1956, Skutch 1945, Cruickshank 1937.
Albinism: Ross 1963.

Swallow-tailed Kite

Natural History: Snyder 1974a, Skutch 1965.
Behavior: Kilham 1980, Lohrer and Winegarner 1980,

Lemke 1979, Buskirk and Lechner 1978, Snyder 1974a, Green
et al. 1972, Nicholsen 1928.
Distribution: Green et al. 1972, Hicks 1955.
Plumage: Snyder 1974a.

Turkey Vulture

Behavior: Jackson et al. 1978, Stewart 1978, Sallee 1977,
Prather et al. 1976, Kushlan 1973, Temple 1969, Loftin and
Tyson 1965, Stager 1964, Owre and Northington 1961.
Plumage: Henckel 1981, McIlhenny 1937.
Taxonomy: Amadon 1977, Wetmore 1964.
Migration: Smith 1980, Stewart 1977, Mote 1969.
Albinism: Allaire 1977, Voelker 1976, Davis 1970, Ross
1963.

White-tailed Eagle

Natural History: Love 1983, Wille and Kampp 1983,
Fischer 1982, Cramp and Simmons 1980, Waterson 1964.
Behavior: Rudebeck 1951.
Status and Distribution: Balch 1982, Roberson 1980,
Hansen 1979, Taverner 1934.
Plumage: Forsman 1981.
Identification: Porter et al. 1981, Waterston 1964.
Albinism: Love 1983, Sage 1962.

White-tailed Hawk

Natural History: Morrison 1978, Stevenson and Meitzen
1946.
Behavior: Stevenson and Meitzen 1946, Friedmann 1925.
Status and Distribution: Morrison 1978, Oberholser 1974.
Plumage: Voous 1968.

Zone-tailed Hawk

Natural History: Millsap 1981.
Behavior: Clark 1984b, Zimmerman 1976a, Hubbard 1974a,
Mueller 1972, Willis 1966, Willis 1963, Huber 1929.
Distribution: Matteson and Riley 1981, Bohl and Traylor
1958, Grey 1917.
Plumage: Huber 1929.

Index

Note: Numbers in **boldface type** indicate illustrations (color or black-and-white plates) at the center of the book; numbers in *italics* indicate pages where the birds are shown in photographs.